Book of Taurus

ן

KABBALISTIC COSMOLOGY
and the
MAGIC OF ESSENTIAL FORM

Rawn Clark

© 2024

BOOK OF TAURUS:
KABBALISTIC COSMOLOGY AND THE MAGIC OF ESSENTIAL MEANING
By Rawn Clark

_____

Dedication

Like the Ancients before me, I have traveled these Paths of Understanding and have come back to tell what I've seen.   But this time, I tell you how to get there in the hope that you too will travel and reach that Brilliant Horizon.

Most of what is written in these pages was first spoken by me in a series of 58 videos posted on my YouTube channel over a period of eight months from September 15th, 2023 trough May 13th, 2024. The series was titled *"Rawn's Kabbalistic Cosmology: From Macrocosmic to Microscopic"* and it used the work of the 182 Gates of the Gra Tree of Life as a guide.

CONTENTS

CONTENTS CONT'D

INTRODUCTION

+++++++++++++++++++++
Understanding (Binah) is the power to see how Essential Meaning
fits together and thus arrive at the right choice.
+++++++++++++++++++++

The "I", or Awareness with a Big 'A', Self-realizes because that is simply the nature of all awareness: Awareness self-realizes. With that grand Self-realization of "I AM" comes awareness that The "I" has meaning, an *Essential* Meaning. The "I" means something; It has a specific structure; a specific nature, color, shape, smell, and character. All of which is of course infinite in nature, scope and variety.

Its process of Self-realization necessitates that all of Its Essential Meaning (EM) *must* express itself (that's what EM does by its very nature) and (again by its very nature) that expression is through the taking of form. *All* EM expresses itself through form and consequently, *ALL* forms express their EM.

And we can perceive this EM communicated by each form . . . Not only *can* we, but we actually *do*, all the time, with each of our perceptions. You see, EM is the basis of *all* perception and *all* communication. Unfortunately modern humans are unconscious of EM and this aspect of natural perception. But have no fear; it is very easy to turn this into a fully conscious part of your every day perceptions!

When you do, the world becomes an open book and you *begin* to *Understand* . . .

For every bit of the EM of The "I" there is a *perfect* form, an *Essential* Form (EF). They go hand-in-hand, each meaning inseparable from its form, in perfect harmony and synchrony. Likewise, every form in our temporal realm (which by nature is a manifestation of a combination of EMs) is the *perfect* expression of its composite EM. Or rather, every temporal form *perfectly* communicates its EM. In fact, every temporal form *is* an Essential Form in its own right due to the *perfection* with which it communicates its EM. In this sense, there is no such thing as an 'imperfect' form! EM can *only* cause forms that are perfect expressions of itself; that is simply the nature of meaning in relation to form.

So when we directly (consciously and intentionally) perceive the EM of the forms around us, we see the objective, absolute, unadulterated, unmitigated truth being expressed by that form in the immediate temporal present moment.

Let that sink in for a moment. Maybe read that sentence again . . .

This changes everything in terms of our powers of perception and of our ability to understand and interact with the cosmos around us. And this is the basis upon which the Magic of Essential Form is built. You see, this is not the flashy kind of "magic" you're probably used to or expecting. There's no impressing others with your supernatural powers, no evoking spirits of Venus or Mars, etc. This is a simple and vastly more important type of magic; one that leads to ***understanding***. Understanding how things fit together and work; understanding the nature of our existence and our part in the cosmos. And, perhaps most important of all, how we can be a better manifestation of our own EM, a better participant in the grand adventure of Self-realizing that we call "the Cosmos".

Humans have this habit of creating symbols that represent things, ideas, etc. that are important to us; a sort of shorthand. As forms, each symbol expresses a certain set of EMs which are perceived by the observer. In this way, our symbols communicate meaning to us.

Some symbols are better, clearer, more accurate and accessible and do a better job of communicating the original intention of their creator. I would say they are more objectively accurate and this is an important distinction to make concerning *human generated* symbolic forms: they are never 100% objectively accurate. This is because EM is too vast to fit within a human construct, especially a 2-d symbol.

Usually they do no more than hint at the intended meaning, they lead us in the right direction and it's up to us to go the extra way. Take the Ankh for example: ♀ Its EM can tell us a lot but it cannot begin to capture the thousands of years of tradition that associates with the symbol. But if you come to it with some understanding of the tradition behind it, the symbol comes to life and speaks volumes. This type of symbol is purely a human construct but if we take one that is more clearly rooted in the natural world, such as that for our Sun ☉, we find a more objectively accurate communication.

In any event, human generated symbols or constructs have their limits compared to natural forms, but that doesn't mean that they don't have their uses. Some in fact are *very* useful due to their comprehensive objectivity but these usually require a fair bit of study beforehand.

One such symbol is the Kabbalistic Tree of Life, specifically the natural array of the Gra Tree. And it is due to how well and how accurately is describes the Cosmos and The "I" in Its wholeness that I have chosen to employ it here in my exposé of the Magic of Essential Form. Through this exploration of the EM of this Cosmic EF you will come to Understand the nature of The "I", of the Cosmos, how it all "works", and how you fit into it All. This is perhaps the ultimate Understanding available to the human being; it allows you to perfectly fit into your existence and opens you to all the "lesser" magics.

PREREQUISITES

There are, of course, some preparations to be made before the main work with the Gra Tree.

First and foremost is your recognition of The "I". It is absolutely vital that you are able to locate The "I" within yourself and are able to perceive it externally to yourself. To that end, I offer you a quote from my little book *"Love Letter To A Dying World"*.

++++++++++++++++++++++

In every book I have read about Kabbalah, Kether has been treated as ineffable, unreachable, as so high above us mere mortals as to be incomprehensible, as god. But I vehemently disagree with this assumption. To my mind, Kether as the Supernal "crown" must be THE most common thing, not the rarest thing. It must be THE most fundamental, simplest, most comprehensible and easiest thing to experience, not the most difficult . . .

Life is THE most common thing in the universe. EVERY thing is alive, is filled with "I"ness. The speck of dust on my computer screen is alive and filled with "I"ness. The fly buzzing around my apartment is filled with "I"ness. The Camellia bush outside my door is filled with "I"ness. The Moon is filled with "I"ness. The small creature swimming about in some distant ocean on some distant planet circling some distant star is full of aliveness and possesses the same "I"ness. There is nothing that exists that is not alive and filled with "I"ness.

By "I"ness I mean the exact same sense of "I" that fills you, that sense of "I" you find when you look inside yourself and set aside your bias for the "me" and "mine". That universal "I" is Kether. It is the crown of existence. It is right there under the surface of you and of everything else that exists in the infinite universe.

"I" is THE most common thing in the universe. This is why it is the first of the sephirot because it applies to EVERY thing. It is supernal and universal, infinite and eternal in scope.

Cast your eyes around the space you are sitting in while you read and realize that EVERY thing you see is ALIVE and possesses "I"ness. Even the things we consider to be inanimate objects are alive with "I"ness. You are truly not alone… You are sitting in a sea of "I".

Practice:

1) Your first exercise is a meditation on the "I". Sit with your eyes closed and look within for the "I". It's not easy to find at first because all your false ideas as to what "I" is will get in the way. You must let go of all your preconceptions, let go of "me-ness" and all the limitations and personalizations of your ideas of "I".

Focus upon your *experience* of "I-ness", that sense and experience of simply being. Let go of everything except "I". You may want to make a mantra of "I", repeating the word over and over to focus your attention.

Carry on in this way until you can sit comfortably in the "I" for at least 5 minutes without interruption. This may take some weeks or months for you to achieve. In all cases you must be patient and persistent in equal measure.

This is a meditation for a lifetime and you should return to it often.

2) The second exercise in an extension of the first. Begin with your eyes closed as before and enter into the "I". Now cast your mind outward into your surroundings and sense the "I" in all things in your immediate environment.

Little by little expand the quantity of the universe included in the perception of "I". Grow your experience and perception of the "I" to include your block, your city, your country, your continent, your planet, your solar system, your galaxy, etc. until it encompasses the whole universe.

Feel the "I" as infinite . . . There is no differentiation to this "I". No "me", no "other", no parts, no individuals, only "I": the One, Unified, Infinite Self.

Continue with this meditation until you can comfortably and quickly perceive this infinite "I".

3) This exercise is a departure from the previous two in that it is done with the eyes open. Sitting with your eyes open, immerse your mind in the "I" and look to your immediate surroundings. Let your eyes rest on one thing and perceive the "I" within it. Survey all the things within your immediate surroundings and perceive the "I" within each.

Now cast your eyes further afield perceiving the "I" within everything you see. You must perceive the "I" within the minutest thing and the largest thing equally.

Experiment in the different settings you encounter until you can easily and comfortably slip into this state of perception at any moment.

4) This exercise is an extension of the previous and is, as it were, a moving exercise. As you go throughout your day, recognize the "I" within each person, animal and thing you encounter. From your own place of perceiving the "I", greet the "I" within this other person/animal/object. You stand as equals, "I" to "I" . . .

+++++++++++++++++++++

The second most important prerequisite is that you learn how to directly (i.e., consciously and with intention) perceive Essential Meaning. You will need to employ this ability throughout your work with the Gra Tree and its 182 Gates. Since probably the simplest and most succinct textual instruction I've written was again, in my little book "*Love Letter*", here's a quote from that chapter:

+++++++++++++++++++++

The "I" is self aware and recognizes itself as both an infinite singular self and as a self composed of an infinite number of parts. It fills each part of itself equally with its Essential Meaning giving each part a life of its own. But the "I" is not a passive thing – it is *expressive*.

Each part, as well as the whole, actively expresses its Essential Meaning and it does so through form – through shape, size, color, duration, etc. So, in this sense, both form and Essential Meaning are also infinite and supernal.

Essential Meaning always expresses itself through form and form is always an expression of Essential Meaning. Where there is life there is Essential Meaning and where there is form there is life.

Chokmah/Wisdom is Essential Meaning and Binah/Understanding is Essential Form. In Chokmah we have the explosion of "I" into an infinite expanse of Essential Meaning and in Binah we find the mother of all forms. Chokmah fills the womb of Binah with the fiery seed of Essential Meaning and Binah in turn gives a watery birth to the universe of things.

Essential Meaning is at the same time a singular infinite thing and a *particulate* thing. There are an infinite number of different types of Essential Meaning just as there are an infinite number and variety of forms. Each form expresses either a single Essential Meaning or a combination of Essential Meanings, establishing infinite variety.

It is by looking though form that we directly perceive Essential Meaning. This direct perception results in an experiential "knowing" of the essence of the thing being examined; thus the title "wisdom" which is a deeper, more comprehensive and immediate thing than "understanding". We can attain an "understanding" of a thing by examining its structure but only when we look *within* its form do we arrive at the deeper state of "wisdom".

Practice:

1) This first exercise will teach you how to directly perceive the Essential Meaning of any form.

Sit in a quiet place where you are assured of privacy. Choose five small objects and place them in front of you.

These objects can be anything so long as they are all markedly different from each other. For example, I have chosen five things from my immediate environment: a black cigarette lighter; a small statue of Ganesh; a pen; a clump of Spanish Moss; and, a small orange stone. They are all quite different from each other in appearance and function.

Now quiet your mind and gaze at each object in turn for a moment or two. Now look again at each object but this time try to perceive how it makes you FEEL.

This is an immediate perception that comes BEFORE you begin to form any thoughts about the object. *It is pre-rational.* Thinking about the object and thinking about your feelings -- even naming your feelings or the object – come AFTER this perception. This is very important and may take some time and effort to master so be patient and persistent with your self.

Repeat this with your five objects until you get the hang of it and can immediately perceive the Essential Meaning in each.

Now choose a different five objects and repeat the exercise until you have perceived the Essential Meaning in each. Consider this exercise a success when you are able to perceive the Essential Meaning of any object placed before you.

2) As before, sit in a quiet, private room and clear your mind. Now methodically, starting directly in front of you and going from one thing to the next around the room, look at each object in turn and perceive its Essential Meaning as before.

In this way, get to know the Essential Meaning of your environment intimately. Does anything clash? Do certain things harmonize more than others? Look at your room as a whole and ask yourself if it suits you.

This exercise is a success when you can perceive the contents of your room as a whole and individually.

3) Now we will take this exercise outside into your normal life.

Prepare yourself by taking a moment to quiet your mind and bring your focus into your body and into the present moment. When you are ready, enter the outdoors and go for a walk. Perceive the Essential Meaning of everything, every person and every being you encounter. Pay special attention to perceiving the Essential Meaning of the people you meet.

You walk amidst a sea of Essential Meaning.

Do not be surprised or discouraged if you are unable to maintain this level of direct perception for more than a few moments at a time. It can be quite disorienting or disconcerting at first but give it time and it will become easier with practice. You can count your work with this exercise a success when you are able to maintain this level of perception for as long as you want, whenever and wherever you want.

+++++++++++++++++++++

The third prerequisite is you must familiarize yourself with the Letters of the Hebrew Alephbet since they play such a big part in everything that follows. I suggest that you study the following chart closely and in detail. It is best if you memorize the Letter shapes, names, meanings and general symbolism.

Hebrew	English	Pronunciation	Meaning	Symbol
א	Aleph	silent letter	Ox or Bull	♈︎
ב	Beth	B as in boy / V as in vine	House	♄
ג	Gimel	G as in girl / G as in George	Camel	♃
ד	Daleth	D as in door	Door	♂
ה	Heh	H as in hay	Window	♈
ו	Vav	V as in vine	Nail	♉
ז	Zayin	Z as in zebra	Sword	♊
ח	Cheth	Ch as in Bach	Corral or Fence	♋
ט	Teth	T as in time	Basket or Coiled serpent	♌
י	Yod	Y as in yes	Finger or Hand	♍
כ	Kaph	K as in kite	Palm of hand	♀
ל	Lamed	L as in look	Ox goad or Staff	♎
מ	Mem	M as in mom	Water	▽
נ	Nun	N as in now	Fish	♏
ס	Samekh	S as in son	Prop	♐
ע	Ayin	silent letter	Eye or Spring or Naught	♑
פ	Peh	P as in park / Ph as in phone	Mouth	☿
צ	Tzaddi	Ts as in nuts	Fish-hook	♒
ק	Qooph	K as in keep	Back of head or Ape	♓
ר	Resh	R as in rain / rolled 'R'	Head or Face	☉
ש	Shin	Sh as in shy / S as in sun	Tooth	△
ת	Tav	T as in tall / Th as in they	Cross, Mark or Sign	☽

The Fourth and final prerequisite is a familiarity with the Gra Tree of Life and its symbology. Ideally, you will already have mastered the direct perception of EM before embarking upon this study since that ability will greatly facilitate your comprehension. What follows then is a summation of *my* Understanding of this venerable symbol, based loosely on the 9 month long video series I posted on my YouTube channel titled "Rawn's Kabbalistic Cosmology: Macrocosmic To Microscopic". Through it, we come to Understand the structure of The "I" or Cosmos.

As you get to know the Tree, you should try to imagine its existence within your own body, giving it a tangible three-dimensional reality. You sort of back-into the 2-d image, placing Kether/Crown above and Malkuth/Domain below, Chokmah/Wisdom at your left temple and Binah/Understanding at your right, etc,. Of course it doesn't actually exist in your physical body, but personalizing it in this way makes the task of integrating these symbols into your conscious mind much, much easier.

Remember: this is *my* Understanding based on almost 40 years of intensive study and it does not correspond exactly to that of many (most?) others! First of all, my understanding is not at all religious in nature and it is bereft of all religious dogma. For me, kabbalah is *cosmology* and describes the structure of The "I" or One Self, the structure of everything that is. This gives me a very different perspective than most and frees me to explore *with* it and *through* it instead of taking it as static dogma.

I have my roots in Hebrew Kabbalah as well as Golden Dawn Kabbalah, so I'm relatively proficient in Golden Dawn Kabbalah and *very* proficient in Hebrew Kabbalah; but this isn't really going to be about either Kabbalah. This is really no less valid than an ancient book that we revere: it is someone *else's* experience. I, though, follow in my hero Franz Bardon's steps and write not only of my own experience, but also offer you a path to gain your own experience for yourself. So, *Rawn's* Qabbalistic Cosmology, okay?

STRUCTURE OF THE GRA TREE
OVERVIEW OF SYMBOLS

Essential Meaning is the language of *all* symbols be they in the form of images, words, ideas, sounds, sensations, etc. As such, symbols (like EM) communicate firstly at the pre-rational level; *then* secondarily, the rational mind takes over and elaborates on that initial perception. We can see here a separation between the true perception and the subsequent interpretation by the rational intellect. Our focus here is primarily upon the initial perception of EM which will then inform our rational exploration; for it is in the EM where the truth of each symbol lies.

So as you read along, you are to directly perceive (with whatever level of ability you possess) the EM of each image and idea that I place before you. As I said previously, this is fundamental to the Magic of EF and you should practice it as often as possible.

The oldest record we have of the Kabbalistic Tree of Life is a first century BCE document called the *Sepher Yetzirah*. But mind you, this is just the oldest existent *copy* and the text itself is undoubtedly centuries, if not millennia, older still. What is presented in the *S.Y.* wasn't suddenly made up the day before it was written! It's far too complex and developed a system for that to be the case.

Because it is so ancient there have been, of course, a multitude of different versions and translations and commentaries published over the past two or so millennia. The very best, most comprehensive and unbiased resource on the *S.Y.* is a book by Rabbi Aryeh Kaplan called "*Sepher Yetzirah: The Book of Creation*". [The Hebrew words 'sepher' and 'yetzirah', in English, are 'book' and 'creation / formation'.] I highly recommend this book!!!

Ostensibly, the *S.Y.* describes the sequence of how the Tree of Life was/is created. But it can also be construed as an instruction manual for a specific magical operation. What that operation pertains to is, of course, open to debate. Some say it describes a path of self-realization; others that it is a creation ritual of sorts; I use its methodology in the creation of my Crystal Golems. Whether or not one uses it in this way, it exists as a *very* cogent explanation of an all inclusive cosmology and that is what we draw upon here.

In the modern day there have come to be several differing versions of the Tree of Life, but the *S.Y.* describes only one of these which, as it turns out, is the least well know to the modern audience. Aryeh Kaplan called it the "natural array" but it is also known as the "Gra Tree", named after an 18th century rabbi who wrote a very important commentary on the *S.Y.*.

The different Trees vary in terms of overall structure and in the assignation of Hebrew Letters to the connections (know commonly as the "Paths") between the Sephirot. *Only* the Gra Tree follows exactly the S.Y. and can thus be seen as the archetypal Tree.

Take a moment to directly perceive the EM in each of these different versions of the Tree.

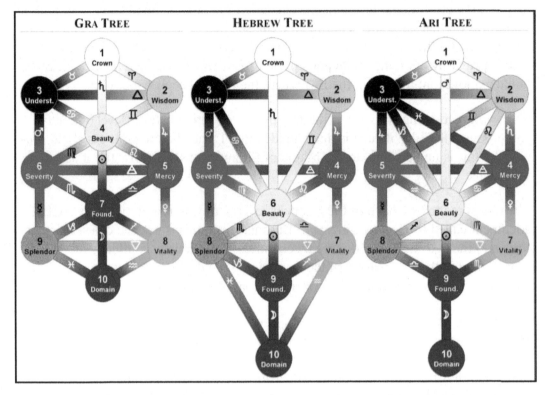

The most familiar shape will undoubtedly be what I've called here "Hebrew Tree" but you are probably most familiar with the Golden Dawn or Western Hermetic version, which makes a mess of the attributions of the Hebrew Letters. Because it's such a mess and entirely misses the message of the symbol, I have omitted it. I present here only those versions of the Tree that follow the proper arrangement of the Letters according to the *S.Y.*.

You can see for yourself that each presents a similar yet different meaning. Each is more or less inclusive than the others for different reasons and in different ways. The most inclusive and integral is obviously the archetypal Gra Tree.

At this point I must remind you that this is just a human construct. Its sole power is in its ability to communicate specific meaning to the human awareness. It possesses no intrinsic power or value of its own. It does not occur anywhere in nature and has absolutely no relevance to anything other than a human understanding. But as a human construct it is, in my opinion, a damn good one! Ha! When you delve into it and open yourself to it, it teaches you endlessly. It is perhaps *the most* objectively accurate and honest depiction of the entirety of the cosmos (i.e., not just the human bits).

Here then is the most complete, and therefore complex, version of the Gra Tree of Life. Its EM draws the perceiver in and grabs hold of the awareness; but in order for this complex symbol to make rational sense, I will need to break it down into its parts and explain each in turn. Fundamentally there are just two parts: the Sephirot and the Connections/Paths, but I will break it down into five parts to make it easier to comprehend. 1) 10 Sephirot; 2) 3 Mother Letters; 3) 7 Planetary Letters; 4) 12 Zodiacal Letters; and, 5) 14 Hidden Paths.

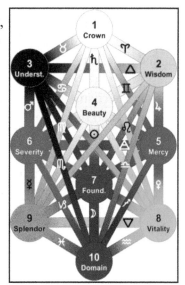

ORIGINS THE SEPHIROT

Cosmology at around the time that the *S.Y.* was written looked something like the image to the right. It depicted 10 consecutive spheres or realms:

Sphere of the Prime Mover

     1) The Prime Mover ("god")
     2) The Fixed Stars (zodiac)
     3) Realm of Saturn
     4) Realm of Jupiter
     5) Realm of Mars
     6) Realm of Sun
     7) Realm of Venus
     8) Realm of Mercury
     9) Realm of Moon
    10) Realm of Earth

To early humans, these "realms" were not planets and stars as we think of them today: they were gods; great, mystical, universal powers that *coincided* with the observed objects that moved through the night sky. They were all aspects of the divine, of "God", not physical planets with specific sizes and compositions, atmospheres and gravity that orbit at specific speeds and distances, etc., that we know today. We must always keep this in mind when working with these ancient symbols! We must think like the ancients who created them if we are to accurately understand them!

Furthermore, it was a *geocentric universe*, not a *heliocentric system*. The human world was at the center or nadir, not the Sun which instead was relegated to the sixth realm.

Nor was their order based on their distance; instead, it was rooted in the *speed* at which they traveled across the sky. Remember, this cosmology was founded upon actual observation by eye, without the use of telescopes.

This is the cosmologic underpinning of western occultism even today. It gives us the order and most especially, the *numbering* of the 7 Planets. Saturn is assigned the number 3 because it's third in order after the Prime Mover and the Fixed Stars; Sun is given 6 because it's 6th in sequence; Moon is 9 and Earth (Malkuth) is 10; all because of this specific *10-based* cosmology. Note that it is not based on 0 through 9, but 1 through 10 (indicating that it most likely predates the invention of the zero).

This is also the cosmological underpinning of the Tree of Life with its 10 Sephirot.

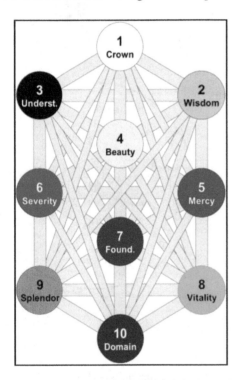 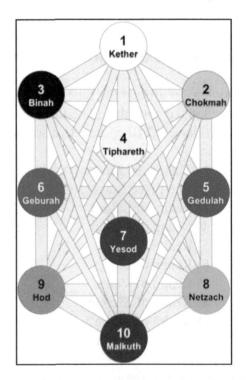

However, and this is a BIG however, the Sephirot do **NOT** equal the Planets! Instead, the Planets are relegated to the vertical connections between the Sephirot.

Read that again and stick it firmly in your head because it means you most likely have to unlearn everything you have been taught about the Tree of Life. One of the gravest errors western occultists have made in their usurpation of the Hebrew Tree of Life is to associate the Planets with the Sephirot! [The second, was how they assigned the Letters to the connecting paths.] The meaning of this symbol is utterly transformed when you remove the Planets from the Sephirot and give the Letters their proper (i.e., their *Hebrew*) assignments.

The meaning of the *numbers* (one of the meanings of the word "sephirot") however, is much the same between the two cosmologies. 1/Kether/Crown is much the same as the 1/Prime Mover; 3/Binah/Understanding is much the same as the 3/*Realm* of Saturn; 6/Tiphareth/Beauty is much the same as the 6/*Realm* of Sun; and, 10/Malkuth/Domain is much the same as the 10/*Realm* of Earth, etc. [Remember: these are the ancient's ways of thinking of the planets as mystical powers.]

The modern, commonly used colors given to the Sephirot are just that, modern. They appear nowhere in the ancient Kabbalistic traditions and probably arise in the western usurpation somewhere between the 14th and 17th centuries A.D.. The reason I say this, is because they come about as a consequence of the erroneous association of the Sephirot with the Planets.

These colors of the Planets actually come from the Alchemical tradition. They are the colors of the oxides (i.e., the rust) of the noble metals assigned to each of the Planets.

PLANET	METAL	COLOR OF OXIDE
Saturn	Lead	Black
Jupiter	Tin	Blue
Mars	Iron	Red (i.e., rust)
Sun	Gold	~none~ so Gold or Yellow
Venus	Copper	Green (i.e., verdi gris)
Mercury	Mercury	Cinnabar Orange
Moon	Silver	Dark Violet or Purple

So they were superimposed on top of the Tree of Life and we arrive at the common colors of the Sephirot. The thing is, even though their association was through an error, they work at a symbolic level for the Sephirot!

And white and gray work symbolically for Kether/Crown and Chokmah/Wisdom respectively. And that is why I use them here.

So, now that you have some idea of the philosophical and structural origins of this symbol, I will turn to explaining a bit about what it actually means.

The Tree of Life is a symbolic depiction of the structure and life of the Cosmos and everything within it. It illustrates a single thing: The "I", if you will, and Its process of Self-realization. The "I" and Its process of Self-realization are infinite. Each of the 10 Sephirot represents a specific stage or phase in that infinite process.

They are each a slightly different type, flavor or level of Awareness. Everything from the Supernal "I" to you and me, are contained in this symbol.

The diagram below illustrates important information about the significance of the Sephirot that you will need to know so do study it closely and familiarize yourself with its details.

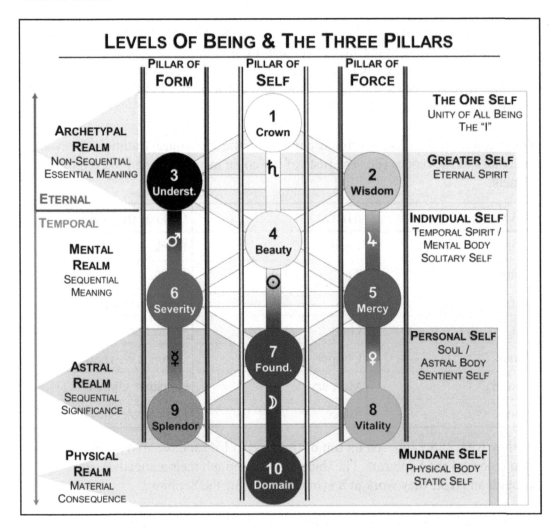

Note that it encompasses multiple realms with the single symbol, each of which is infinite in its own right. Each Sephirot contains everything "below", *within* itself, echoing the ten concentric circles of the past. This is an important aspect of the cosmology of the Tree: infinities within infinities, each of which contain infinities.

THE TEN SEPHIROT

Something you must understand about the Kabbalistic Tree of Life: it's not based on supposition, theory, fantasy, etc. It's based on factual human experience. Ancient masters of Wisdom, if you will, actually touched upon that highest, most inclusive level of Awareness and essentially came back from that experience with notes. "I saw this, I did this, I experienced this and perceived this, etc." *That* is where the Tree of Life and the Sepher Yetzirah come from: from factual human experience of these higher states of Awareness.

They charted the *wholeness* of that Awareness. Not just the most inclusive, expansive part; but all the other parts that make up the whole body of Awareness too. And in that process, they came up with this description and this illustration of the structure of the Awareness they had discovered.

Furthermore, this is all based on *repeated* human experience of these various realms / types / stages / phases of Awareness. This wasn't just a one-off where one person went and had these experiences, came back and wrote about them. No, these experiences have been repeated over and over throughout human history by thousands, if not millions, of people.

The Tree of Life is basically a map. It says "you are here" and "you can go anywhere within this body of Awareness", *and* it shows you how to get there. In effect, it's a map that comes with an instruction manual! (In fact, one way to interpret the Sepher Yetzirah is as a set of instructions.)

1 – Kether

Those ancient ones titled the highest, most inclusive aspect of what they perceived as "Kether", which means "Crown" in English. Look at the Essential Meaning of this image of Kether with that lone white sphere at the very top.

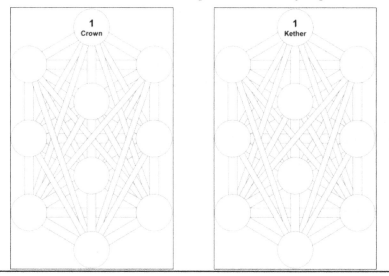

As I said, Kether means Crown. It's something that stands *above* human consciousness; something different; another order of consciousness above our sequentialized, brain-bound awareness. Not separate, but definitely different.

We choose the color white to represent Kether only because the more accurate symbol is impossible to depict in two dimensions. The true "color" of Kether is Brilliance: a light so bright that it has no color and no opacity. It is the Brilliant "light" of pure, infinite Awareness itself.

We humans pretty much universally perceive Awareness as Light. As an all-permeating Light in which *everything* exists all at once. There is no sequence here; no time; no before or after; no tomorrow or yesterday; no time at all, only *Now*. In Kether, it's *all* here *now*. The concept / experience of perpetuity or eternity doesn't even exist. At this level it just simply *is*. Absolutely *every* thing that *is*, everything that has being, exists simultaneously, *now*. At this uppermost level of Awareness, there is no differentiation, no parts of Self here, just The One Self of the absolute Unity.

What lies beyond that One Self is completely unknown. The ancients called this unknowable region the "Ayin soph aur", or *Light without end*. It is so radically different a state than Awareness that we have no words or even concepts to describe it so there is no point in trying to discuss it here.

Kether itself (*every*thing that exists), by nature, *has* to be the most common thing in the universe and therefore, *the* easiest thing for us to connect with. This is the sense of "I-ness" that we all experience within our own awareness. *Every* thing that exists experiences this exact same sense of I-ness, of being, because Kether *is* everything and is *in* everything. You are always rooted in your "I", yes? In fact, it's were you live each moment of your existence. Kether has always been right there inside you; so close you didn't even notice it!

When you follow that internal sense of I-ness inward and upward you are led to Kether / Crown and the sense of an infinitely large Self. That Awareness is an infinite expanse of Brilliance, filled with infinite power. It contains within itself *all* that exists and it exists within every thing. Everything is *made of* Awareness . . .

This pristine state of undifferentiated oneness is of course only part of the picture. While it does exists, there is no denying that the rest of the manifest cosmos most definitely is differentiated. The miracle is that *they both exist simultaneously* and without negating one another. Kether recognizes this fact.

It is the nature of Awareness, *all* awareness, to self-realize. That's just what Awareness does in all of its manifestations and Kether, *The One Awareness*, is no different in this regard.

2 – Chokmah

The very first thing that happens in that process of The "I" Self-realizing is that Kether acknowledges that it exists, that it has being. Its being is infinitely complex, infinitely varied, yet infinitely simple at the same time. Mainly, that being has *meaning*. It *means* something and each of its infinite number of parts have meaning. This is Chokmah / Wisdom and the birth of Essential Meaning.

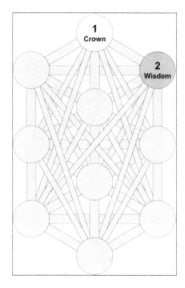 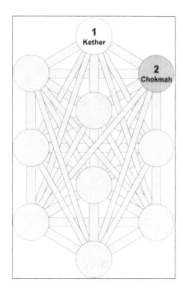

In Chokmah, the whole of Kether, the whole of The "I", is translated into EM which nets an infinite number of parts. In Chokmah, The Unity of Kether becomes the "Unity of Parts"; still undifferentiated and unified but well on their way to ultimate differentiation and manifestation.

From Chokmah one can "see" and "sense" the whole temporal, sequential universe below; thus it *knows* the *whole* score, not *just* the pristine Unity of The "I". It *knows* what all of its parts, all of that infinite number of bits of EM, become.

3 – Binah

The thing about meaning is that by nature, meaning *must* express itself and that expression is *always* through form. Where there is meaning, there is form; and, where there is form, there is meaning. Form is the expression of meaning and since we're talking about *Essential* Meaning here, its expression is, of course, through Essential Form. This is Binah / Understanding.

 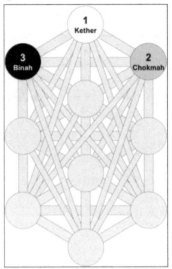

Let's look at the difference between these two terms: Wisdom (Chokmah) and Understanding (Binah). Wisdom is automatic; it's a certain type of knowing that's spontaneous and complete in itself. You don't have to do anything to create it.

Understanding on the other hand, is a *process*. We *come to* an understanding by putting together several pieces of knowledge. It is *sequential*, whereas Wisdom is *non*-sequential.

The EM in Chokmah itself is un-differentiated; there are no little bits of EM that make up the whole. *But*, and it's a big 'but', Awareness in Chokmah "sees" that there are an infinite number of parts that make up manifest universe "below". In other words, in its process of Self-realization, The "I" recognizes that all of its EMs have shapes, sizes, colors, sounds, distinct characteristics, *form*. It's this realization that is Binah / Understanding.

All form exists in Binah but in an un-differentiated state. Form itself is infinite and eternal while each individual form is temporary, so in Binah one sees an infinite ocean of forms that are constantly changing. No one form lasts for more than an instant. Thus Binah is a realm of constant and infinite change.

All of those infinite number of forms are not only potentials that may some day manifest: they are *inevitable*, and it is this inevitability of Form that causes EM to begin to coalesce and clump together in Binah.

Remember, each Sephirot is a stage or phase in the Self-realization of The "I" so they are *active* states, filled with the movement of Awareness and its evolution. Each contains more than just a static state that sees no further than its own domain. Each sees and anticipates what is "below", what is within itself.

The need of EM to express itself is *so* intense that manifestation becomes inevitable and Binah gives birth, so to speak, to all of that infinite number of forms and thus causes the temporal realm of sequence to come into manifestation. The only way that The "I" *can* fully Self-realize is through temporal manifestation. That's just the way it is; that's the *nature* of Awareness.

As I said, EM begins to coalesce in Binah and those groupings begin to form discrete awarenesses that become more and more concrete, eventually forming what I call "Greater Selves", also known as "Holy Guardian Angels". Each of the infinite number of Greater Selves exist at the lowest, densest level of the Supernal / Eternal realm and are composed of a limited and very specific set of EMs, making them utterly unique.

4 – Tiphareth

Their specific EMs are so heavy with the need for the next step in self-expression that they burst forth and form the temporal, sequential realm of differentiation. They are birthed as the children of the Greater Selves; as the solitary individual reflections of The "I" that are infinite in number. What Binah gives birth to is Tiphareth / Beauty.

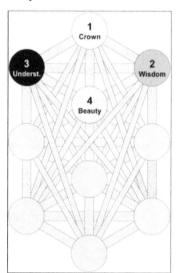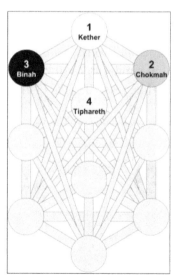

The best way to explain is with the mystical phrase "I am that I am":

Kether is The "I" of the phrase and Chokmah is the "I Am", the Self-realizing "I".

The question "which am I" is answered with Binah and the "I am *that*!". The pronoun 'that' implies two things: 1) specificity (one thing over another thing) and, 2) multiplicity (one out of many things). In other words, the first hints of differentiation.

Which leads us to "I am *that* 'I am'" and Tiphareth. The 'that' referred to takes differentiated form <u>as a specific 'I am"</u> or quantity of self-realizing awareness amid other such self-realizing awarenesses. Indeed, Tiphareth is a realm filled with an infinite number of little reflections of The "I" or Kether, an ocean of "I am"s. And each one of those little reflections is an expression of a specific, unique portion of Essential Meaning.

All together, that infinite number of little reflections make up the entirety of the infinite temporal realm. Each little "I am", each little self-realizing quantity of awareness, is autonomous and lives with the realization that it is surrounded by *other* "I am"s just like itself yet separate from itself. Both differentiation and duality, 'self' versus 'other', are born with Tiphareth.

From this point onward or downward in the Tree, everything pertains to each and every one of these solitary awarenesses in Tiphareth **_and_** to the collective whole or general cosmos. So each Sephirot from here on out takes on a sort of dual significance: one that is personal *and* one that is universal.

5 – Gedulah

Since the natural state of Awareness is unification, each of the solitary awarenesses expresses an innate "urge to merge". But here in the sequential realm, true unification is impossible and so the solitary selves *collectivize*. At first this collectivization is rooted in similarity or alikeness and everything aligns in an infinite sequential continuum of alikeness. This is Gedulah / Mercy.

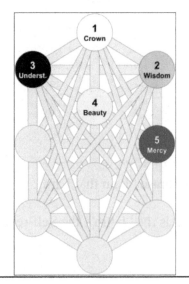
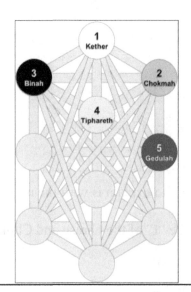

6 – Geburah

At the same time, that whole collective of solitary awarenesses realizes that, though everyone is alike, everyone is *also* different; ever so slightly different. That continuum of alikeness opens into a continuum between alikeness and difference. At one end is Gedulah / Mercy and at the other, Geburah / Severity.

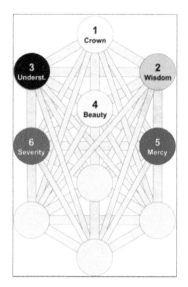 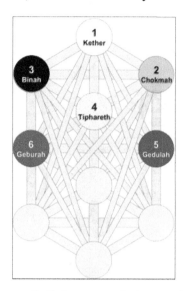

So in Gedulah we have collective awarenesses of all shapes and sizes and flavors; such as human collectives, star collectives, mineral collectives, etc., ad infinitum. In Geburah we have highly individualized awarenesses, each an utterly unique and necessary part of the cosmos; each intimately aware of the power and EM that it alone expresses and brings to the collective awarenesses that it is a part of.

The term 'Severity' here refers to the root meaning 'to sever or cut off the unnecessary'. This severing reveals the true power of *all* the solitary selves; and places 'self' and 'other' in a bright new context of *contrast* instead of homogeneity.

Yet for all the great power that each individual alone possesses, it has relevance *only* in relation to the collective. When isolated from the collective, that power turns upon itself and becomes a self-destructive, cancerous force: this is the challenge of Geburah. Gedulah challenges the solitary self's sense of individuality and uniqueness, while Geburah challenges its sense of collectivity and connection with 'other'.

7 – Yesod

The effect upon the process of self-realization is that the solitary self, that little reflection of The "I", becomes more defined, more identified with its uniqueness and the specific quantity of EM it is destined to express. From this point forward, existence becomes about the relationship between 'self' and 'other'; and Geburah, just like Binah above, gives birth to the vehicle each Solitary Self will need in order to navigate this new reality: the "Sentient Self" of Yesod / Foundation.

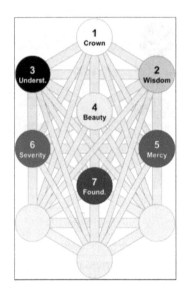 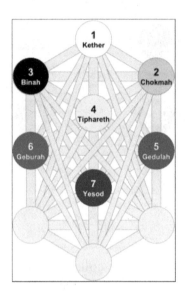

At a more universal level, this is the Mental Realm of Tiphareth/Gedulah/Geburah giving birth to the Astral Realm of Yesod.

In the Supernal (eternal, non-sequential) Realm of Kether/Chokmah/Binah we have Essential Meaning and infinite change; in the Mental (temporal, sequential) Realm of Tiphareth/Gedulah/Geburah, we have transformed EM into *subjective* meaning ("my meaning" vs. "your meaning") and introduced infinite sequence; now, in the Astral Realm of Yesod/Netzach/Hod, meaning becomes *significance* and (eventually) we encounter infinite duration. The awareness is now utterly consumed by this interaction between 'self' and 'other' and in order to navigate that constant barrage self must be able to perceive that significance: to see it, smell it, touch, hear it, etc.

Significance is all about the impact that 'other' has upon 'self' and that 'self' has upon 'other'. The greater the impact: the greater the significance. To the human (astral) psyche, all significance is given an emotional valuation; hence the exaggerated, fanciful, colorful, bucolic or horrific appearance of the Astral Realm to human vision. To a human Sentient Self, all appearances are based upon how **we** *feel* about what we perceive. Perception thus informs us about 'other' *and* about 'self', in pretty much equal measure!

8 – Netzach

At a personal, human level *and* at a universal level, this interaction between 'self' and 'other' happens through *resonance*: I affect you and you affect me. This is Netzach / Vitality and that fundamental '*urge to merge*' that permeates all Awareness.

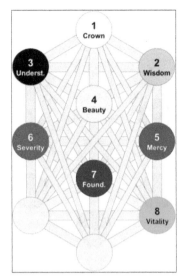 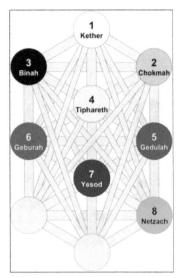

I translate the Hebrew 'Netzach' as 'Vitality' because it is filled with the vital energy of the interaction between an infinite number of sentient selves. Every instance of resonance is an exchange of energy between a 'self' and an 'other', a give and take of little bits of the astral self. In this way, through resonance, *all* things are connected; which of course is a lesser form of the collectivity of Gedulah and the Unity of Chokmah.

Resonance is an act of opening the boundaries of 'self' to 'other' and taking on characteristics of that 'other'. 'Self' empathizes with 'other' and comes to understand 'other' in new ways. And also, 'self' realizes itself more deeply. This is how The "I" Self-realizes through Its microscopic parts, so to speak; through the minutia of the temporal reality; through every little interaction.

9 – Hod

However strong that '*urge to merge*' may be, there is an equally strong instinct of *self-preservation*; of ensuring the survival of the self's uniqueness and its purpose of expressing its own unique EM. 'Self' can only open itself to a certain degree before its own self-identity is lessened and when the 'self' is threatened in this way, it resorts to *dissonance,* the opposite of resonance. Thus a continuum is formed between the resonance of Netzach and the dissonance of Hod / Splendor.

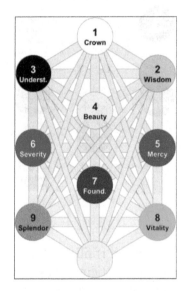 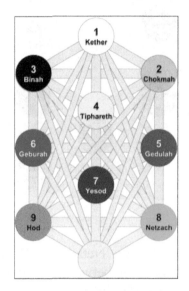

For the most part, dissonance is a *choice* made by the Sentient Self: it's automatic only when the threat to 'self' is dire. Resonance is the opposite: it's automatic and seldom truly by choice. So with Hod, we have the introduction of self-directed choice where the individual is deciding for itself for the first time!

This is a *major* development in the evolution of the Self-realization of The "I"! It's a step on par with the explosion of The One into The Many with Tiphareth, when The One Self became an infinite number of little reflections . . . In fact this is where the name Hod or Splendor in English comes from: it complicates the universe so dramatically and multiplies the options within each moment of time space to such a degree that only "Splendor" can describe its appearance. It dazzles the eye and boggles the mind! Self-determination changes everything.

By *choosing* dissonance, one is saying "***This*** is me!" and is halting all resonating with 'other', maybe even creating conflict with 'other'. It is an extreme act of self-realization through self-assertion. It is a radical expression of the Sentient Self's own EM in its purest form.

Hod represents the rational intellect and the deciding or choosing mind. This is an entirely subjective aspect of awareness and a "lower" manifestation of Mind (Tiphareth), based upon astral significance. Every judgment and choice made by the ration intellect is rooted in significance and based upon our interaction with 'other'.

10 – Malkuth

In universal terms it's like all those little fishes in the ocean have all grown up and are now ready to spawn, all at once. It's a moment of infinite potential and another step change of great magnitude . . . And so Hod (like Geburah and Binah before) gives birth to a new level of existence: Malkuth / Domain and the material realm.

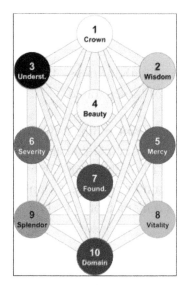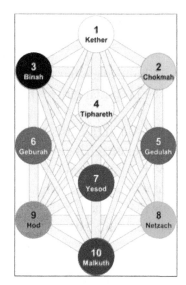

Absorb the EM of this image for a few moments. Notice the absolute symmetry and harmony. Notice that Malkuth is an exact mirror image of Kether and notice how the *whole* Tree empties into and flows into Malkuth.

Malkuth is the *whole* Tree existing right Now, all at once and materially. It's not "just the material realm": it's *all* the realms together in the same moment of Now. *All* the realms, *all* the aspects of Awareness, exist simultaneously in and permeate every atom of Malkuth.

Needless to say, Malkuth is *the* most complex manifestation of The "I". It is where we live and breathe and have our being but it is also us: *we* are part of Malkuth and I'm sure you know just how complex you are! Ha! Now multiply that by infinity and you begin to get some idea.

Malkuth is infinitely complex; yet at the same time, infinitely simple. It just depends upon what aspect of Awareness it is perceived with. Ultimately its simplicity derives from the fact that it just *is*. *This* is what the Self-realization of The "I" looks like; *this* is how it plays out in "real time": as *our* world, *our* Now.

The astral Sentient Body gave us the senses to navigate though the maze of inter-action with 'other' and now, the physical Static Body of Malkuth provides us with everything we need to both express and perceive within the material realm. The term "static" alludes to the great Mystery of Malkuth: how time becomes matter.

Time is composed of three factors: Number one is *change* (the interaction between Chokmah and Binah); number two is *sequence* (the interaction between Gedulah and Geburah); and number three is *duration* which is derived from the interaction between Netzach and Hod (the time it takes to reach the decision of dissonance). Space however, is composed of the same three factors plus one more: *continuity*; which is brought with Malkuth.

There is time without space but there is no space without time. Time-space is the proper term since in spatial terms, the two cannot be separated.

The Static Self of Malkuth exists within a present *Now* moment of time *and* space. Everything is constantly changing and that change is sequential and has duration **but** it is only ever experienced (i.e., lived in and through) *Now*. One is always in a present moment when experiencing anything. In other words, it's only the present moment of *Now* that actually exists: the past is only memory and the evidence of continuity, and the future is just fantasy.

The only thing that actually, objectively exists, exists *Now* and only *Now*. Aware-ness in all its forms, experiences its existence *Now*.

Because of how we perceive that *Now* with our human brains, 'a moment' lasts on average a few nanoseconds before our brains start processing another image of the *Now*. So we are aware of only snippets of *Nows* all strung together in sequence which give us the *impression* of the flow of time. Conversely, the perception/experience of time in the astral, non-physical realm (where we are not relying on our *brains*) does not come with a rigid progression and time can compress and ex-pand at unexpected intervals. In other words, that singular *astral Now* moment can encompass varying amounts of change; or rather, varying amounts of change can be perceived within the confines of a singular *astral* present *Now* moment. But in the *physical* present *Now* moment of time-*space*, this is not true.

The Great Mystery of Malkuth has to do with the material duration of that one sin-gle solitary present moment of *Now* in which everything exists.

If you were to dive into the *Now* moment with your mind, you would find that it gets ever smaller and smaller, briefer and briefer, and you can go on forever. In point of fact, it is infinitely-finite . . . That's the crux of the Great Mystery. You can, quite literally, go on for *ever*.

The present moment is so brief that it happens *between* changes; it happens *between* sequence; and it must of course have absolutely no *duration*. Logically this means that it doesn't exist since all three of these things are infinite. Where the true Mystery lies is that this impossible, infinitely-finite Now moment is a direct doorway to Kether.

Ponder that for a time, please. The infinitely-finite temporal *Now* of time-space is the same as the infinitely-*infinite* supernal **Now** of Kether.

Of course we humans in general do not live in that Awareness that unites us with Kether; but it is nonetheless always there and readily available to *every* thing that exists in the cosmos. Yes, even little old you reading these words right *Now*, all this time after I typed them with my little fingers (right *Now* for me). <grin>

So, moving beyond the deeper Mystical meaning of Malkuth, let's get back to the general overview of what Malkuth means.

Malkuth is the whole point of everything from Tiphareth on. It is both the bodies in which *we* incarnate *and* the bodies in which the rest of the cosmos (all of those original Solitary Selves in Tiphareth) incarnate. The *infinite whole* of the physical Universe is included here. One of the things it tells us is how we, as Sentient, Solitary Selves, are *bound* to our Static Selves for the *duration* of our incarnation.

I will use the following image by way of a brief explanation:

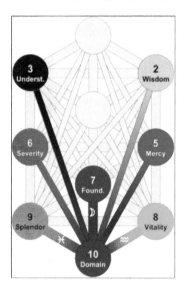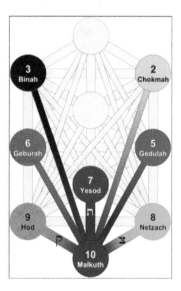

These are all the influences from the other Sephirot that form Malkuth. Each represents a way in which each awareness is bound to its physical form. This is how Awareness takes material form.

In order:

2>10) This is the influx of the specific quantity of EM that you are expressing during this incarnation. In humans (and all organic life) this manifests as our DNA which determines everything about our physical body. In mineral life it manifests as molecular structure; for beings of light, in frequency, etc.

3>10) This is the input of Karma and of continuity. It is that path that you *must* follow in this incarnation in order to self-realize.

5>10) This is the quantity and quality of your connection to the various collective awareness of which you are a part. This shapes how well you get along with others.

6>10) This is the quality and quantity of your connection to your own, unique and innate power; as well as your relationship to power in general throughout your incarnation.

7>10) This is the descent of Awareness itself (being Kether-Tiphareth-Yesod) into the physical body. This is the incorporation or integration of the higher Mind into the lower intellect. Awareness now enjoys (and becomes addicted to) physical sensation.

8>10) Through this avenue, significance becomes physical sensation and resonance becomes physical energy. In humans and many other creatures, this is expressed as emotion. This solidifies and facilitates our interactions with 'other'.

9>10) For humans this is the rational intellect integrating into the brain specifically. For that part of the universe that doesn't have brains, the integration is with whatever serves as their particular interface (based upon 2>10). Again for humans, this brings with it the birth of the subconscious aspect of awareness which is crucial in this process of integration. This connection of the rational intellect with the brain, by way of the subconscious mind, is the final binding that locks us firmly into our incarnation.

THE MOTHER LETTER PATHS

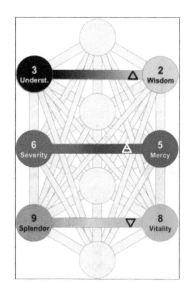
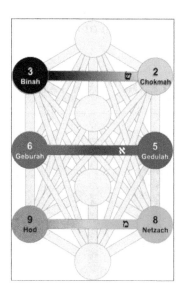

Observe the EM of these images. Notice what it brings in terms of nascent structure.

The three horizontal Paths (connections between Sephirot) are assigned to the so called *Mother* Letters: Shin / Fire to the supernal Path connecting Chokmah to Binah; Aleph / Air to the mental Path connecting Gedulah to Geburah; and, Mem / Water to the astral Path connecting Netzach to Hod.

Remember, the connecting Paths represent the *movement of Awareness* between Sephirotic states, so the movement between these states is special to have warranted the assignment of the *Mother* Letters. These are the three basic, rudimentary building blocks of existence: the three primordial Elements. These are *not* the Elements we manipulate in Bardon's work; instead, they are what he called the "Philosophical Elements" that stand above and behind the working Elements. Essentially, they are the EM of the working Elements.

The cosmic Fire, Shin, is the most powerful, undeniable, primordial movement of EM from Chokmah in its urge to express itself, toward Binah and the state of Essential Form. Shin is the infinite continuum of meaning/form and change, and exists within the supernal realm.

The cosmic Air, Aleph, is the balance between the collectivizing nature of Awareness in Gedulah and the equally potent individualizing nature of Awareness in Geburah. It is the thread that unites the two natures. Aleph is the infinite continuum of alikeness/difference and sequence, and exists within the mental realm.

The cosmic Water, Mem, is the powerful current leading the astral self along its path of self-realization, from the openness of Netzach to the solidity of Hod. Mem is the infinite continuum of resonance/dissonance and duration, and exists within the astral realm.

THE DOUBLE OR PLANETARY LETTER PATHS

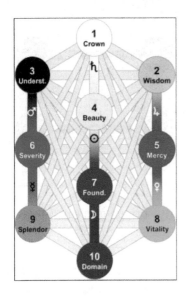 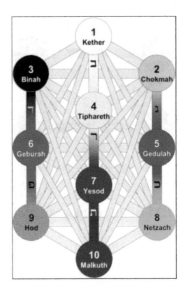

Pause again and observe the EM of this new development. Notice that these Paths are perpendicular to the Mothers and represent something quite different in nature, another order of Awareness.

The seven vertical Paths are assigned to the "Double" or Planetary Letters. Read from top-to-bottom and right-to-left, they are arrayed in the traditional occult order of Saturn, Jupiter, Mars, Sun, Venus, Mercury and Moon.

They are called the *Double* Letters because they each represent two (related) sounds when spoken, depending on the inclusion of certain points when they are written. Furthermore, through their relationship to the Planets, they each have a positive and a negative (*double*) planetary character.

You **_must_** remember here that the Planets are powerful beings or gods, not mere rocks rotating around the sun as they are today! *Each of the ancient gods was known by their personalities.*

The Planetary Paths are bridges between realms: Beth/Saturn, Gimel/Jupiter and Daleth/Mars unite the Supernal and Mental realms; Resh/Sun, Kaph/Venus and Peh/Mercury unite the Mental and Astral realms; and Tav/Moon unites the Astral and Physical realms.

Additionally, the vertical Planetary Paths form the *Three Pillars* alluded to before:

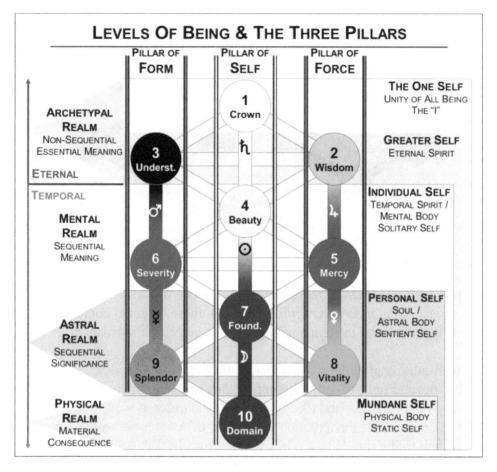

In combination with the horizontal Mother Letter Paths, the vertical Planetary Paths afford a good bit of stability to the structure of the Tree and establish the *separation* between all the Sephirot (stages or types of Awareness).

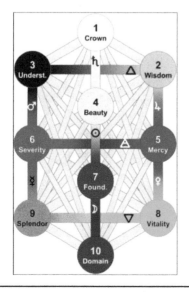
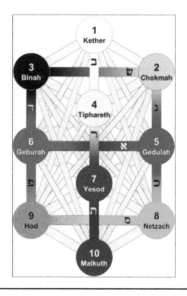

THE SIMPLE (ELEMENTAL) OR ZODIACAL LETTER PATHS

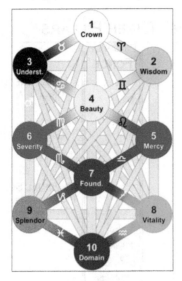 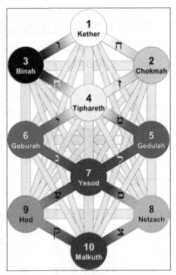

Again, please study to EM of these images and notice the drastic development of *movement* and *circulation* and *rhythm*. See how these diagonal connections bind the whole together with the dynamic threads of symmetry and balance

These twelve diagonal Paths are assigned to the signs of the zodiac. Read from top-to-bottom and right-to-left, the Simple (they have only one sound) Letters appear in aleph-betical order and the zodiacal signs in order as well, from Aries through Pisces. Half of them pertain to the shift of Awareness within a specific realm and half to the shift between adjacent realms. In fact, each of the four zodiacal Elements have their own type of function.

Earth   Fire

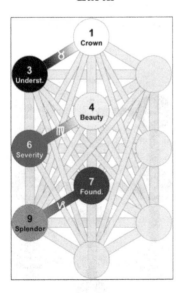 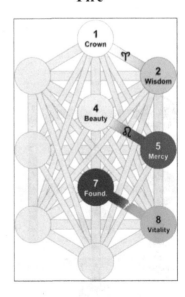

<table>
<tr><td align="center">**Water**</td><td align="center">**Air**</td></tr>
</table>

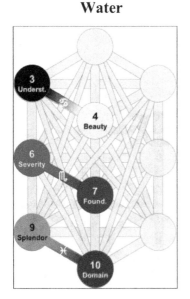 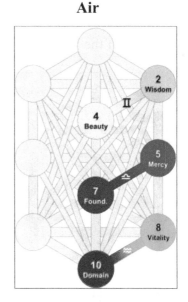

Starting at the bottom-right of the previous page, all three of the Fire sign Paths pertain to an initial shift of awareness within one realm, from the middle Pillar of Self to the outer Pillar of Force. This shift is always a powerful self-realization of some sort, which gets things really moving.

Next in sequence are the three Earth sign Paths in the lower-left image of the previous page. Like the Fire sign Paths, these pertain to the shift within one realm, only this time they flow from the Pillar of Self to the Pillar of *Form*. They answer and balance the Fire sign Paths and always pertain to *Form* and its solidification.

Together, the Fire and Earth Paths help *form* the two poles of the three continuums: Shin, Aleph and Mem.

Next are the three Air sign Paths. These Paths, along with the Waters which follow, each mark a shift of Awareness between one realm and the realm immediately below. They also all (along with the Waters) participate in the creation of the next station along the Pillar of Self. Coming from the Pillar of Force, the Air sign Paths all bring an important and transformative realization to the new level of Self.

Last, but by no means least, are the three Water sign Paths leading from the Pillar of Form. These three Paths are the "mothers" of each new level of Self below Kether: Cancer/Cheth gives birth to the Solitary Selves of Tiphareth/Beauty; Scorpio/Nun gives birth to the Sentient Selves of Yesod/Foundation; and, Pisces/Qooph gives birth to the Static Self of Malkuth/Domain. They provide the finishing touch to the formation of each of these Sephirot and, having traversed them, the Awareness awakens in a new body.

Put the ten Sephirot, the three horizontal Mother Letters, the seven vertical Planetary Letters and the twelve Zodiacal Letters all together and we get this, the standard Gra Tree image of the "32 Paths of Wisdom":

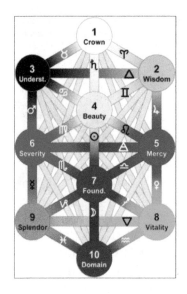 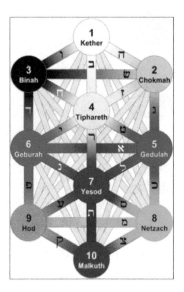

This is a visual representation of the thirty-two Paths of Wisdom encoded in the Torah, Genesis I. But, (again, a **BIG** *but*) this is *not* the *whole* Tree: there are fourteen additional connections between Sephirot in this symbolic structure that have yet to be taken into account.

THE HIDDEN OR UN-LETTERED PATHS

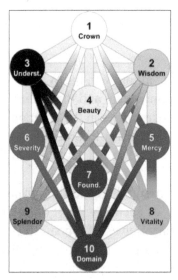 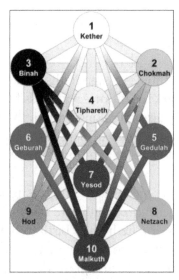

These connections have no Letter association, nor do they have any specific symbols attached to them such as signs, Elements or planets. Thus they cannot be described in the same way as the rest. They are not mentioned *directly* in any ancient writing that I've encountered. At the same time, there are many innuendoes, many allusions and hints to their existence sprinkled throughout the literature, even the Sepher Yetzirah, if you know what you're looking for. But these hints say nothing about their meaning; only that they exist and are significant.

There is Mystery to these Paths unlike any of the others. That Mystery is that one must explore them, must make that shift of Awareness *for oneself*. Their meaning is revealed *only* though their traveling.

These Hidden Paths make connections that none of the others do. They are all diagonal in excess of 45 degrees and all cross realms in new ways. Two of them even connect the tops and bottoms of opposite Pillars! Another two connect the Supernal realm *directly* to the Physical. *All* of them are transformative experiences.

Added to the *32 Paths of Wisdom* Tree, we get the Complete Tree:

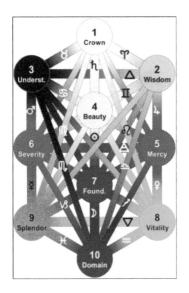 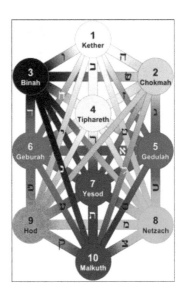

Every connecting Path has a dual nature: it serves as the *creator* of a lower Sephirot and as an emanatory *power* of a higher Sephirot. For example, the Path of Heh/Aries *creates* Chokmah and is a *power* of Kether.

THE CREATORS: All the Paths that create the lowest Sephirot pictured.

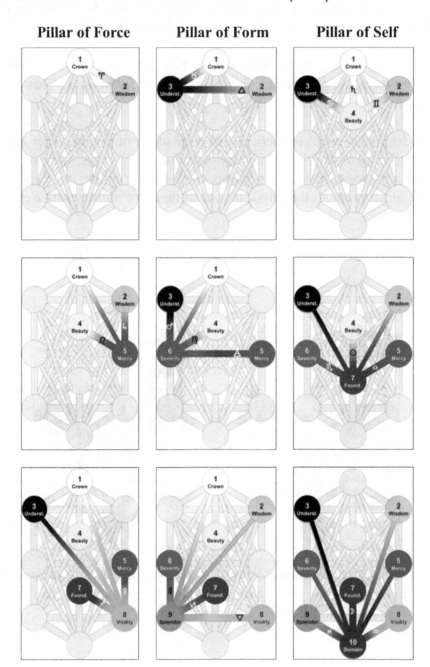

Pillar of Force	Pillar of Form	Pillar of Self

THE POWERS: All the Paths that emanate from the highest Sephirot pictured.

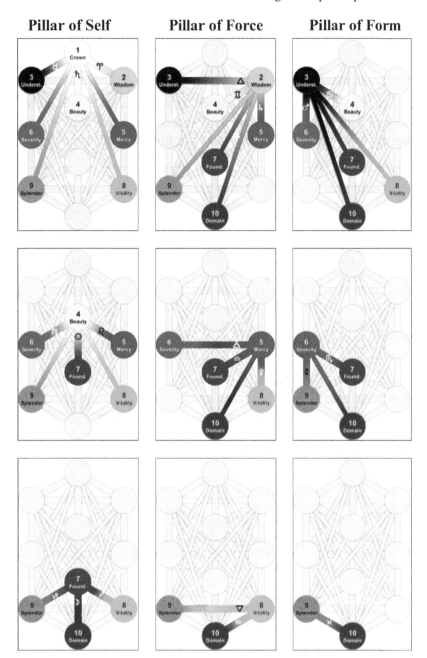

Pillar of Self   Pillar of Force   Pillar of Form

GENERATING THE GATES

The sequencing of the 182 Gates of the Gra Tree (and the 231 Gates of the Hebrew Tree as well) follows a *Creative Sequence*. That is to say, top-to-bottom and right-to-left the Paths that create each Sephirot, along with all the Paths above, are what form each Gate in sequence. Thus there are no Gates of Kether since Kether is not created by anything higher. Therefore, the first Gate is a Linear Gate of Chokmah: Kether> Heh/Aries> Chokmah (top-left of previous page).

As we progress through the Tree, the Gates become more complex and involve up to six Paths and Sephirot. Gate shapes are: linear (two Sephirot and one Path), triangular (three Sephirot and three Paths), quadrangular (four Sephirot and four Paths), pentangular (five Sephirot and five Paths), and hexangular (six Sephirot and six Paths).

Each linear Gate sets the stage for subsequent triangles, quadrangles, etc. Let's take the Gates of Tiphareth as an example. Here are all the Gates of Tiphareth in order (presented top-to-bottom but *left-to-right* for the English reader):

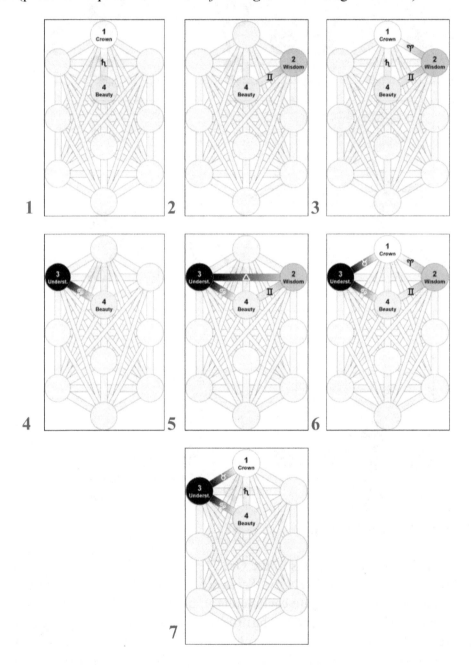

Before we arrive at the Gates of Tiphareth in the Creative Sequence, Binah and Chokmah have already been created, so the Tree that the new Gates will be added to looks like this:

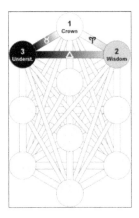

So these three Paths of Heh/Aries, Vav/Taurus and Shin/Air have already been activated and any new linear Gates are able to make more complex Gates (triangles and quadrangles) with them. To illustrate: In figure 1 above, the linear Gate of Kether> Beth/Saturn> Tiphareth does not form any Gates (i.e., *geometric forms*) with what is already there, but with the addition of the linear Gate of Chokmah> Zayin/Gemini> Tiphareth (figure 2), a triangular Gate is subsequently formed with the inclusion of the Path of Heh/Aries which exists already (figure 3).

While all seven are considered *Gates of Tiphareth*, within that total we can define further sub-sets. Figure 1 would be a *Gate of Beth/Saturn* and figures 2 and 3 would be Gates of Zayin/Gemini – Zayin being the Path that generated the subsequent geometric form(s). This generative Path determines the sub-set and is always the starting point when working a Gate. For example in figure 3, the sequence of this Gate goes like this: Chokmah> Zayin/Gemini> Tiphareth> Beth/Saturn> Kether> Heh/Aries> Chokmah.

This is considered the Gate's *forward* or *primary* motion but, when *working* a Gate, one follows its forward motion first and then back-tracks, going in the opposite direction till once again reaching the starting point. By doing this, each Path is experienced from two different perspectives: forward and backward.

Working the Gates & The Magic of Essential Form

So what do I mean by *working* a Gate? Why would you want to do it and what does the Magic of Essential Form have to do with anything? What the heck is this Magic anyway? Well, I believe I can answer all these questions at once, because to *work* a Gate is to practice the Magic of Essential Form.

Have you ever heard of "path-working"? It was a popular technique several decades ago (I don't know anymore) at least, in the Golden Dawn-ish magical "community" applied mostly to working with the Tarot and the Tattvas, etc. One took either a mental or astra-mental journey into the Tarot imagery and followed the "path" presented. Basically one steps into the mental or astra-mental projection of the Tarot card and goes for a walk of discovery, letting the symbolism guide you along. This turns out to be a valid technique that can lead to many insights that are otherwise difficult to attain to – as long as you're careful to discern between self-delusion or fantasy and actual insight.

You *can* benefit from path-working or not and it all depends on you and how well you know yourself.

The Magic of Essential Form and Gate-working are similar to path-working. The main difference is the incorporation of Essential Meaning and letting that drive the *Form* of your experience/journey. With Gate-working, EM is the teacher and the director that informs the whole experience. And when combined with the Magic of Essential Meaning and its ability to *become* EM, working the Gates becomes truly transformative, expands one's Understanding exponentially and can even have powerful effects upon one's surroundings.

What one does when working a Gate is begin by immersing oneself in the EM of each Sephirot and Path(s) involved in the Gate. If you are able, you should even *become* these various EMs. Then incorporate all the intellectual information you know about the respective Sephirot and Path(s). Let *both* the EM and the intellectual information fill your awareness.

Then project your awareness (higher mind) into the EM of the starting Sephirot, letting the EM and intellectual storehouse dictate the scenery (if any) and events as *you* make the *shift in awareness* from one Sephirotic state to the next. As you make that shift in awareness, travel along the Path to the next Sephirah. And so on until you reach the end; and then, reverse direction and make all those shifts in the opposite direction.

A Gate working is *always* followed with a period of reflection and integration so that the information gleaned will be retained and actually mean something other than just an interesting experience. No matter what your particular level of ability, working a Gate *always* teaches you something new (usually lots of things).

The first working of a Gate you will probably be stumbling around a bit in unfamiliar territory and that is why I recommend working each Gate at least three times in succession for your first experience. The second time you'll be a little more sure-footed and on the third go 'round, you'll be relaxed enough to look around and take more of it in.

The *magic* part of that process occurs when you project your awareness (your mental body) into the EM of the Sephirot and travel *through* various EMs of other Paths and Sephirot. <u>You are giving form to the EM</u>; or rather, you are providing the mental substance that the EM will in-form. The EM will resonate with what is within your intellect and teach you new things.

That is the Magic of EF in a nutshell: we turn EM into a *form* in the same way that we turn the Philosophical Elements into substances that we accumulate and project, etc. And since EM *always* expresses its meaning, we learn from the experience and our Understanding grows.

The Magic of EF is all about Understanding or Binah and the reason I have called this the *Book of Taurus* is because the Path of Vav/Taurus is the avenue by which Kether initially creates Binah. I have applied this magic to the Gra Tree of Life because it is itself a sort of Essential Form and makes a good training ground (aside from what you will learn from the Gates themselves about the Cosmos); but this magic can be applied to any symbol or symbol set. Just combine the EM with your intellectual understanding and go for a journey within it and through it.

COMPREHENSIVE COMMENTARY

UPON ALL 182 GATES
PLUS THE 10 SEPHIROT

I HEREBY PRESENT TO YOU, FOR THE FIRST TIME EVER, MY WRITTEN PRACTICAL COMMENTS ON ALL 182 GATES OF THE GRA TREE OF LIFE, PLUS THE 10 SEPHIROT. MANY OF THESE COMMENTS COME FROM MY PRIOR YOUTUBE VIDEO SERIES BUT HAVE BEEN ENTIRELY REWRITTEN, MAKING THESE MY *FINAL* WORDS ON THE MATTER.

IT HAS TAKEN ME ALMOST 40 YEARS OF STUDY AND 30 YEARS OF DEDICATED PRACTICE WORKING THE GATES TO BE ABLE TO WRITE THESE WORDS FOR YOU. I HOPE THEY GUIDE YOU WELL!

KETHER / CROWN

כתר

KEYWORD: "I"

So I've introduced you to the Tree of Life symbol in general and its five parts; now my plan is to take you through the 182 Gates (plus the 10 Sephirot) in detail. The order we will follow is called the Creative Sequence. However, this doesn't *really* happen sequentially, instead it happens all at once; it just is and always has been. But in order to comprehend it with our sequentialized awareness, we need to approach it in this way of sequence; otherwise it's simply too much for us to hold in our minds all at one time.

We start at the beginning of the sequence with Kether but it's not just the beginning: it's also the *whole* of the sequence wrapped into one.

In truth, the figure on the left is the *same* as the figure on the right. The figure on the right exists *within* the figure on the left. The *whole* of the figure on the right is *within* Kether. Look at the EM of both figures and Understand how this is so.

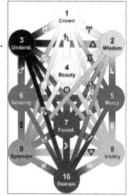

Everything is contained within Kether and everything is Awareness. It happens all at once and without any sequence or time. It has no beginning, nor end; it just is. This means there is no *singular act* of creation . . . no big bang, etc.

While keeping this in the back of our minds, we must now turn to treating Kether, like all the Sephirot, as an arbitrarily defined static state of awareness in order to understand it in the broader context. You'll have to bear with me because it is *very* difficult for me to describe Kether as a *static* state since it encompasses an infinite number of perspectives. It's hard for me to wrap my words around both simultaneously!

Kether means "crown" and represents the *static* state of The One Awareness or "I". A crown sits atop, above the *normal* awareness of the human head; it's a separate type of awareness. But a crown is just a pretty piece of jewelry if it's not sitting on a head and making a queen or king. It *confers* the powers of a monarch upon the chosen one and is the true source of all their powers of rulership. In fact, all coronation rituals are rooted in the act of connecting the monarch-to-be with the higher powers held within the crown.

The higher power conferred by Kether is the unified Awarenesses of **ALL** that exists. In other words, Kether is _ALL_ Awareness, in one and all at once, eternally. I call this The "I" or The Unity or The One Self. Imagine the awarenesses of every one of the infinite number of things that exist in the whole of the infinite Universe, all joined together as one: that is Kether. And since every mental, astral and physical thing is made of the stuff of Awareness, you also have to include the whole of the infinite *manifest* universe as well into your conception of Kether.

Static Kether is an *undifferentiated* state of "I"ness. It does not think of itself as being a combination of an infinite number of parts: it sees itself as One Thing. It *is* The "I"; the same "I" you have learned to connect with inside yourself. But The "I" inside of you is just the first touching of Kether; just a bit of the eventual experience. Our descent from Kether through the body of the Tree, will teach us the fullness of Kether, bit by bit.

So, there's the static Kether in which the Awareness just *is*; but there are two more perspectives within that static state. The first is Kether looking "outward" (or "upward" in the Tree diagram) to whatever lies beyond or 'other than' itself (called *Ayin Soph Aur* by the ancients). The human mind cannot possibly comprehend the *Ayin* because it logically cannot exist since Kether itself is **ALL** that exists and the Ayin cannot be any part of Kether. It cannot exist, plain and simple, and our minds cannot deal with the non-existent; we cannot even find words to begin describing it. <u>Only Kether can comprehend the *Ayin*</u>.

The other perspective is looking within or *Self-Realization*. It is the *nature*, the primary urge and characteristic of all awareness, to self-realize. That's just what Awareness does: it self-realizes.

To truly rise as a human consciousness to Kether is an interesting experience. Many say it's not possible or it's dangerous and you'll lose yourself, etc. But this is simply not true and whoever tells you this is either uniformed or trying to dissuade you from experiences that it's your birthright to have. Your awareness is tethered to your physical body until your incarnation ends and you will *always* to return to it, no matter where you travel with your spirit (mind). Furthermore, it is the "goal" or "fate" of *ALL* awarenesses to return to their source in Kether, never a death sentence! Another way to say it is: <u>Kether is rooted in Malkuth</u>, always.

For me, and I suspect for most humans, the experience of Kether is one of Brilliance. There is an infinite whiteness to the light, without any definition at all. There is the sensation of spatial infinite-ness and eternal Now-ness. And then, when I look within, the whole Tree and the whole Cosmos open up before me.

Then Self-Realization begins and leads to Chokmah . . .

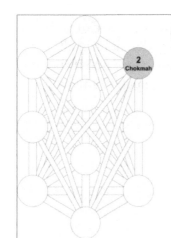

CHOKMAH / WISDOM

חוכמה

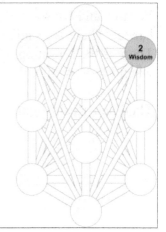

KEYWORDS: "I *AM*",
ESSENTIAL MEANING,
KETHRIC BRILLIANCE

Where Kether *is* Light, Chokmah is *filled with* Light; and whereas Kether is "*I*", Chokmah is "I *am*". The "I" has recognized that it *exists*: it has *be*ing and its being *means* something. [I suggest you meditate long and deep over these two sentences before continuing. It is vital that you Understand what is being said here.]

The light that fills Chokmah is called the *Kethric Brilliance*. This Brilliance is caused by the "I" Awareness moving as it were, toward Self-realization. All movement of the "I" Awareness within ItSelf causes the Kethric Brilliance to appear. One can even say the KB *is* the movement of the "I" Awareness.

This Brilliance illuminates the meaning of The "I" and The "I" sees every detail of its infinite Being within Chokmah. What it sees is its *Essential Meaning*, the meaning that is the *essence* of all its infinite parts, the meaning that is true for *every* part of ItSelf.

The "I" realizes that it is also a *Unity of Parts*, infinite in number and variety. It is the *whole* of existence and while it is undifferentiated in Chokmah, it sees all of its differentiated parts manifest "below" in the temporal realm.

Chokmah, like Kether, also has three perspectives: Looking "upward" to Kether it feels no separation; looking around itself it sees that it is a Unified whole of infinite parts; and, looking "downward" it sees all of its infinite number of parts, *all* of its EM, spread out before it in various stages of differentiation and manifestation.

Static Chokmah *is* EM; undifferentiated but with full awareness of its inevitable differentiation. EM is *objective* meaning. It's not *your* meaning or *my* meaning: it is *every*thing's meaning. It is infinite and eternal; supernal and temporal. And EM is not a passive thing: it actively seeks to *express* itself. EM *must* express itself as part of the Self-realization of The "I".

This static state of Awareness is given the name Chokmah (or *Wisdom* in English) because, to the human mind, this is a state of pure *knowing*, of always having the right information and of seeing to the very heart of every matter. There is nothing that the Chokmah awareness does not know and so when the human mind merges with Chokmah, *all* knowledge becomes available.

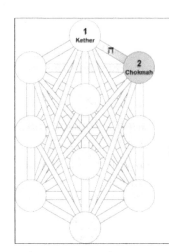

GATE #1

ה HEH (WINDOW)

ARIES ♈

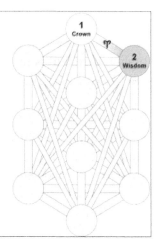

Sequence: Crown <ARIES> Wisdom

Return: Wisdom <ARIES> Crown

Keyword: Self-realization

This is probably *the most* power-filled Gate you will ever experience; but it will probably be years from now before you will fully comprehend it! Ha!

Heh is the first movement of The "I", the initialization of Its Self-realization. As such, this is where the KB is born and at the terminus of this Path in Chokmah, the EM arises. In other words, this is *really* important stuff! Perhaps <u>*THE*</u> most important stuff as it marks the very birth of the manifest Cosmos.

This is indicated by the assignation of the zodiacal sign of Aries: cardinal Fire, ruled by Mars and the birth of the cycle of 12 signs. Like Aries, it's very forceful in nature; it does not hesitate but rather flows immediately toward its goal. There is simply no denying its will to Self-realize.

Heh / Aries represents that movement in the Awareness of The "I"; that "turning of its head" toward Self-realization and recognizing that it does indeed exist. It is the very beginning of Self-discovery. From a sequentialized human perspective, the Awareness of The "I" illuminating ItSelf in this way is *the most* creative act. Thus this is the Gate of creation and creating and will eventually confer these powers to the traveler. It will also confer all the powers of Aries beyond creativity.

To begin, you must imbibe the EM of this Gate's image and sharply focus your mind on the contents of your intellectual understanding of all the components of the Gate. When you feel ready, mentally *step into* Kether. By "step into" I mean raise your awareness to your "I" and literally imagine yourself standing in Kether, surrounded by Brilliance.

At *every* step of the way throughout your journey you *must* seek to perceive the EM of your surroundings and of the concepts presented to you. <u>At *every* step</u>!

Once oriented, you must make that Heh / Aries shift in the Awareness of The "I" as it recognizes that it exists, that it has being and that it means something. In actuality, that shift is instantaneous but you should strive to slow it down and savor (and learn from) every moment.

Eventually you arrive in Chokmah to the fullness of your realization. You see and feel the wholeness of your EM, chomping at the bit to express itself. You feel yourself to be the Unity of Parts and feel your state of undifferentiation. Then you look "down" and see the differentiation of the infinite manifest universe below.

When you are ready, return your gaze "up" to Kether. Feel its closeness: it's just a mere turn of the head away. Remember and feel what you went through along the Path of Heh / Aries to get here from Kether. See and feel the KB raining down upon you.

Now pass back "up" (against the natural flow) from Chokmah to Kether until you stand in Kether once again. *Feel* the difference between these two Sephirotic states. Study that difference! And feel every inch of that transition as you pass between the two.

Reacclimatize yourself to Kether and note the differences, if any, in your experience of Kether now that you have worked this Gate. Look "back" at Chokmah and note how, if at all, this feels different than the first time you looked over.

When you have absorbed all that you can (or when you feel ready at any rate), return to a normal state of awareness and move immediately into contemplation of your experience. Write down any salient points if that is your inclination. The point here is that **you must always integrate your experiences of Gate working into your normal awareness**. If you do not do this final step, much will be lost and your transformation will be slowed, so please never neglect it!

I recommend that you work this Gate at *least* three times before moving on to another.

In this process you need to trust yourself and trust the intelligence or spirit of Tree (its EM basically). There is no 'right' or 'wrong' in this work: your experience will be what it *will* be and that will be as it *should* be! Don't judge and expect: just *learn*. To *learn* from the Gates is, after all, the whole point. Oh, and of course, to *enjoy* yourself!

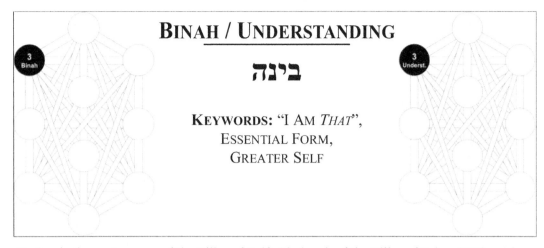

BINAH / UNDERSTANDING

בינה

KEYWORDS: "I Am *THAT*",
ESSENTIAL FORM,
GREATER SELF

Kether is the root source of the Pillar of Self; Chokmah of the Pillar of Force (EM); and now we have Binah as the root source of the Pillar of Form (EF). The point (Kether), the line (Chokmah) and the triangle (Binah). This is the archetypal triune set of relationships in the Tree, echoed by Tiphareth-Gedulah-Geburah and Yesod-Netzach-Hod.

EM *must* express itself. It literally shouts its meaning to the cosmos and in so doing, it Forms the cosmos. Binah then is the *expression* of Chokmah's EM and EM *always* expresses itself through Essential Form. Binah *is* EF; the perfect compliment to Chokmah's EM. Neither can exist without the other.

Binah is where EM begins to take expression through form and the forms in Binah are as infinite in number as the particles of EM in Chokmah. In Binah, specific forms are infinitely finite in Duration (in fact there is no duration here) and forms are always changing. Change here, is infinite and specific forms are only fleetingly temporary. But *Form* itself, like change, is infinite and eternal.

There is no sequence to the Forms forming in Binah and no true differentiation; just infinitely changing shapes and sizes, colors and textures, etc. It's fascinatingly frenetic.

Although the foundational, root state of Awareness is Unification and Oneness (Kether), the process of Self-realization that The "I" has embarked upon requires a self-examination of *all* Its parts. This necessitates a splitting apart of the Unity of EMs, a process of defining and differentiating; and that begins here, in Binah.

At first, Binah appears dark and this is because all of the KB streaming in as EM from Chokmah is absorbed and transmuted into Form. But this is only an initial experience which changes over time as one acclimates. You see, Binah has all these layers to it, all these levels of in-forming and increasing distance between those particles of EM that were United in Chokmah.

Those layers will help me explain Binah. At its highest, most rarified level Binah looks "upward" to *both* Chokmah (its immediate predecessor) and Kether. From Chokmah it receives a powerful *rush* of EM and from Kether is receives a purifying influx that guarantees the absolute *rightness* of all its Forms. Both come with KB: the influx from Kether with the purest form of KB; and, that from Chokmah, transformed into EM and therefore not as bright.

At the, shall we say, 'static state' level to which we refer by the label 'Binah', we have the darkened tumult of forms, not a one of which we can pin down and truly identify.

Slightly "below" this level, the Unity's *urge to merge* starts to take hold amidst this process of spitting apart, and similar (in the broadest sense) EMs start to gather together. This marks the onset of the formation of what I call *Greater Selves*. As we penetrate deeper and deeper into the layers of Binah, these Greater Selves become more and more specific in their composition of EMs. Eventually we start to see Greaters that portend things that inhabit the material realm; such as a Greater of planetary bodies, of stars, of various minerals, of various species of plants and animals, etc., etc., ever more specific as we descend.

Eventually we reach a point where everything becomes too close to differentiation for the supernal realm to support and Binah gives birth to the temporal, sequential realm of differentiation (Tiphareth). Thus *every* thing in our realm has <u>a</u> Greater Self in Binah that gave birth to its own Solitary Self or Temporal Mental Body.

The personal Greater Self in Binah is also known as The "Holy Guardian Angel" in some traditions but this is too impersonal for my tastes. Each GS gives birth to (or *projects* into the temporal realm) many Solitary Selves throughout the infinite stream of time-space, all for the purpose of incarnation. In this way, The "I" Self-realizes through <u>personal interaction with itself</u>.

We have an extremely intimate relationship with our personal GS. It is the little voice inside that tells us right from wrong and that is always guiding us along the way. It is a guardian angel in that sense but it is also a very strict task-master that accepts only our best effort. In other words, it is the long arm of karma or *universal necessity*, always correcting our footsteps when we stray from our path. So Binah is where we go when we wish to commune directly, face-to-face with our GS.

The Solitary Selves projected by a GS are aspects of its own quantity or arrangement of EM, so each Individual's character reflects that of the GS. The Individuals actually make up the GS or rather; the GS projects the *whole* of itself into the temporal realm by way of its Individuals. In other words, the GSes are the *substance* of the temporal realm and they inhabit this substance with their Awareness. They are *always* aware of every second of their material manifestations because they *are* their manifestations; they *are* the Awareness within each one of us, living every moment of our existences. We are each little bits of our GS made manifest.

Binah is also the birth place of *continuity;* a force closely akin to karma that glues changes together and which matures along with the temporal realm.

With the experiencing of the Binah state of Awareness you may come to understand the nature of Form and, most specifically, how EM becomes EF. This is the Mystery of the sequence from "*I*" to "I *am*" to "I am *that*".

Binah, like all of the Sephirot of the Pillar of Form, gives birth to the next level of Self along the central Pillar of Self. She represents Supernal Fertility and is known as "The Bright Fertile Mother".

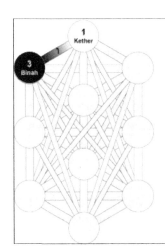

GATE #2

ו VAV (NAIL)
TAURUS ♉

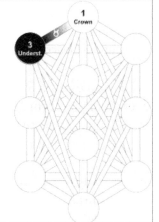

Sequence: Crown <TAURUS> Underst.

Return: Underst. <TAURUS> Crown

Keyword: Perfection

The Hebrew 'Vav' means *nail* in English: something that binds one thing to another. To this is assigned the zodiacal sign of Taurus (fixed Earth), which is ruled by the planet Venus. From this alone we can see the influences of earthy groundedness and innocent beauty.

Add to this the fact that it represents the shift in Awareness from Kether to Binah, and we see that here The "I" comes to rest in the natural beauty of its own Form. There is a sense of gentle satisfaction in the successful expression of its EM; a majestic and glorious sort of peacefulness.

Ultimately, this Gate is about the *perfection* of all the forms of Binah and of the process of transforming EM into EF. Each form is a *perfectly* correct and utterly clear expression of each particle of EM. *Perfectly*! This is the perfection of Nature herself: it could be no other way.

Working this Gate brings many realizations about the nature of Form, its origins and the inherent perfection of *all* forms. One also comes to see and Understand the *aliveness* of all forms. This Gate is especially beneficial to anyone involved with the creative arts!

The working method is exactly the same as the last Gate of Heh / Aries.

To begin, you must imbibe the EM of this Gate's image and sharply focus your mind on the contents of your intellectual understanding of all the components of the Gate. When you feel ready, mentally *step into* Kether. By "step into" I mean raise your awareness to your "I" and literally imagine yourself standing in Kether, surrounded by Brilliance.

When sufficiently oriented, look "down" to Binah and try to sense what that transition in states of Awareness feels like. Begin walking down the Path of Vav / Taurus toward Binah, from the state of undifferentiated Oneness into infinite Form. Learn from every step along the way.

What does this Path have to teach you about Form and its relationship with Awareness and EM? How does The "I" become Form and why? Take your time in this descent and learn everything you can.

When you eventually arrive in Binah, feel the relative solidity and the way that the ever-changing forms envelop you, giving voice to all your Meaning. Look "down" into the temporal cosmos and realize just how intimately The "I" is connected and involved in every moment of its existence . . .

When ready, look "upward" to Kether and travel back, against the natural flow of Vav / Taurus. Feel all Form and need for Form drop away as you return to the infinite simplicity of The Source: Kether. Does it feel any differently upon your return than when you started?

As before, repeat this Gate at least three times before moving on to another.

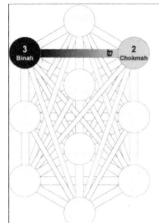

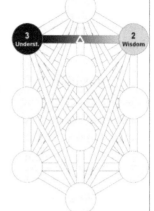

GATE #3

ש SHIN (TOOTH)

ARCHETYPAL FIRE △

Sequence: Wisdom <FIRE> Underst.

Return: Underst. <FIRE> Wisdom

Keyword: Supernal Fire

The Hebrew 'Shin' means *tooth* in English. What does a tooth do? I grinds our food down into small bits so that we can digest it and make use of in the maintenance and growth of our bodies. It plays a big part in maintaining our physical aliveness. The Path of Shin has much the same function: it is the insatiable desire within EM to express itself through EF; thereby turning EM into something that will enable its own further Self-realization through Form. It begins the process of breaking up the Unified EM of Chokmah into its infinity of parts; so that it may become the infinity of forms in Binah. Through Shin each little particle of EM manifests this unstoppable desire to express itself and cumulatively, they form Binah. Shin is Chokmah's "birth canal" for Binah.

Shin is the Mother Letter of the *Supernal Fire*; such is its level of energy and frenetic desire of all that EM to express itself. The Supernal Fire is the orgasmic explosion of that Unity of Parts into an infinite number of parts, infinitely changing. Here too is the birth of *Infinite Change* as well as *Infinite Continuity* (which gives Meaning to all those changes).

Change is the aliveness of EM by way of the fact that it needs an infinite number of forms to fully express itself, and only through Infinite Change can that infinity be achieved in the temporal realm. And Infinite Continuity is those treads of EM that run through everything and bind all the temporal moments together into a singular Now.

Shin is really the driving force, the energy that moves it all forward, of the entire tree. It is the <u>will to Self-realize</u> inherent to The "I" and to Awareness ItSelf. It is *the* strongest power, period. And Self-realization . . . is twin to Self-expression: the one necessitates the other.

Of the three Paths thusfar, Shin has the strongest directional flow to it (from Chokmah toward Binah). You will likely be swept away by it the first time you experience it and it will take some focused will to slow your progress. And slowing your progress will be necessary to give you time to absorb some of what is happening;

otherwise it goes by too swiftly for comprehension. It's sort of like a massive river flowing into the sea: it's all rush, rush, rush till you get to the sea, then it's "ahhhhhh, at last" and relaxation as you merge with the ocean of Form in Binah.

This connection between Chokmah and Binah is called *Chashmal* ("speaking silence") in certain Kabbalistic texts in order to point out a very powerful type of magic that is learned here. This is the Universal Language that does not require words (though words are often a part of its speaking). With this language it is possible to communicate directly with *any* thing, be it person, animal or stone. This is the language of EM which expresses itself through forms of *every* kind. It is constantly being spoken by everything, everywhere. Only, very few humans know it even exists!

The first part of learning to speak this language, is to train yourself to *hear* it; or rather, to *perceive* it. This is, of course, the direct perception of EM with which you are already familiar and actively using. Working this Gate will open you to the possibility of also *speaking* in EM, for if you do take your time and slow your passage, you can learn a great deal about the mechanics of transforming EM into EF.

Because of its strong directional flow, you may find the journey back to Chokmah from Binah difficult at first. All it takes is determination and persistence and you will soon manage it (and eventually master it).

Working this Gate is just like the last two linear Gates so I won't describe the whole process again. You can easily figure it out for yourself. The only real difference is that you start out in Chokmah instead of Kether: you "step into" it just as you did before.

And as usual, the rule of three repetitions applies.

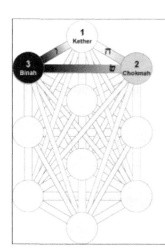

GATE #4

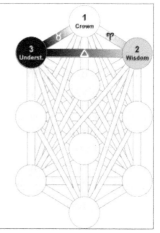

Sequence: ↻ Wisdom <FIRE> Underst.
<TAURUS> Crown <ARIES> Wisdom

Return: ↻ Wisdom <ARIES> Crown
<TAURUS> Underst. <FIRE> Wisdom

This is the first triangular Gate out of 54, and it's the archetype of the three upward pointing triangles on the Tree: the *Supernal Triangle*. This triune set of relationships, between Paths *and* Sephirot, is echoed at all three levels. The foundation of each triangle is a Mother Letter and that infinite continuum between Force and Form; initiated by a Fire sign and perfected by an Earth sign.

This is considered the <u>second Gate of Shin / Fire</u> since that is the "lowest" Path in the Gate and is the second Gate starting with Shin. Thus Chokmah and the Path of Shin will be our starting place.

Working a Gate with 3, 4, 5, or 6 sides is naturally more complex and involves a mixing of perspectives and states of Awareness that a linear Gate does not. This mixing of multiple states is the whole goal of working the more complex geometric forms. It's a process of integration wherein you learn how *all* the aspects of The "I" work together as One. The integration of each additional perspective broadens your experience of each part. It also makes each part you touch upon a more permanent and stable aspect of your character.

This Gate will teach you about the triune nature of The "I" and, in time, how to make use of that knowledge. By uniting these three Sephirot, you will stabilize and mature your conception, perception and experience of the Supernal Realm within your awareness.

Since this is our first triangle and therefore more complex, I will talk you through its working as I did with our first two linear Gates.

To begin, you must imbibe the EM of this Gate's image and sharply focus your mind on the contents of your intellectual understanding of *all six* components of the Gate. When you feel ready, mentally *step into* Chokmah. You stand amid an infinite ocean of EM. *See* and *feel* its unending expanse and infinite variety, all waiting, needing, chomping at the bit to express themselves. They *must* express themselves! Feel that explosive energy, ready to burst.

Then let it burst and travel with the powerful outflow of Fiery Shin into Binah. You arrive transformed into infinite Form; rising and falling in ever changing shapes and sizes and colors. You have brought Chokmah with you into Binah and now, as that conjoined Chokmah-Binah Awareness, you look "up" to Kether and travel against the flow along the Path of Vav / Taurus.

This is a return home, as it were, to the Infinite Simplicity of The "I"; a letting go of all hints of Form. You have brought Chokmah and Binah into Kether with you and now your Awareness encompasses all three simultaneously. [Note: This simultaneity of Awarenesses might take a while to get used to. Nonetheless it is well worth mastering!]

Now, as The "I"-Chokmah-Binah, look "down" to Chokmah and renew your process of Self-Realization. Reaffirm your identity as "I *Am*!" as you pass along the Path of Heh / Aries. Let those Creative juices flow as you descend into infinite EM. In what ways does Chokmah feel different now that you've been around once?

When you are ready, you must return in the opposite direction around the triangle. Be ready for new lessons along the way!

From Chokmah, pass "up" against the flow, along the Path of Heh / Aries to Kether, letting go of even Meaning. Then "down" (with the flow) along the Path of Vav / Taurus; immersing yourself in the outpouring of perfection into Binah and its infinite tumult of ever-changing Form. Then you must make your way against the natural flow, "up" the Path of Shin / Fire for a final return to Chokmah and undifferentiated EM.

Take careful note of how your experience of Chokmah has changed (if at all) since the beginning of this Gate. Repeat at least three time per usual.

TIPHARETH / BEAUTY

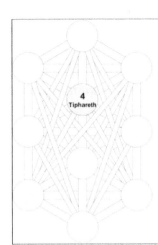

תפארת

KEYWORDS: "I AM *THAT 'I AM'*",
SOLITARY SELF

Differentiation. That's an interesting word, an interesting concept, especially in the context of a Universe that up until this point has been totally *un*differentiated. It is a radical shift, one that changes *everything*.

The "I", in its process of Self-realization, must now explode or shatter (both images have been used by the ancients) into an infinite array of different parts; each of which is a unique expression of specific parts of the Unity of EM. The Unity *must* now become *manifest* as an infinity of parts. At first, that manifestation is as little bits of Awareness, little reflections of The "I", which I call the *Solitary Selves*.

Each Solitary Self is a discrete, autonomous awareness in and of itself. Hand-in-hand with this explosive splitting of The "I" Awareness comes – *for the very first time* – cognizance of 'other', as the Solitary Self finds itself standing in an infinite universe filled with 'other' little reflections of The "I" just like itself. 'Self' is suddenly surrounded by 'other'; and from this moment on, the Self-realization of The "I" is all bound up in the relationship between 'self' and 'other'.

Each Solitary Self of Tiphareth *knows* that it is made of exactly the same "I"-stuff as 'other' and recognizes its unity with all its fellows, but at the same time it recognizes its own uniqueness. It alone in all that infinity of Solitary Selves expresses this one selection of particles of EM, in this specific ratio, etc. It is both unique *and* alike, simultaneously.

Each of the Solitary Selves is, in effect, a small version of "the "I". That's why we say: "I" for Kether, "I *am*!" for Chokmah, "I am *that*" for Binah, and "I am *that 'I am'*!" for Tiphareth. Each Solitary Self is an *"I am"* in its own right and the whole infinite number of them together constitute The "I". In other words, The "I" has become manifest *as* Its parts; or at least with Tiphareth it has taken the first steps toward that end.

An important lesson about the nature of The "I" and Awareness is that its process of Self-realization necessitates that it encounter itself as 'other' in order to truly get to know itself. It has to see itself from the *out*side as well as the *in*side; and the only way it can achieve that is through splitting itself into parts *and inhabiting all of those parts*. It's ingenious!!! And it *is* Beautiful . . .

So all those Greater Selves in the lowest part of Binah feel the great heaviness of their EM and its need to express itself *more*, ever *more* and in ever new ways. The Greaters *must* and *cannot* do otherwise than empty their contents out and form (Binah is the Mother of Form) a universe that is fully differentiated; where all if its EM can differentiate and express its fullness.

And so the universe of an infinite number of Solitary Selves is "born". *Every* thing that exists mentally, astrally and physically, has a Solitary Self "above/behind/within" it: it is a thing's *temporal mental body*. [The *eternal* mental body is the thing's Greater Self.]

This means that there exists a "phase" or "area" within which the *un*differentiated transitions into a *differentiated* state; where the *inevitable* becomes the *actualized*. We have come to call it the Akasha or the Abyss and numerous other names depending on how it is conceived. I prefer *Akasha* because it sounds nice and is non-adversarial. <grin>

Many think of Akasha as a substance but it is not. It cannot be accumulated or projected in the way of an Element or energy and is, in fact, more properly *a state of being*. One *enters* the Akasha and one projects *into* the Akasha, usually for the purpose of realizing a noble desire of some sort. When an empowered act of will is introduced into the Akasha, into that phase of reality where possibilities become probabilities become inevitabilities become actualities, then that desire can do nothing other than descend through the layers of manifestation. This is a Law of Nature (which is another way of saying "that's just the way it is").

This "zone" of Akasha exists metaphorically between Binah and Tiphareth or, more accurately, between the supernal triad and Tiphareth (i.e., below the Path of Shin / Fire). This zone represents a radically different mode or level of manifestation of Awareness; so different that it is most often experienced as some sort of barrier, or vast black gulf or Abyss to *human* awareness. This is the origin the idea of it being an Abyss and why one of the names of Binah is *Dark Sterile Crone*.

Basically, it requires a different part of our awareness, of *Mind*, to cross the Abyss than we're used to using. The experience is so foreign to our norm that it seems impenetrable at first, but *not* insurmountable. The trick is to genuinely let go of *all* expectations and *all* preconceptions and just *be* in the Now.

Tiphareth and in fact *all* the Sephirot (and Paths) from here on in, have a dual significance: both <u>universal</u> and <u>personal</u>. It pertains the movement of The "I" Awareness throughout ItSelf *and* it pertains to *you personally* and to every Solitary Self. This is truly a dimensional shift in the Tree!

As your Greater Self in Binah, you make that radical shift and squeeze a bit of yourself down into the differentiated state of Tiphareth as just one teeny tiny Solitary Self. Actually your Greater projects countless Solitary Selves but our discussion here concerns just *you* and *your* solitary Self.

You stand shoulder-to-shoulder amid an infinite ocean of 'other' Solitary Selves. You realize that you are all connected through The "I" and that little reflection you each carry; and yet you are alone, in yourself, by yourself, surrounded by a unknowable 'other', *lots* of 'other'. You feel oddly alone and yet intimately connected, both equally and at the same instant.

The Universal implication is that The "I" has split ItSelf into an infinite number of differentiated parts *all* of which (the *whole* infinity) are having the aforementioned realizations about 'self' and 'other'. The Universe is readjusting ItSelf.

When you look "down" from Tiphareth, the whole of the manifest universe lies below you. The part of you most closely connected to your Greater Self still sees the wholeness of time and its infinite duration; but this fades and you quickly begin to experience the minutia of time-space and your single "present" incarnation (to which you are rooted).

The upper level of Tiphareth equates to the Fire region of your temporal mental body (or just Mental Body); that most volatile part of your awareness that can reach into the supernal realm and touch the Greater and The "I". The main body of Tiphareth (and all of its *Powers*) equates to the "downward" looking Air region of your Mental Body; involved in naming, deciding and thinking and all the things we equate to the intellectual functioning of awareness.

This is that Self that incarnates into a human body, over and over throughout the stream of time-space. It will put on a new Astral Body and then a new Physical Body each time; but that comes later and doesn't concern us just yet.

When you look "up" from Tiphareth, especially if you inhabit just the Fire region of your Mental Body, you will see that your connection with The "I" is immediate and there is no barrier. It is just as intimate and accessible as your incarnation: <u>you are rooted in *both* places</u>! Furthermore, your relationship with Binah and Chokmah is just as intimate and immediate, though indeed different.

For an incarnate person, Tiphareth is a sort of *refuge* from the complexity of involvement in temporal existence; a place of calm and perspective – its greatest gift to the incarnate is its *perspective*! It is the equivalent of the *Depth Point* in Franz Bardon's *Initiation Into Hermetics*.

The static state of Tiphareth is called "*Beauty*" in English because it is a truly BEAUTIFUL (all CAPS!) sight to see; that infinite ocean of little reflections of The "I". Simply beautiful, no other word will do.

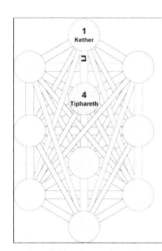

GATE #5

ב BETH (HOUSE)

SATURN ♄

Sequence: Crown <SATURN> Beauty

Return: Beauty <SATURN> Crown

Keywords: Immanence, Limitation

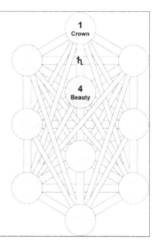

The fifth Gate is a linear Gate for the Path of Beth. 'Beth', in English, means *house*. It is the first letter of the Torah and it's said to "contain the whole Torah", such is its importance. Another indication of its significance is its attribution of the Planet Saturn, the outermost planetary Sphere. In other words, it marks a boundary and a limit to human awareness. It is the Great Limiter, Death personified.

That is certainly how the Path of Beth appears from its terminus: at one end is life as we know it and at the other, Supernal end is the Great Unknown. And because the human rational intellect is incapable of looking into the Supernal, it has been labeled as forbidden and dark, *saturnine* and unreachable other than in death. It marks a line in the sand between the known and the unknowable parts of the cosmos.

However, if we rip away all the superstition and myth, we see that this Path is nothing more, *and nothing less*, than the descent of The "I" from Kether *directly* into the infinite ocean of Solitary Selves. It is the light that fills each little reflection. In other words, the Path of Beth tells the story of the *immanence* of The "I" within the entire cosmos.

Immanence is a fundamental concept to the Kabbalistic Tree of Life! The Tree is a diagram of this immanence: it shows the way that The "I" Awareness not only spreads throughout the whole body of the cosmos; but how it *causes* the whole cosmos. And where that act of immanence occurs, where it all actually happens, is in Beth. This is where the action is.

To truly understand this Path we must start in Kether, *as* The "I" (as the Gate does). The "I" looks "down" and in so doing, It flows into the sequential universe "below": <u>for wherever the attention of The "I" focuses, the totality of Its Awareness also flows</u>. This is automatic and occurs the instant the attention turns; and, it happens in a flash of no duration.

Of course, in *working* the Gate we want to slow this act of immanence down and savor it! This is much more easily done than what was experienced with the Path of Shin; all it takes is a bit of intention and planning beforehand.

Slowing it down, we first experience a pull from "below" as if its inevitability and necessity is calling to us. As we descend (and it is with a definite feeling of *descending*) the feeling becomes one of *splitting through multiplication*. Almost exploding into an infinity of little bits. Each of the parts is both a *part* of The "I" **and** contains the *whole* of The "I" at the same time.

Halfway through Beth we cross over the Path of Shin / Fire and this has a great influence upon the process of immanentation. At this point, The "I" takes on the properties of both Chokmah and Binah: it *becomes* those particles of EM which are differentiating. It's a fiery explosion of Kethric Brilliance and EM intermixed. The rest of the descent is a time during which all those bits mature and coalesce into the Solitary Selves of Tiphareth.

Simultaneously with all this expanding and exploding, there is the pervasive sense of squeezing oneself into a very, very small container! Infinity is squeezed into a finite "house" (Beth) -- you have to remember that, not only is a *part* of The "I" present within each Solitary Self: the *whole* of The "I" is there also.

At the end of the "downward" journey of Beth, Tiphareth will be a much different experience!

The return or "upward" against-the-flow journey that completes the Gate is one of liberation, Unification and return to Source. [This is why Franz Bardon's *IIH* is associated with this Path.] During the "upward" journey, you have the opportunity to understand everything about the specific collection of EMs that you personally express and are manifesting: you can trace their whole path of evolution from undifferentiated to ultimate differentiation. The "upward" goal is, of course, the other side of Saturn not often talked about: Union with The "I"

From this Gate you will learn all about immanence and its infinite ramifications. You can also learn much about how Life creates, enters and inhabits Form. And finally you will learn about the *fact* of ultimate spiritual liberation and the primacy it holds within the human psyche.

But probably the greatest lesson of all is just how accessible, how close-at-hand The "I" is to each and every thing in the Cosmos: it is **not** some distant, unknowable deity!

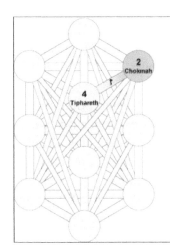

GATE #6

ז ZAYIN (SWORD)

GEMINI ♊

Sequence: Wisdom <GEMINI> Beauty

Return: Beauty <GEMINI> Wisdom

Keywords: 'Self' and 'Other'

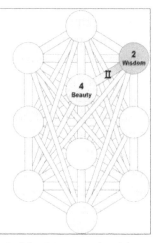

The association of the zodiacal sign Gemini (mutable Air, ruled by Mercury) with Zayin (*sword* in English) pretty much says it all. Zayin introduces the concept of 'other' and the relationship between 'self' and 'other', to the mix. As I said earlier, all of the Air signs bring something out of left field, something not really expected and quite different, always something consequential.

We're talking about the flow of EM from an undifferentiated state in Chokmah into a differentiated and fairly complex state of combination in Tiphareth. As it descends into differentiation by this Path it goes through stages: First stage is groupings of like EM; second stage of finer groupings; third stage where grouping become even more refined and starts to incorporate EMs that are not alike; and the final fourth stage of Tiphareth where the groupings are complex and finalized combinations of EMs of varying kinds (but with an underlying commonality).

The finalization process results in discrete Individualized identities (Tiphareth). As a consequence of differences in the EM composition of these identities, they each experience and perceive their shared alikeness, but more importantly, or more *consequentially*, they also perceive their differences and individual uniqueness. This causes there to be a sort of schism in the formerly Unified state of awareness and we end up identifying first 'self' and then 'other'. This makes for the necessity of *relationship* between 'self' and 'other' which sort of takes over further development. Everything below Tiphareth concerns this growing dynamic between 'self' and 'other'.

Thus the association with Gemini, the Twins, and the two-faced Janus head. And also the association with the sword imagery of Zayin: a two-sided implement.

It's interesting to note that the impetus or driving force behind this descent is the Path of Beth. That transformative descent of The "I" into Tiphareth causes a simultaneous decent from Chokmah (Zayin) and Binah (Cheth) into Tiphareth.

Working this Gate on the descent will teach you about the mechanics of the transformation from undifferentiation into differentiation; and, about how your specific cluster of EMs come to be and the ways you are related to others.

The return journey "up" against the flow will be all about the *un*-differentiation of your differentiated 'self' identity. At some distant point in your existence this will naturally occur but in the mean time, you have the opportunity to make this an act of self-will. Willfully dismantling your identity as 'self' in this manner is psychologically cleansing and liberating. Through this practice you can unite your awareness with Chokmah / Wisdom. You will also learn far more about yourself through this process: sort of like a student watchmaker who must take the watch apart to learn how it's put together.

Hidden within this Gate there sits a very potent magic having to do with the creation of discrete identities using EM.

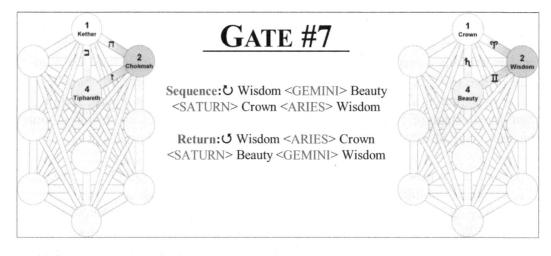

GATE #7

Sequence: ↻ Wisdom <GEMINI> Beauty <SATURN> Crown <ARIES> Wisdom

Return: ↺ Wisdom <ARIES> Crown <SATURN> Beauty <GEMINI> Wisdom

This is the second of the two Gates of Zayin and our second triangular Gate. It starts of course in Chokmah with the passage down to Tiphareth.

From this Gate you will learn all about the dynamic between the descent of The "I" via Beth into Tiphareth and why/how it drives that of Zayin. You will learn exactly how vital this dynamic of 'self' vs. 'other' is to the Self-realization of The "I" -- The "I" *must* confront ItSelf *as* 'other' to *fully* Self-realize. You will find that it is an inevitability inherent to the Path of Heh and that initial movement toward Self-realization.

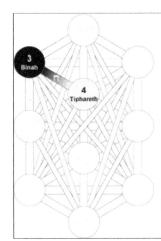

GATE #8

ח CHETH (CORRAL, FENCE)

CANCER ♋

Sequence: Underst. <CANCER> Beauty

Return: Beauty <CANCER> Underst.

Keywords: Creation of sequential realm
and Solitary Self

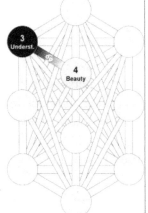

Cheth means *fence* or *corral* in English and is assigned the zodiacal sign of Cancer, the cardinal Water sign ruled by the Moon. Cancer is the Crab and crabs are known to lay an immense number of eggs at a time, up to several million over their lifetime. Each female crab is *born* with all her eggs and she releases some of them periodically as she ages. She releases them is a giant swarm of tiny little eggs into the Great Ocean basically to fend for themselves, come what may. There is no better descriptive symbolism than this for the Greater Selves of Binah in the human lexicon!

To the Greaters, the Path of Cheth is the umbilical cord and birth canal through which they give birth to the Solitary Selves which form Tiphareth. They cast their spawn throughout the stream of time-space and – here's the Mystery – each of their developing, evolving "eggs" is responsible for its own choices. In other words, she places them (us) in the hands of fate to determine our own way for ourselves, just like crab-mother does with her eggs.

The big difference between crab and Greater is that the Greater *inhabits* her own offspring. The Greater Awareness is *immanent* to all of her Solitary Selves, at the same time and eternally. She incarnates *through* her Solitary Selves. And, like Zayin, there is a transition from a relatively undifferentiated state into a differentiated state as the Greater, in effect, breaks or divides into parts. And just like The "I" in relation to each of its reflections, *both* a part of the Greater *and* the whole of the Greater exists within each of her Solitary Selves.

That transformation, that step in the Self-realization process of The "I", occurs right here in Cheth.

This is the Solitary Self's connection and immediate access to its Greater Self and to the realm of the Greaters. The Greater basically touches the Fire region of the Solitary Mental body. So this Gate is of special importance as it will connect you with your Greater Self; a connection that will prove itself to be of inestimable value!

From a Universal perspective, this Gate is about the birth of the sequential realm; about the finalization of that explosion of The One into The Many. You can learn, in detail if you wish, all about the mechanics of this transition.

From a personal perspective, the "downward" (with the flow) working of this Gate will bring an understanding of the nature and make up of your part of your Greater Self; and how, where and why you fit into the Greater's expression of its EM. You can learn all about the mechanics of that process and perhaps even how to make use of its magic.

The "upward" return journey (against the flow) is an *expansion* of awareness. Eventually, you can learn to actually merge your awareness with your Greater and see the temporal realm through your Greater's eyes, so to speak, even to the point of acting as your Greater Self.

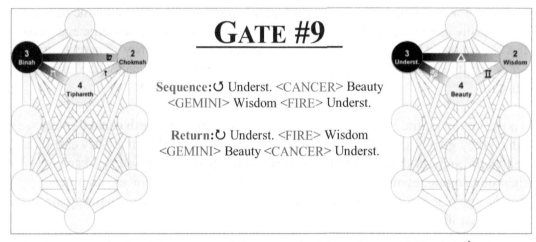

GATE #9

Sequence: ↺ Underst. <CANCER> Beauty <GEMINI> Wisdom <FIRE> Underst.

Return: ↻ Underst. <FIRE> Wisdom <GEMINI> Beauty <CANCER> Underst.

This is our third triangular Gate and the second of four Gates of Cheth (5th of 7 Gates of Tiphareth). We start of course in Binah and follow Cheth into Tiphareth.

The forward flow of this Gate takes you first (*with* the Flow) through the process of Forming your Solitary Self; then (*against* the flow) through the process of dismantling your EM and returning to the Source of the Unity of EM; and finally of engendering (*with* the flow) all the Forms of Binah. With the return flow, this process is reversed: you pass (*against* the flow) back to the source of EM; (*with* the flow) as your EM is distilled out of the Unity of EM; and finally, (*against* the flow) disassembling your self to return to the Mother of All Form, Binah and your Greater Self.

The effect of this Gate is to unite the two poles that form your Solitary Self, *through* the Fire that powers the descent into incarnation. This strengthens the constitution of your Solitary Self as well as making you more flexible and fit for the challenges of incarnation ahead. It teaches you about the symbiotic relationship of EM and EF.

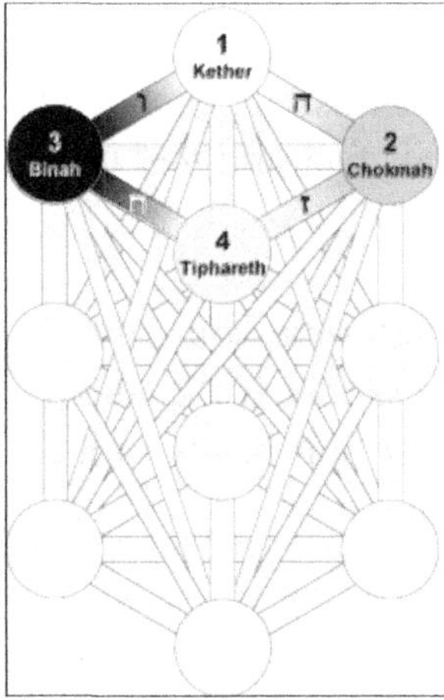

GATE #10

Sequence:↺ Underst. <CANCER> Beauty <GEMINI> Wisdom <ARIES> Crown <TAURUS> Underst.

Return:↻ Underst. <TAURUS> Crown <ARIES> Wisdom <GEMINI> Beauty <CANCER> Underst.

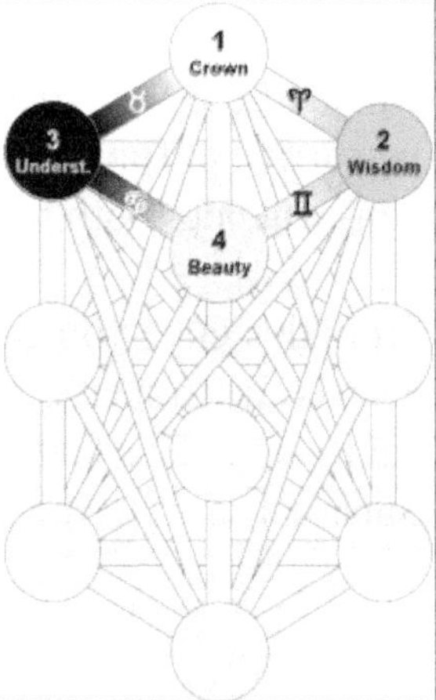

This 6th Gate of Tiphareth (and third of Cheth) is our very first quadrangular Gate. As to be expected, the quadrangles are a bit more complex than the triangles. You have to juggle yet another set of symbols and take a step further, so to speak. In comparison, the triangles are simpler and more focused Gates, while the quadrangles all tend to be more balanced and generalized. The quads always mix at least two levels of Self and sometimes three; while the triangles either one or two.

This particular quadrangle outlines the upper quad *of three* in the Gra Tree. It basically (with Shin and Beth) encompasses the Supernal Realm *and* the birth of its progeny, Tiphareth. In other words, it's the Supernal *plus* its transition into the Mental, sequential realm. It establishes the four archetypes of the Sephirot which echo in each of the following quads of the Tree. Thus: Tiphareth becomes the Kether archetype of the second quad and Yesod the Kether archetype of the third quad; Gedulah the Chokmah archetype of the second quad and Netzach of the third quad; and so on down the line. The relationships between Sephirot in the first quad are echoed in each subsequent quad.

Tiphareth in the first quad is subtly different from Tiphareth in the second quad; and likewise, Yesod in the second quad is subtly different from Yesod in the third. In the second quad, Tiphareth rules the Mental Realm and gives birth to astral Yesod; in the third quad, Yesod rules the Astral Realm and gives birth to material Malkuth.

So back to the Gate at hand: As usual we start in Binah as our Greater Self and pass *with* the flow into Tiphareth and become our Solitary Self. You will note that in this Gate, two of the Paths are traveled *with* the flow and two *against* the flow. This sequence is interesting and has a lot to do with the Gate's significance: forward is with-against-against-with and reverse is against-with-with-against. Each left-right half of the Gate is experienced differently; once with the flow and once against.

The quad you are forming with this Gate encompasses Shin and Beth and the whole of the Supernal Realm, and you should (will) be aware of this fact each time you arrive in Binah. You will do well to pause and focus on this fact and *feel* its consequences both times.

From this Gate you can learn all about the Supernal Realm. With time you may even come to merge your awareness with that Infinite Awareness that *is* the Supernal Realm. This Gate also has the effect of binding your Solitary Self firmly to its Supernal root, to the point that you will never loose sight of it.

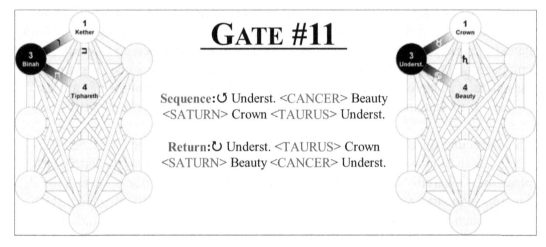

GATE #11

Sequence: ↺ Underst. <CANCER> Beauty <SATURN> Crown <TAURUS> Underst.

Return: ↺ Underst. <TAURUS> Crown <SATURN> Beauty <CANCER> Underst.

Here is our 4th triangular Gate, 4th of Cheth and 7th (last) of Tiphareth.

It is an echo of the triangular Gate #7 only this time; it has to do with Binah and EF instead of Chokmah and EM. You will learn how that descent of The "I" along Beth drives *both* Cheth and Zayin; how they balance each other, and how they are *both* simultaneous with Beth. You will also receive a gift from working this Gate in the form of understanding the *absolute* perfection of your own form: mental, astral *and* physical.

GEDULAH / MERCY

גדולה

KEYWORDS: ALIKENESS, COLLECTIVITY, SEQUENCE

Our next static state stop along our path of the Self-realization process of The "I" is Gedulah / *Mercy*, also known as Chesed / *Loving Kindness*. If you meditate on these terms you will see that they both speak of <u>affinity</u> and <u>compassion</u> which I distill into a single word: *alikeness*.

The natural, primordial or resting state of Awareness is unification. Awareness has an inbred *urge to merge* and that is the Solitary Self's first inclination. But, the Solitary Selves can no longer merge in the same way that they're used to (Kethric Unification) and the closest they can come is to *collectivize*. They recognize their degree of alikeness to 'other' and, due to the Law of the Mental Realm in which they exist ("like attracts like"), they collect or gather together with them. The more alike, the greater the attraction and closer they gather together. This produces a continuum of alikeness.

As a consequence, *sequence* becomes part of the reality of the Cosmos. This very important and rather momentous! We have here, the emergence of two new highly consequential factors pertaining to this all important relationship between 'self' and 'other': *alikeness* (the *urge to merge*) and *sequence* (forming an infinite continuum).

Each of us has a certain set of 'other' Solitary Selves that we experience similarity or alikeness with. We are thus involved (whether we are aware of it or not) in numerous collectives of awareness. For example, we all share in the collective of human awareness. We are all somewhere along that infinite continuum of alikeness of each collective. It is important to note that when you yourself experience one of the continuums on which you stand, <u>the continuum will always start with you</u>. This points to the fact that from the personal perspective, the relationship with 'other' is always ***yours*** and no one else's. We each enact this same drama of 'self'/'other'. In Gedulah/Mercy, the focus is: 'self' ***AND*** 'other'.

This is, and always will be, our starting point and fall-back position in our relations with 'other'. Remember that . . . Remember also that each Sephirot contains within itself all that follows in the Tree. This means that this *urge to merge* and to always *remember the collective*, <u>always</u> takes precedence over the Solitary Self's uniqueness and independence.

From the Universal perspective, Gedulah represents the whole infinite body of Solitary Selves aligning itself by virtue of degree of alikeness into an infinite, sequentialized continuum. From this perspective, the whole infinite body becomes a single *collective of parts* in mimicry of the higher *Unity of Parts* (Chokmah).

In Gedulah, you can expect to encounter all of the various collectives of which you are a part. These collectives are arrayed by virtue of their specificity or inclusiveness. In other words, within the broader human collective, you will find your national collective and within that, your regional collective, etc. There are layers upon layers of collectivity in Gedulah!

Through Gedulah you can get to know all about each of your collectives and even participate at a conscious level if you wish. You can also learn about collectives to which you do not belong. Also you can, if you really work at it, even become a master of the Mental Realm *Law of Attraction* (like attracts like); if nothing else, you can at least learn about this Law and its consequences.

In closing, I cannot fail to mention one of the primary consequences of this Law: so called *Divine Providence*, the universal provider. At the Universal level, this Law means that <u>every part of the Cosmos takes care of every 'other' part</u>. In real time terms, this means that *all* of your <u>needs</u> are met by the Universe, *always*. This is simply how the Cosmos is constructed, its nature. There's nothing really "divine" about it, it's just the way things work. And it's true for *every* thing that exists; all of our *needs* are always met. The problem is in not recognizing what our true **needs** are and not recognizing the hand of the Cosmos in all things.

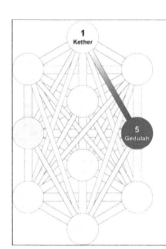

GATE #12
HIDDEN PATH: 1>5

Sequence: Crown <HP:1-5> Mercy

Return: Mercy <HP:5-1> Crown

Keyword: Urge to Merge

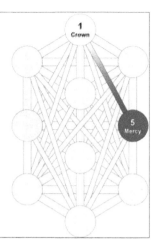

This is the first of the *un-Lettered* or *Hidden* Paths. That means it has no standard attribution and remains undescribed in that way. I can describe each of them to a certain degree, but for the most part they must be experienced to truly reach an understanding.

An interesting feature of the Hidden Paths is than they *all cross multiple Lettered Paths* (from two to five); whereas only three Lettered (Planetary) Paths cross one Lettered (Mother) Path each. Otherwise the Lettered Paths do not cross each other. Many are crossed by Hidden Paths but that is far different than Lettered Paths crossing each other (for instance when Beth crossed Shin previously). In general, <u>these crossings by the Hidden Paths effect only the Hidden Paths and not the Lettered Paths</u>.

This Linear Gate of HP:1>5 is the source of that insatiable and primordial *urge to merge* I've spoken of in relation to Gedulah. It is, in effect, a *blessing* from Kether upon both the Universal and the personal aspects of Gedulah. The downward (with the flow) passage crosses first Shin and then Zayin; this gives it a boost of power (Shin) and that rationale of the 'self'/'other' dynamic (Zayin), in light of which that *urge to merge* becomes most relevant. On the return (against the flow) passage these two crossings mark different stages in the process of letting go of 'self' identification.

Working this Gate will inform you of everything there is to know about that *urge to merge*: its overall importance within the sequential realm and how to make use of it.

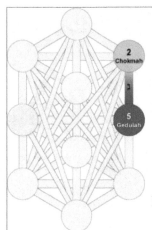

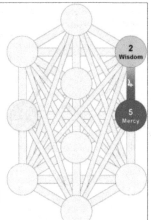

GATE #13

ג GIMMEL (CAMEL)

JUPITER ♃

Sequence: Wisdom <JUPITER> Mercy

Return: Mercy <JUPITER> Wisdom

Keywords: Providence, Symbolic forms

The Hebrew *Gimel* means "Camel" in English and is a Double Letter assigned to the planet Jupiter. In astrology, Jupiter is the "Great Benefic" and is thought to bring good fortune and ease. Its 12 year cycle around the zodiac also marks an important cycle in human growth, so it's the first of the *human* planets really (Saturn being *beyond* human experience). Gimel *brings* the Jovian energy *into* Gedulah; so Gedulah does have a Jovian aspect to it, but Gedulah is **not** Jupiter itself. It is *more than* Jupiter!

The Paths of Jupiter and Mars (Daleth) are significant for the fact that they bring a Supernal influence deep into the sequential Mental Realm. Consequently they are equally complex and multifaceted!

From the Universal perspective what is happening here is the whole infinite body of the *Unity* of Parts and its undifferentiated EM, is differentiating into an infinite number of *collectivized* parts. This is an aspect of the Akasha and is its primary function so to speak. In working this Gate, one of the first things you can learn about is the transition from undifferentiated to differentiated and *why* collectivization occurs.

From this sprout several other functions; the most important of which is Divine Providence. At its root, this Universal provision for the remedy of *all* need comes from the nature of Chokmah as a *Unity* of Parts or *Unified* Awareness. It acts as *one* thing, not as many things acting together. This unification-of-action carries over into the sequential universe as *collective concern* and providence, wherein each looks out for every 'other': every part or 'self' works *with* every 'other' in mimicry of Chokmah's Unity.

Working this Gate you will learn all about the workings of this providential mechanism; how to immediately recognize its hand, and how to accurately discern between 'desire' and 'need'. You will see the vastly beautiful and infinitely complex web of interdependence that forms our Cosmos!

Jupiter is said to be expansive and this is another function of Gimel. As that Unified, undifferentiated state of Chokmah transitions to the differentiation of Gedulah, there is a multiplying (by infinity) explosion into parts simultaneous to what we witnessed in Beth/Saturn specifically. This is the One becoming the many. It has the effect upon the process of Self-realization of increasing the self's opportunities to self-realize through the agency of 'other'. You will learn here just how important this is and why collectivization is its natural byproduct!

Franz Bardon's *Practice of Magical Evocation* is said to correspond with this Path (by way of the Tarot) and this brings me to the final function of Gimel that I want to discuss: namely, EM acquiring *symbolic* form. By '*symbolic* form' I mean the Philosophical Force that underlies all forms. These '*symbolic* forms' have an *aliveness* to them by virtue of the purity and forcefulness of their EM here (especially in Gedulah). So, in Gedulah it is possible to encounter these '*symbolic* forms' as symbolic creatures; hence evocation.

But, and here's *another* BIG 'but', since this is the "upper" part of the Mental Realm where the Law of Attraction holds sway above all others, it is sublimely easy to create any appearance you want and thereby attract any corresponding EM to inhabit your creation. In order to evoke, you must inhabit the evocationists level of Mind (at least the solitary Air region of the temporal Mental Body) and this is a very powerfully creative aspect of human consciousness. In other words, *self-delusion* is most often the case here and instead of encountering the *objective* '*symbolic* forms', we encounter our own *subjective* creations.

I advise against using the working of this Gate for the evocation of <u>known</u> (i.e., you find them in a grimoire of some sort) entities until such time as you have absolutely mastered yourself. However, it works very well for general exploration of this level of '*symbolic* forms' which is best accessed in the traversing of Gimel itself. If you approach it without expectations and preconceptions, you will then surely encounter these beings (for they do express an *aliveness* at this level) in their *objective* forms. Eventually, when you are well practiced at setting aside your own biases, wants and desires, you can enter with the will to encounter specific forms of EM without danger of subjectification.

Of course, when you have reached a state of absolute self-mastery you can use the working of this Gate to reach any known or preconceived entity; and, if you want, you can purify them by bringing forth their objective forms. [Often this generates a surprising result where the two stand in very sharp contrast!]

The return (against the flow) travel in the Gate is all about returning to the state of Unified EM in Chokmah, from a place of differentiation and collectivity. You will learn all about the descending process in reverse, and if you pay close attention, you will see each of its definable layers. This will be very educational and you can even learn to tarry at specific levels to absorb more deeply.

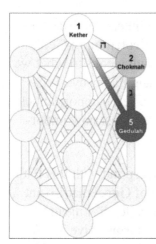

GATE #14

Sequence: ☋ Wisdom <JUPITER> Mercy
<HP:5-1> Crown <ARIES> Wisdom

Return: ☋ Wisdom <ARIES> Crown
<HP:1-5> Mercy <JUPITER> Wisdom

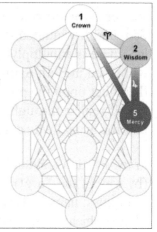

This Gate starts and ends in Chokmah and augments two main attributes of Gimel by placing them in context with the Path of Heh/Aries and the HP from Kether. Thus we see that both the 'urge to merge' and Universal providence are a 'gift' of Kether; or rather, they are aspects of the emanation of Kethric Brilliance. You can learn much about the KB and its mastery though this Gate.

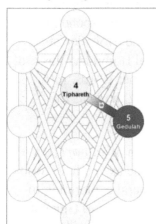

GATE #15

☊ TETH (COILED SERPENT)

LEO ♌

Sequence: Beauty <LEO> Mercy

Return: Mercy <LEO> Beauty

Keywords: Very best of 'self'

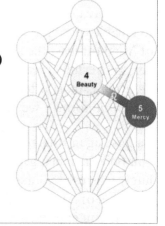

Teth means *basket* or *coiled serpent* in English and is associated with the zodiacal sign Leo, the Lion; the fixed Fire sign ruled by the Sun. All of these symbols speak very clearly the significance of the Path of Teth.

Teth is the Solitary Self coming into *and completing* Gedulah. It wishes to contribute the *very best* aspect or face of itself to the collective awareness. It arrives in true leonine fashion with mane ablaze in all its glory! It wraps itself in a beautiful handmade basket of the finest quality and waits like a coiled serpent within, ready to unleash its pent-up power. Its power shows itself as eye-thrilling sunlight; the Light of the Solitary Self in echo of the Kethric Brilliance and the Path of Heh above.

From a Universal perspective, this is the spirit with which the whole infinite body of Solitary Selves within Tiphareth collectivizes in Gedulah. And at the personal level, it is this same spirit of appreciation for 'self' and respect for the collective with which each Solitary Self enters into participation with the collectivity of Gedulah.

Each Solitary Self brings its *very best* to the collective and thus completes Gedulah.

GATE #16

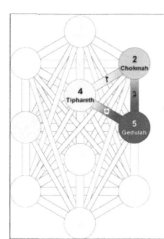

Sequence: ↺ Beauty <LEO> Mercy <JUPITER> Wisdom <GEMINI> Beauty

Return: ↺ Beauty <GEMINI> Wisdom <JUPITER> Mercy <LEO> Beauty

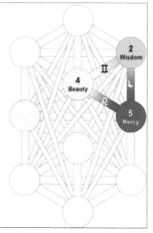

Here we see and come to Understand the sense of respect or reverence for the collectivity of Gedulah that underlies our bringing only our best face forward as we enter the Sephirot. Because the relationship between 'self' and 'other' (Zayin) is so pivotal and essential to our overall Self-realization, *only giving our best will do.* At the same time, giving *our best* is a vital part of the functioning of Universal providence (Gimel).

This Gate, along with the two that follow, present important lessons we *must* learn in moving forward: lessons about the supremacy of the collective and that *urge to merge.* Human beings on the whole have forgotten this fact, much to our own and the planet's detriment! So it is vital that we not make the same mistake over and over again, especially as we move into the parts of Self-realization that have to do with our individual uniqueness and power.

GATE #17

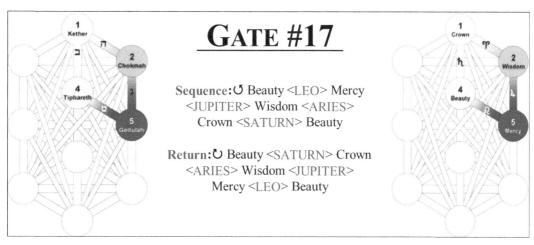

Sequence: ↺ Beauty <LEO> Mercy <JUPITER> Wisdom <ARIES> Crown <SATURN> Beauty

Return: ↺ Beauty <SATURN> Crown <ARIES> Wisdom <JUPITER> Mercy <LEO> Beauty

This Gate brings the same lesson as the previous but takes it to the higher octave of Kether, Heh and Beth.

GATE #18

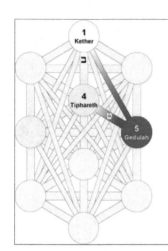

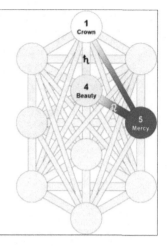

Sequence: ↻ Beauty <LEO> Mercy
<HP:5-1> Crown <SATURN> Beauty

Return: ↻ Beauty <SATURN> Crown
<HP:1-5> Mercy <LEO> Beauty

This Gate brings a blessing from Kether that teaches exactly how fundamental always being *our best* selves is to the descent of The "I" into manifestation as a Solitary Self. This ability to intentionally bring *our best* to the collective is truly an aspect of Divine Providence.

GEBURAH / SEVERITY

גבורה

KEYWORDS: POWER, UNIQUENESS

In its process of Self-realization through contextualizing itself with 'other', the Solitary Self recognizes that, along side being essentially the same and alike 'other', it is also *different* from all 'other'. Its *uniqueness* or difference has always been there; it's just that it has been overshadowed by the fact that uniqueness is not, in and of itself, a unique thing! *Every* thing in the Cosmos is utterly unique! It is therefore utterly *alike* every 'other' thing in this respect! <Ha!> And, it's *only* because of its having to contend with 'other' that the 'self' even comes to realize its own uniqueness: only because of the contrast!

Geburah is the Self-realization of the individual's own utter uniqueness; and like-wise, the utter and complete uniqueness of every 'other' that exists. This means that each and every Solitary Self has something utterly unique to offer to the col-lective of the Cosmos, its own "part to play". Each individual 'self' possess a spe-cial power that only it possesses. That power is fully realized here in Geburah. At the Universal level, the whole infinite body of Solitary Selves realizes its *collective* power simultaneously; and at a personal level a Solitary Self comes to recognize its own uniqueness and its own power. Thus Gedulah equals power, uniqueness and the beginnings of self-determination.

The Hebrew word 'Geburah' means *severity* in English. This is meant in the "to sever" sense, not the "severe" aspect: with Geburah, what is unique is exposed and the extraneous is cut away. There is a consolidation and focus happening here as with all Sephirot on the Pillar of Form.

This Sephirot is also called 'Pachad' which means *fear* or *awe*. This refers to the vision of a Solitary Self's true unique power, as well as to the Power of Geburah as a whole. It is truly intimidating and awesome!

However, the power of the individual Solitary Self comes with a caveat: **it is rele-vant only in context with the collective**. When used solely for *personal* welfare or gain, the individual's power becomes cancerous and self-destructive. But when used on behalf of *all*, it becomes an Essential Force, a necessary and required con-stituent of the Cosmos. Sadly, this is where humans have gone astray . . .

One of humanity's greatest errors in terms of Geburah is its association with warfare and the binding of the concept of personal power, strictly to *power over* instead of *power with*. On the contrary, the *objective* Geburah is a positive, nurturing and protective force of the collective *at all times*. The *objective* Geburah is never destructive – the 'paring away' of severity is only for the health of the collective and to expose the underlying power of its members. Geburah is 'power *with*', not 'power *over*'.

Standing as your Solitary Self (Mental Body) within Geburah you will immediately feel your radiant power and you will recognize its uniqueness. You will naturally be facing toward Gedulah at first but you are free to move as you please. You feel a sense of solidity that you haven't felt before; an increased sense of 'self'. You now possess something all of your own: your unique power. You begin to feel self-determined.

Looking 'up' towards Gedulah, you are immediately connected with your collectives. This will naturally captivate the majority of your field of view, so to speak; but behind Gedulah are also influxes from Tiphareth, Binah and Kether that you will need to explore.

Looking 'down', you see the Astral Realm forming below and you feel a very strong and undeniable gravitational pull into incarnation.

In Geburah you can learn everything there is to know about your own unique ability and power and its practical applications. Eventually you may be able to wield that raw Power from Geburah itself. You also have the opportunity to learn about 'power' in general: how it functions, its mechanics, how to defeat or increase it, and how to wield it.

Most of all you can learn about your own uniqueness: where it originates, why it originated, and what part it plays in the collective.

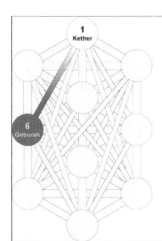

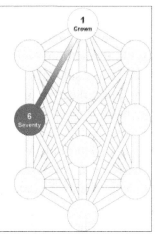

GATE #19
HIDDEN PATH: 1>6

Sequence: Crown <HP:1-6> Severity

Return: Severity <HP:6-1> Crown

Keywords: Blessing of Power
& Uniqueness

This is a blessing from the Source of All Power and All Uniqueness: Kether. You will learn about the true origin of your power and uniqueness and the *necessity* of it being personalized through you and all 'other' in the process of Self-realization.

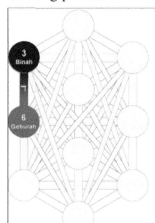

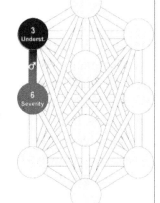

GATE #20
ד DALETH (DOOR)
MARS ♂

Sequence: Underst. <MARS> Severity

Return: Severity <MARS> Underst.

Keywords: Individuation,
Impress from Greater Self

The Double Letter 'Daleth' means *door* in English and **is ascribed to the Planet Mars**. Almost everywhere in modern occultism you will instead find *Venus* associated with the Letter Daleth because of the Tarot attribution of The Empress card. This stems from two sources: first is the mess that western occultists have made of the attribution of Hebrew Letter to the Paths of the Tree; and second, is a lack of understanding of the ancient *non-militaristic* significance of Mars.

Mars *has* to be attributed to Daleth in the *original* Hebrew Tree, there's no two ways about it; and Daleth *has* to connect Binah with Geburah, again no two ways about it.

Next comes the militarization of Mars. This was really a great pity. It came about during the period in human development/history when, en masse, we began to move away from power _with_ toward power _over_. When kings and queens and tzars, etc. took over and started making war on each other is when Mars became the *God of War* (they needed to turn war into a matter of worship in order to retain power over the masses).

At that point we lost touch with what our power was really for: the collective. And we lost touch with the *objective* Mars of the ancients who was about Power With, Protection, Nurturance, Strength, Support and Uniqueness. Now all we are left with is silly little boys and girls running around in lock-step, killing each other and our collective future; and greedy little despots directing their little suicidal games . . .

That's what noble Mars has become. Even the name we use in the modern day: "mars", is a Greco-Roman perversion! Unfortunately it's all I have to use, so use it I shall, albeit reluctantly.

It's my belief that the cosmology of the Tree of Life reaches back to that ancient time thousands of years ago, when *our* "Mars" was a Noble force for the collective good. In that context, the Daleth/Door pairing with Mars makes sense and fits perfectly into the Tree here, between Binah and Geburah. [It even rectifies the Tarot attribution of The Empress to Mars: Mars rules Aries/Heh, the Emperor in Tarot, and surely an Empress rules her Emperor! Ha!]

Daleth is the Path or conduit (doorway) by which the Greater Self impresses its specific quantity of EM upon each Solitary Self. It reinforces what was received from Cheth/Cancer and brings it to the forefront of the individual's attention. Where Cheth/Cancer *creates* the Solitary Self, Daleth/Mars puts a final stamp of uniqueness to it. It does so in order to prepare the Solitary Self for incarnation. Our Greater Self always has its finger on the button of our unique power, so to speak, and is always urging us to use our power in productive ways and for the collective good.

Through working this Gate – <u>if you manage to let go of your ingrained militarized, misogynistic programming around Mars</u> – you *can* learn everything there is to know about *our* Noble Mars and what the true intent of Power is. You will also learn even more than you have previously about the specific "recipe" of EMs which constitute your being and about how that quantity fits within your Greater Self. In other words, you can learn one hell of a lot about yourself that you probably wouldn't have learnt otherwise, elsewhere.

In harmony with The Empress of the Tarot, Daleth is the *doorway* through which the Greater Selves plant the seed of Uniqueness into each of their Solitary Selves in full expectation that it will bloom and bear fruit through incarnation. The recognition of uniqueness changes everything in the relationship between 'self' and 'other' and renders the 'self' even more capable in navigating its way around an evermore complicated existence.

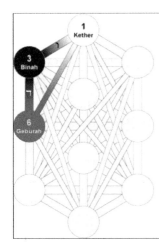

GATE #21

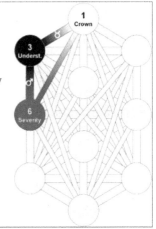

Sequence: ☋ Underst. <MARS> Severity <HP:6-1> Crown <TAURUS> Underst.

Return: ☊ Underst. <TAURUS> Crown <HP:1-6> Severity <MARS> Underst.

This Gate shows that the imprint from Binah upon Geburah has its root in Kether and is in fact part of a blessing from Kether.

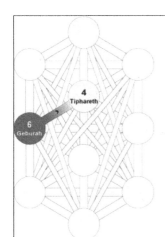

GATE #22

ר YOD (HAND, FINGER)

VIRGO ♍

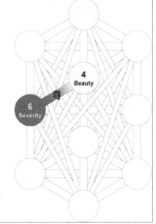

Sequence: Beauty <VIRGO> Severity

Return: Severity <VIRGO> Beauty

Keywords: Analysis and rectification

Yod is the *10th* Letter of the Hebrew alephbet and as such (per Kabbalistic Gematria) it carries a sense of completion with it, a sense of finality and fulfillment. Yod is also the mutable Earth sign of Virgo, ruled by Mercury and translates as *hand* or, more often, *finger*.

Virgo is "The Virgin" but 'virgin' meant something somewhat different to the ancients than it does in the modern day. It refers specifically to a young woman in the prime of her life and has nothing to do with whether or not she has had sex. She is said to "be of childbearing age", meaning that she is fertile while implying that she has not (yet) given birth.

This is meant as an agricultural symbol of mid-summer, turning towards autumn: when the fruit is ripening on the branch and the grain is maturing and it's just beginning to be harvest time. It is a time when the crop is watched closely and evaluated for that optimal moment for reaping. The *hand* holds it and the *finger* points out the various tell-tale signs of either ripeness or immaturity. It is a time of *nearing completion* and *critical evaluation*, all in the pursuit of perfection.

Of course the Yod/Virgo has essentially the same function in the Tree. It connects Tiphareth (the seat of the Solitary Self) with Geburah (the seat of the individual's unique power) and represents a self-critical *proving* of the individual's uniqueness. The unique power of the individual is tested and examined by the Solitary Self for its rightness and is readied for the challenges of the future. This again is an echo of Vav/Taurus above; thus 'perfection' is replaced with 'fitness' and 'readiness'.

This is a natural, ongoing self-regulating process of *all* awareness as it double-checks itself and makes sure that it always presents its *very best* (Teth/Leo) to the collective. It combines self-analysis with self-rectification (the former being pointless without the latter).

The working of this Gate gives you the opportunity to examine your own unique power and evaluate how you measure up to its potential. Traveling in *both* directions doubles the clarity of your perspective on yourself. This is also the place and time to make any improvements to your character that seem appropriate!

This process of self-rectification is extensive as illustrated by the three Gates that follow.

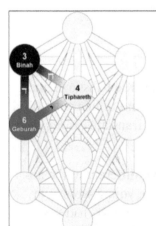

GATE #23

Sequence: ☽ Beauty <VIRGO> Severity <MARS> Underst. <CANCER> Beauty

Return: ☽ Beauty <CANCER> Underst. <MARS> Severity <VIRGO> Beauty

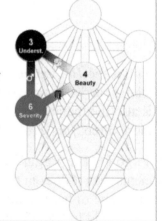

With this Gate the individual's unique power is "tested" or evaluated against the primary (Cheth/Cancer) and secondary (Daleth/Mars) impresses from the Greater Self upon the Solitary Self. You must submit to *both* directions for the testing to be complete. Take your time and look closely at yourself in all honesty.

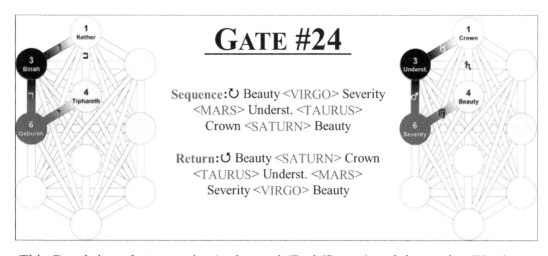

GATE #24

Sequence: ☽ Beauty <VIRGO> Severity
<MARS> Underst. <TAURUS>
Crown <SATURN> Beauty

Return: ☽ Beauty <SATURN> Crown
<TAURUS> Underst. <MARS>
Severity <VIRGO> Beauty

This Gate brings that saturnine 'strictness' (Beth/Saturn) and the taurian (Vav/Taurus) 'need for perfection' to the process of self-rectification specifically. It reminds us of the Kethric blessing that moves through the *whole* Tree; and says to us that it is the Awareness of The "I" that is Self-rectifying here.

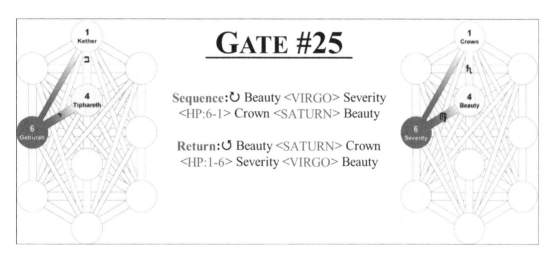

GATE #25

Sequence: ☽ Beauty <VIRGO> Severity
<HP:6-1> Crown <SATURN> Beauty

Return: ☽ Beauty <SATURN> Crown
<HP:1-6> Severity <VIRGO> Beauty

This is the final, Kethric stage of this period of self-analysis and self-rectification. This completes the process and the individual is deemed 'ripe'. There is a sense of judgment here and of having been judged.

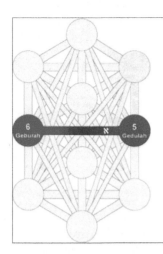

GATE #26

א ALEPH (Ox)

ARCHETYPAL AIR △

Sequence: Mercy <AIR> Severity

Return: Severity <AIR> Mercy

Keywords: Alikeness/Difference,
Subjective Meaning/Archetypal Form

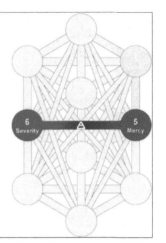

'Aleph' is the Mother Letter of Primordial Air and translates into English as *Ox*. In fact, the Letter itself looks an ox yoke: an apparatus that enables an ox to pull a cart or plow. This is 'ox' as a beast of burden, a domesticated animal that has no will of its own and only follows the will of its "master". It is the same with physical air: it moves only when a force makes it move, otherwise it is at rest and calm.

Air, of course, is essential to human life and we cannot exist for long without it. Aleph is the same: it is only through recognizing our uniqueness that we have independent life; it is only through this separation or differentiation between 'self' and 'other' that we become individualized.

Aleph *is* the infinite continuum between Gedulah/Alikeness and Geburah/Difference. At one end of this continuum we share commonality and at the other end, we are each unique. The directional flow of the Path is interesting. The 'forward' direction is that of the natural sequence of the process of Self-realization, but its force is mild; and the 'reverse' direction meets with no appreciable resistance, unlike with Shin/Fire where the flow is quite strong. So, it is easy for awareness to flow back and forth between these two poles of Gedulah and Geburah.

Furthermore, it is a _sequential_ continuum of graduated degrees of alikeness/ difference. This paints the whole rest of the Tree with the brush of sequence and the Mental Realm becomes the Realm of Sequence. Underlying sequence, of course, is *continuity*: the force which binds each successive increment along the continuum to the next. Sequence and continuity go hand-in-hand.

Aleph will later be crossed by Resh/Sun (Tiphareth to Yesod) marking the *exact* center of the Gra Tree, so Aleph also carries this "center of things" significance with it. In fact, Aleph is the 11th Lettered Path, which means we've now covered half of the Hebrew alephbet. The Aleph-Resh crossing is a very important point or moment in the Tree and we will come to that later in our discussion of the Gates of

---

Yesod; nonetheless, it does have an impact at this stage. As you pass along this Path in either direction, you will come to a place of pausing midway and this is the crossing point of perfect balance between the two poles.

In the Supernal Realm we had *Essential* Meaning and *Essential* Form as the two ends of the continuum of Shin/Fire. Here in the <u>Mental</u> Realm, these have both evolved and become *Subjective* Meaning (my truth and your truth, our truth and their truth) and *Archetypal* Form at each end of the continuum of Aleph/Air. This pattern repeats again in the Astral Realm which surrounds the Mother Letter Mem/Water.

In the Sepher Yetzirah, Aleph is spoken of as the "covenant" between man and IHVH. This covenant is nothing other than the free and easy connection between the Solitary Self's unique power and the collective. Through this promissory agreement, The "I" gives *meaning* to our power and consequently, *life* to our material existence.

Working this Gate is to reaffirm our participation in this Philosophical covenant. We can eventually become masters of this continuum within our selves, easily negotiating that union of 'self' with 'collective'. You will learn all about your connection to all of the various collectives you are part of; how to increase and nurture that connection and how to buffer it when necessary. You will also learn how your power and uniqueness are dependant upon your connections; how your collective membership determines your power and how it influences its strength or weakness.

All of this is further elucidated by the six Gates of Aleph that follow.

Aleph and its Gates complete Geburah and our whole attention turns toward our relationship with 'other'. It becomes our overriding focus in all that follows.

GATE #27

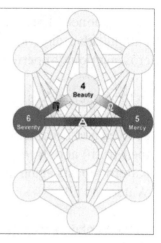

Sequence: ↻ Mercy <AIR> Severity <VIRGO> Beauty <LEO> Mercy

Return: ↻ Mercy <LEO> Beauty <VIRGO> Severity <AIR> Mercy

Interestingly, this Gate is really about the meaning we bring to the Path of Teth/ Leo and not Aleph/Air: here we define what "my very best" *really* means. Working this Gate will bring you to a *perfected* Understanding of exactly who you are in relation to your commitment to your collectives and exactly what your unique gift is about.

On another note, as the Mental triangle (akin to the Supernal triangle), this Gate can also educate you about the nature of both subjective meaning and archetypal form. It will explain how the evolution from their supernal corollaries (EM and EF), to their Mental manifestations, is necessitated by the splitting of Awareness

GATE #28

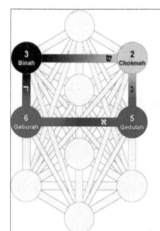

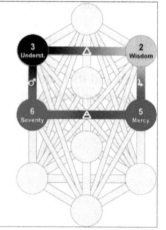

Sequence: ↻ Mercy <AIR> Severity <MARS> Underst. <FIRE> Wisdom <JUPITER> Mercy

Return: ↻ Mercy <JUPITER> Wisdom <FIRE> Underst. <MARS> Severity <AIR> Mercy

This Gate is all about this transformation of EM and EF into their Mental Realm corollaries. *But*, there is a bit of mystery here. By all appearances you would naturally assume that EM flows down the Pillar of Force into Gedulah via the Path of Gimel/Jupiter and that EF flows down the Pillar of Form into Geburah via the Path of Daleth/Mars, no? Well, it's a bit more complicated than that! Ha!

What actually happens is EM (which is purely objective by nature) becomes *subjective* meaning in Gedulah <u>because of what happens in the Pillar of Form</u> with the

Path of Daleth/Mars; and furthermore, EF (again, an objective thing) becomes *archetypal* form (a subjective thing) in Geburah <u>because of what happens in the Pillar of Force</u> with the Path of Gimel/Jupiter. Meanwhile, 'archetypes' are more naturally an aspect of Gimel and 'subjectivity' more naturally an aspect of Daleth! So there is a sort of cross-pollination and reversing of poles as it were, in this transition between supernal and mental. *This is a very important lesson*!

Working this Gate reveals this mystery of cross-pollination and shows how the Aleph/Air continuum is indeed the child of the Shin/Fire continuum.

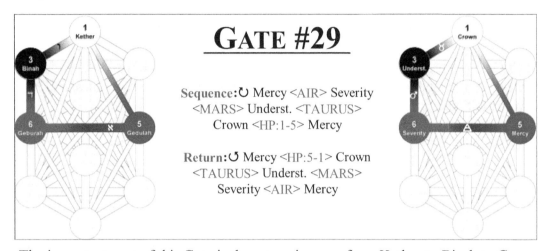

GATE #29

Sequence: ↺ Mercy <AIR> Severity <MARS> Underst. <TAURUS> Crown <HP:1-5> Mercy

Return: ↻ Mercy <HP:5-1> Crown <TAURUS> Underst. <MARS> Severity <AIR> Mercy

The important part of this Gate is the return journey from Kether to Binah to Geburah. This is where all the action is really happening and it has to do with how major a part Kether plays in the purification of the individual's uniqueness and power. Thus, collectivity itself is blessed by Kether through this purification.

From working this Gate you will learn the mechanics of this Kethric intervention.

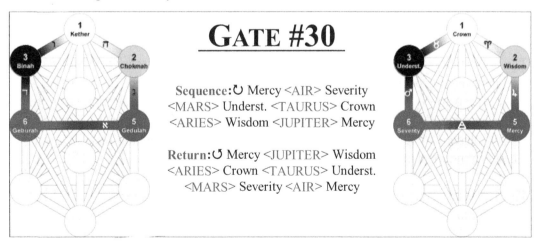

GATE #30

Sequence: ↺ Mercy <AIR> Severity <MARS> Underst. <TAURUS> Crown <ARIES> Wisdom <JUPITER> Mercy

Return: ↻ Mercy <JUPITER> Wisdom <ARIES> Crown <TAURUS> Underst. <MARS> Severity <AIR> Mercy

This very balanced Gate, if done with the proper mixing and multiplying of awarenesses as you go around, will transform your Gedulah self. It serves as an initiation into Gedulah of sorts.

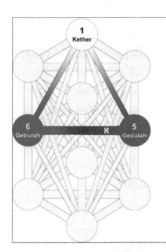

GATE #31

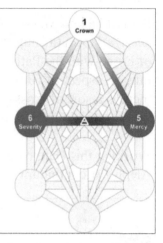

Sequence: ↻ Mercy <AIR> Severity
<HP:6-1> Crown <HP:1-5> Mercy

Return: ↻ Mercy <HP:5-1> Crown
<HP:1-6> Severity <AIR> Mercy

This Gate is a great blessing upon both the unique self of Geburah and the collectivizing self of Gedulah; as well as the interaction between these two poles, and between 'self' and 'other'.

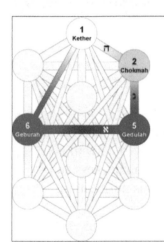

GATE #32

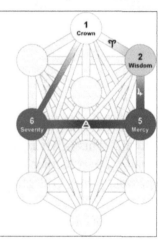

Sequence: ↻ Mercy <AIR> Severity
<HP:6-1> Crown <ARIES>
Wisdom <JUPITER> Mercy

Return: ↻ Mercy <JUPITER> Wisdom
<ARIES> Crown <HP:1-6>
Severity <AIR> Mercy

This is a mirror of Gate #29.

The important part of *this* Gate is the forward journey from Kether to Chokmah to Gedulah; most especially the Paths of Heh/Aries and Gimel/Jupiter in both directions. It has to do with how major a part Kether plays in the quality and strength of the individual's ability to collectivize. Thus, the unique power of the individual is itself blessed by Kether through this clarification. From working this Gate you will learn the mechanics of this Kethric intervention.

This is the last Gate of Geburah and of the Mental Realm. In a way, it completes a phase in *our* Self-realization and readies us for our next step: into the Astral.

YESOD / FOUNDATION

יסוד

KEYWORDS: SIGNIFICANCE,
SYMBOLIC MEANING,
SENTIENT SELF, ASTRAL REALM

After the individuation of Geburah, a new level of Self *must* emerge in order for The "I" to continue its process of Self-realization. From this point on, that process is all bound up in the relationship between 'self' and 'other' and so the Solitary Self requires several additional attributes in order to accommodate this change in focus. Furthermore, its immediate goal is incarnation into material form and this necessitates some sort of way for mind to inhabit physical substance in such a way that mind will be able to navigate and interact in this new physical world.

The logical solution for The "I" is to adopt an *interface* that Mind can attach itself to and fill *and*, it must be a substance that once filled with Mind can attach to and fill physical matter. We call this the Astral substance, a type of *proto-matter* that is capable of combining both Mind and matter. It is affected by Mind and affects matter; it is the glue that holds matter together into the forms we are accustomed to. [Every physical thing has an astral template or substrate.]

This interface is 'Yesod' or *foundation* in English; for it is the literal foundation of the physical realm and everything in it. It is what enables Mind to inhabit matter. And, it is important to understand, it exists only because Mind is on the path to incarnation: as soon as an incarnation ends, the astral template disintegrates. It has no other importance than as an incarnational medium for use by Mind and it has no life of its own. It is temporary.

In the Supernal realm we have *Essential Meaning* and *Essential Form*; in the Mental realm we have *subjective meaning* and *archetypal form*; here in the Astral realm, meaning and form have evolved still further and because existence is all about interaction between 'self' and 'other', we now have *significance* and *symbolic form*.

Life in the astral is personal. All interaction with 'other' has a relative importance to us personally; in other words, *significance*. Every interaction generates some degree of significance so significance is the medium of exchange, so to speak, in astral realm.

Perceiving this new substance of significance takes a new set of senses: the astral senses of clairvoyance, clairaudience, clairsentience, etc. Therefore we call our astral body the Sentient Self; with it we can navigate through the whirlwind of significance we encounter.

Significance is a reaction, a personally subjective valuation, not an objective fact. It's based on how we *feel* about a given thing or situation but is nonetheless instigated by an objective thing or occurrence (an EM of EF). These new senses perceive *both* the objective impetus (EM/EF) *and* the subjective relevance (significance). In other words, each perception by the astral senses informs us about 'other' *and* 'self' in equal measure! This is *why* The "I" operates through this mode in its Self-realization.

Since every perception by the Sentient Self is wrapped in a personal feeling and is in effect an *interpretation* of the objective root, it fits the definition of a symbol; and so all form in the astral realm is symbolic. In fact, compared to the physical realm, the astral realm generally appears quite fanciful, colorful and musical, magical and fantastic to the traveler. Every thing carries a vibrancy to it, an aliveness that is palpable.

So, the Sentient Self is a body (astral body) that the Solitary Self (mental body) must put on in order to fit into and connect with its eventual physical body. The aim is to enable Mind to move around, perceive and interact with its environment in the physical realm. The senses that formed in the astral body translate very directly into our five physical senses; and the (astral) emotions that we experience manifest themselves immediately though our nerves and hormones, etc. I'm always just blown away by how utterly ingenious this scheme is and how perfectly it achieves the melding of "I" and matter! Ingenious!

At any rate, my point was that it is the *Solitary Self* that inhabits the Sentient and physical bodies. They are not separate bodies. The astral self exists *only* because of the Solitary Self and the physical exists *only* because of the Solitary self <u>and</u> the astral self. Another way of putting it is: physical body = physio-astra-mental body; and astral body = astra-mental body. A mental body can exist without an astral or physical body; there is no astral body without a pre-existing mental body; and there is no physical body without an astra-mental body. <u>Astral is an intermediate substance</u>.

So, the Sentient Self stands in a infinite realm of 'other' and must navigate through an infinite number of encounters and interactions, all perceived through a lens of significance and symbol. Ponder that for a minute or two.

Your whole existence is about 'self' and 'other'. Your experience of 'self' is one of discovering who you are in relation to 'other'; how you measure up and how you feel about your interactions. It's a new sort of introspection or self-awareness for the Solitary Self.

The astral body interacts with 'other' through *resonance* and self-regulates interaction though the opposing pole of *dissonance*; all of which entails a *high* degree of self-determination and autonomy. This all begins here in Yesod and will develop further on when we come to the Powers of Yesod, Netzach and Hod.

It needs to be noted that everything from here on (Yesod included) disintegrates at the end of each incarnation and reforms anew each time the Solitary Self reincarnates.

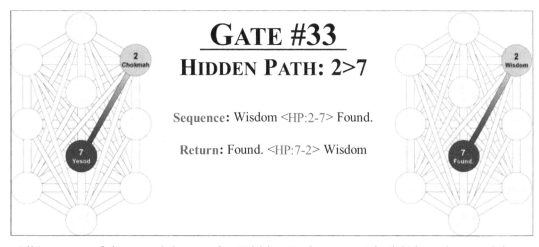

GATE #33
HIDDEN PATH: 2>7

Sequence: Wisdom <HP:2-7> Found.

Return: Found. <HP:7-2> Wisdom

All but two of the remaining twelve Hidden Paths cross Aleph/Air and two of them even cross over the Aleph-Resh Crossing. In the eight of these that originate in the Supernal realm, this crossing of Aleph/Air is a point at which things transition from Supernal to sequential. It is always distinct and noticeable and often the most educational part of the journey.

In this Gate the Unity of Parts is descending into your Sentient Self; imbuing it with your unique set of EMs that are responsible for setting the whole tone of your interactions with 'other'. As you first cross over Teth/Leo (descending with the flow), your EMs begin to group together; and with the Aleph/Air crossing, they finalize their separation into your unique astral form. The process is reversed during the 'against the flow' ascent back to Chokmah.

Working this Gate will clarify and strengthen your astral expression of your EM. You will also learn about the connection between objective EM and subjective significance; and you will increase the objective purity of your astral perceptions.

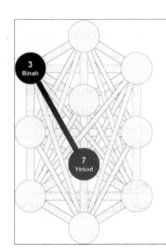

GATE #34
HIDDEN PATH: 3>7

Sequence: Underst. <HP:3-7> Found.

Return: Found. <HP:7-3> Underst.

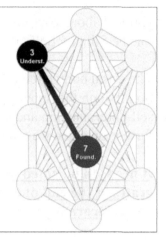

This the second of the karmic Gates. The connection between Binah and Yesod represents the imprint of your astral karma of this present incarnation. All things physical have a mental, astral and physical karma. The mental level karma is transmitted via Cheth/Cancer into Tiphareth with the initial formation of the Solitary Self; the astral karma is transmitted here with this Hidden Path; and the physical karma via HP:3>10.

Now, by 'karma' I mean something very specific and it has to do with Universal *continuity* stemming from Binah. It first manifests in the sequential realm and touches every moment of its mental, astral and physical existence: it is the root of sequence itself. This <u>Force of Continuity</u> binds everything together, every moment, every action, every cause and consequence, every thought and feeling, every atom, etc.

That great force combines with the equally powerful Force of Universal Providence and the result is 'karma'. Karma is the continuity of the Universe seeing to it that exactly *what* you <u>need</u> is provided exactly *when* you <u>need</u> it and in the exact *way* you <u>need</u> it in the present moment of time-space. In the human experience that is experienced as either convenient or inconvenient, good or bad and most often as something coming from "out there" in the Universe as a higher judgment of some kind. In point of fact, it is intimately our own, formed exclusively by our own actions and decisions; and therefore, <u>under our control</u>.

As a Greater Self 'descends into' / 'creates' / 'projects parts of itself into' the sequential realm and forms Solitary Selves, it immediately begins a thread of continuity (Cheth/Cancer) that persists with each Solitary Self throughout its entire existence. This particular Path is your thread that connects to your astral body and manifests as your astral karma (i.e., related to your emotions and your character).

Working this Gate on the descent (with the flow), you may feel the intersection with Yod/Virgo as a sort of focusing and when you cross Aleph/Air you will definitely feel everything come into sharp focus. On the return (against the flow), you should feel the crossing of Yod/Virgo more significantly and I advise you to tarry there and examine what's happening at this juncture.

This Gate is a very important Gate in so far as Understanding your own karma, at least its astral component in this lifetime. These are very valuable lessons that shouldn't be missed! [Believe me; it will make life easier as you get older! Ha!]

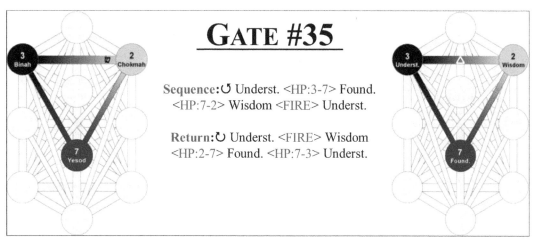

GATE #35

Sequence: ↺ Underst. <HP:3-7> Found. <HP:7-2> Wisdom <FIRE> Underst.

Return: ↻ Underst. <FIRE> Wisdom <HP:2-7> Found. <HP:7-3> Underst.

This Gate clarifies the connection between EM and karma, specifically as it pertains to your astral body. It also shows how it is powered by the Shin/Fire dynamic between Chokmah and Binah. With this knowledge you will better understand your own karma.

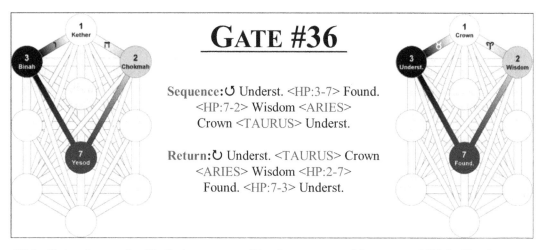

GATE #36

Sequence: ↺ Underst. <HP:3-7> Found. <HP:7-2> Wisdom <ARIES> Crown <TAURUS> Underst.

Return: ↻ Underst. <TAURUS> Crown <ARIES> Wisdom <HP:2-7> Found. <HP:7-3> Underst.

This Gate shows the Kethric source of both your astral karma and EM. Furthermore you will see how the aim of your karma is to perfect your expression of your EM.

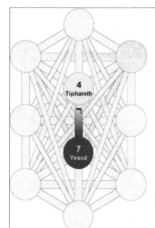

GATE #37

ר **RESH** (HEAD, FACE)

SUN ☉

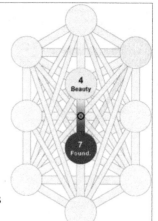

Sequence: Beauty <SUN> Found.

Return: Found. <SUN> Beauty

Keywords: Face, Conscious awareness

The Hebrew Double Letter 'Resh' translates as *face* or *head* in English and is attributed to the Sun. This is the *conscious awareness* of the Solitary Self descending into Yesod and putting on its astral body. Like the Sun, the conscious awareness rules and is the center of gravity of the personal or astral self. It is the sustaining, radiant power to which the other planets (Venus, Mercury and Moon) bow down and owe their lives. This is literally the *face* we present to the world.

As noted before, where the Resh/Sun crosses Aleph/Air is the absolute center point of the Gra Tree, the point of perfect balance halfway between Tiphareth and Yesod. This crossing is a major point of transformation in Awareness where the conscious part starts to manifest as *sub*-conscious (astral) and *un*-conscious (physical); both of which are necessary modifications for success in relating to 'other'. This interaction between 'self' and 'other' is so overwhelmingly complex that the conscious mind alone cannot handle all of it all at once so parts have to be shunted off to sub- and un-conscious levels of awareness.

Of all the Paths that cross Aleph/Air, this crossing is the most noticeable and dramatic. When working this Gate you will notice two distinct phases to Resh/Sun. The first half (of the 'with the flow' descent) is filled with a sense of perfect clarity and intention; the second half, with a sense of putting on new clothes as you descend fully into Yesod. By the time you reach Yesod you are fully swathed in several layers and even have on rubber boots for trudging through the mud! Ha!

The return 'against the flow' ascent is a matter of stripping away all your layers of protection and returning to your naked Solitary state of awareness and full consciousness. When you reach the crossing point of the return there is a sense of a heavy weight being lifted or of stepping out of a quagmire and suddenly being able to move freely. And when you once again reach Tiphareth, there is a sense of great clarity.

By working this Gate you learn all about the nature of the astral awareness, its connection to the *conscious* awareness, and the reasons behind the sub- and un-conscious layers. You may even learn to master the astral self here and to truly shape it *consciously* for yourself; otherwise its formation is automatic and unintended. This is the quintessential Gate of character transformation . . .

GATE #38

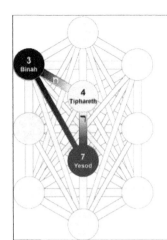

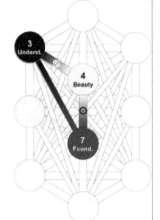

Sequence: ↻ Beauty <SUN> Found.
<HP:7-3> Underst. <CANCER> Beauty

Return: ↻ Beauty <CANCER> Underst.
<HP:3-7> Found. <SUN> Beauty

This Gate is all about the degree to which your Greater Self influences the descent of awareness from Tiphareth to Yesod; specifically, the role of karma in this equation and the way that it shapes this descent. Variations in this descent affect the shape of one's material existence during each incarnation. Working this Gate teaches you still more about your karma, the reasons behind it and its goals.

GATE #39

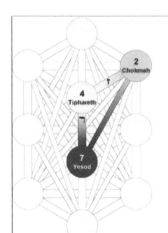

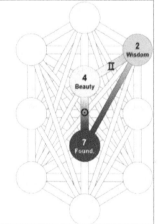

Sequence: ↻ Beauty <SUN> Found.
<HP:7-2> Wisdom <GEMINI> Beauty

Return: ↻ Beauty <GEMINI> Wisdom
<HP:2-7> Found. <SUN> Beauty

Oddly enough, this Gate is about the differences in EM between 'self' and 'other'. The most important part of this education is found in the Path of Zayin/Gemini and its comparison to the strictly personal HP:2>7. Only a small portion of the stream of EM radiating from Chokmah into Tiphareth is destined for your own Solitary Self and the rest splits off to all the 'other'. The EM that passes via HP:2>7 is your portion alone, specifically that part most relevant to your astral being. By comparing these two streams you will learn a great deal about your own EM and its relation to the 'other' you encounter in this lifetime.

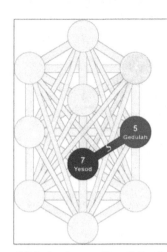

GATE #40

ל **LAMED** (OX GOAD)

LIBRA ♎

Sequence: Mercy <LIBRA> Found.

Return: Found. <LIBRA> Mercy

Keyword: Equilibrium

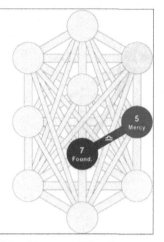

This is the zodiacal Path of Libra, the cardinal Air sign ruled by Venus. The Letter 'Lamed' translates as *ox goad* in English and actually resembles an ox goad in shape. Symbolically then, it gives direction to the Aleph/Air (which means *ox*).

Lamed is also said to be the *serpent uncoiled* which it also resembles. As Teth/Leo is known as the *coiled serpent*, this symbolically infers that Lamed is the power of Leo unleashed upon Yesod. In other words, the *very best* of 'self' conferred by Teth/Leo to the collectives in Gedulah by the Solitary Self, is now forwarded to Yesod and the astral self.

That input of the *very best* from the Solitary Self, having been processed through the collectivity of Gedulah, is hereby transformed into a force of *compassion, co-operation* and *balance* or *equilibrium*. This is what is communicated by Lamed/Libra to Yesod.

This Path is basically an instruction from the Gedulah collectives to the formative astral self that is should always strive for balance and equanimity in all its interactions with 'other'. That remains a basic impulse of the astral self and can be seen throughout the astral realm in the way that most astral beings treat one another: interaction always begins with openness. To anyone who can perceive EM, there is no way to hide or camouflage or pretend in the astral realm since one's essence is visible to all plainly expressed through one's astral form; so really, honesty up front is the only reasonable approach. This sort of public nakedness, as it were, leads to a natural form of compassion for 'other'.

Through working this Gate you have the opportunity to examine this urge within yourself and 'other', and to know its implications (which are far reaching). This is a Force that can be mastered to the extent that you will be able impact, and even cause, the resolution of most conflicts.

GATE #41

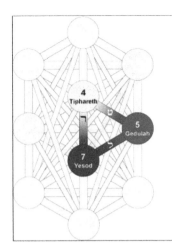

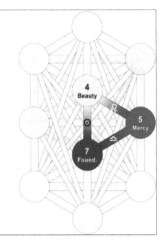

Sequence: ☋ Mercy <LIBRA> Found.
<SUN> Beauty <LEO> Mercy

Return: ☋ Mercy <LEO> Beauty
<SUN> Found. <LIBRA> Mercy

This Gate amplifies and clarifies the reflection of the *very best* of 'self' from Tiphareth, through Gedulah and into Yesod. Working it helps to stabilize the integration of Solitary and Sentient Selves.

GATE #42

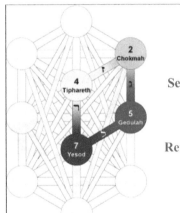

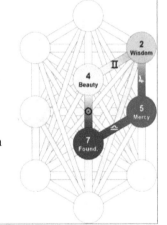

Sequence: ☋ Mercy <LIBRA> Found.
<SUN> Beauty <GEMINI>
Wisdom <JUPITER> Mercy

Return: ☋ Mercy <JUPITER> Wisdom
<GEMINI> Beauty <SUN>
Found. <LIBRA> Mercy

This Gate shows how fundamental compassion and equanimity are to the ever-present interaction between 'self' and 'other' in the astral realm. The need for equilibrium has its root in Chokmah and working this Gates will strengthen and clarify its astral manifestation.

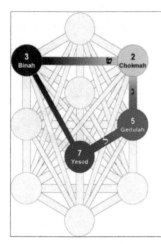

GATE #43

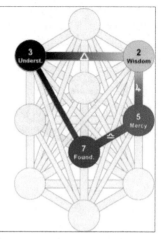

Sequence: ↺ Mercy <LIBRA> Found.
<HP:7-3> Underst. <FIRE>
Wisdom <JUPITER> Mercy

Return: ↻ Mercy <JUPITER> Wisdom
<FIRE> Underst. <HP:3-7>
Found. <LIBRA> Mercy

This Gate, along with the following two Gates, speaks about the connection between the personal karma and this urge to equilibrate. In this case, the driving power behind this need is revealed as Shin/Fire and by working this Gate you can harness this great power, thus increasing your ability to bring balance into all your interactions with 'other'.

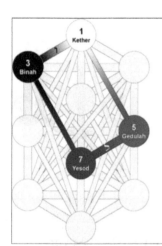

GATE #44

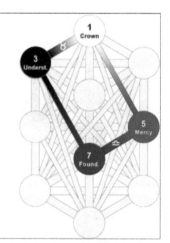

Sequence: ↺ Mercy <LIBRA> Found.
<HP:7-3> Underst. <TAURUS>
Crown <HP:1-5> Mercy

Return: ↻ Mercy <HP:5-1> Crown
<TAURUS> Underst. <HP:3-7>
Found. <LIBRA> Mercy

This shows you how your karmic pathway is a blessing from Kether meant for your process of perfecting your self-expression, specifically as it pertains to astral interaction with 'other'. It all comes down to treating 'other' with compassion and as an equal and working this Gate will show you how (and why) that is possible in *all* situations.

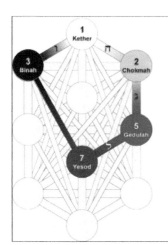

GATE #45

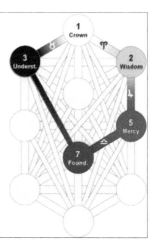

Sequence: ↻ Mercy <LIBRA> Found.
<HP:7-3> Underst. <TAURUS> Crown
<ARIES> Wisdom <JUPITER> Mercy

Return: ↺ Mercy <JUPITER> Wisdom
<ARIES> Crown <TAURUS> Underst.
<HP:3-7> Found. <LIBRA> Mercy

We see here that when we intentionally make compassion an act of our highest creativity, it will invariably have a positive and quickening effect upon our karmic life-path. Through working this Gate we can make use of this dynamic and powerfully effect not only our karma, but more importantly, our ability to clearly follow the dictates of our path.

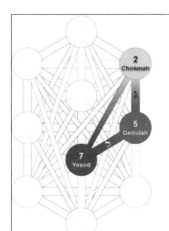

GATE #46

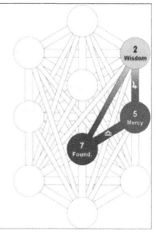

Sequence: ↻ Mercy <LIBRA> Found.
<HP:7-2> Wisdom <JUPITER> Mercy

Return: ↺ Mercy <JUPITER> Wisdom
<HP:2-7> Found. <LIBRA> Mercy

EM is the most determinative factor in our being who we are and by working this Gate, we come to understand the ins and outs and implications of this fact. The overriding message of the '*urge to merge*' and of collectivization comes from Chokmah ultimately; here you will learn *why* that is and why it *must* be the case.

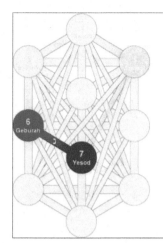

GATE #47

נ NUN (FISH)

SCORPIO ♏

Sequence: Severity <SCORPIO> Found.

Return: Found. <SCORPIO> Severity

Keyword: Self-determination

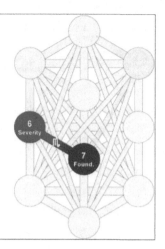

The Hebrew 'Nun' means *fish* in English which is appropriate seeing as this is the Path of Scorpio, a fixed Water sign ruled by Mars. This *fish* is the self that inhabits the Watery astral region of Mem/Water below and is the *perfect* life form for this task. In fact, this *fish* symbolism sets the symbolic stage for what comes next: Mem/Water, Tzaddi/Aquarius and Qooph/Pisces.

Aside from the Watery symbolism, fish also carries with it the symbolism of both abundance and fertility. Abundance by way of the sheer number of fish in the sea and the great schools that they travel in: fertility by way of their use as fertilizer of crops at the time of planting seeds.

Like the cardinal Water sign Path above (Cheth/Cancer) is to Binah, Nun/Pisces is the Path by which Geburah gives birth to a new level or type of self, the Sentient Self. All of the Water sign Paths are, in effect, birth canals and all of the Sephirot of the Pillar of Severity are mothers of a sort. Every one of these mothers provides the finishing touch that completes each new level of Self.

Here there is no multiplication or explosion of numbers as there was with Cheth/Cancer; instead, all of the power of Geburah is focused into one single manifestation. That immense power that manifests *astrally*, is the individual's uniqueness transformed into an immensely potent *significance*. This charge of significance is so great that it manifests as *self-determination*. Of course this makes everything infinitely more complex now that every astral thing has the power to determine for itself how it will interact with 'other'. It all suddenly becomes unpredictable and up to the whim of each individual.

This is where the Scorpio symbolism shows itself; for self-determination is much like the scorpion's sting or at least the threat of stinging that the scorpion presents. Will the scorpion sting or not? It's up to the scorpion to decide and that complicates all interactions within the astral realm.

So Nun/Scorpio is our own power of self-determination and it is all based upon relative significance. Our evaluation of the relative significance of each 'other' we encounter determines our course of action. Relative significance of course has to do with the differences and similarities between our own unique powers and traits and those of 'other'; hence its root in Geburah.

The sign of Scorpio traditionally comes with sexual overtones and what this is referring to is the astral nakedness I mentioned earlier. The significance communicated by your Geburah self is so strong that it is completely visible to all 'other' in your astral form. It cannot be hidden and so the individual has no choice but to confront its own shame for its actions. In effect the astral self has none of the privacy we are accustomed to in the material realm. When I look at a person's astral form *everything* about them is made plain.

The Path of Nun/Scorpio marks a couple of important milestones in the development of the Tree. First of all it completes the second quadrangle which transitions from the mental realm to the astral realm; or from the Air region to the Water region of the Mental Body. The second feature is that it provides the final connection in the upper hexagon of Kether, Chokmah, Binah, Gedulah, Geburah and Yesod. The significance of these two milestones will be explored through upcoming Gates.

Working this Gate will teach you everything there is to know about your own power of self-determination. On the descent from Geburah toward Yesod you will experience an increase and focalization of your own uniqueness and a growing sense of self-assurance; and on the return, a sense of letting go of a great and heavy responsibility, and of returning to simple power.

The greatest lesson here is about the implied responsibility that self-determination confers. You now have the power to do harm to 'other', along with the consequent duty to do no harm and to use your power always for the common good. In other words, you now have the ability and freedom to do great damage to your own karma! Or not; it's all up to *you* now . . .

GATE #48

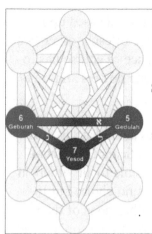

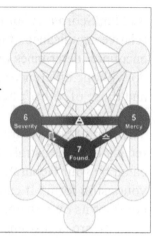

Sequence: ☋ Severity \<SCORPIO\> Found.
\<LIBRA\> Mercy \<AIR\> Severity

Return: ☋ Severity \<AIR\> Mercy
\<LIBRA\> Found. \<SCORPIO\> Severity

This Gate, and the six that follow, are all about the important connection between the Lamed/Libra and Nun/Scorpio, between the need for compassionate balance and the power of self-determination.

The important thing to keep in mind is that the Pillar of Mercy and all that comes from it, is always superior and always takes precedence to the Pillar of Severity and all that comes from it. In other words, Lamed/Libra is more important that Nun/Scorpio as it relates to their interaction. Nonetheless, in an odd twist of meaning, they are completely and perfectly balanced, and that is the lesson of this Gate. They are in point of fact, balanced *through* Aleph/Air and that infinite continuum of alikeness/difference.

Through working this Gate you will learn in detail about this connection and its perfect balance. Working in both directions builds a certain *stability* into the astral self and subsequent personality structure.

GATE #49

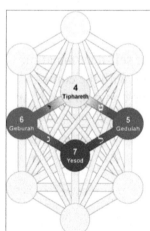

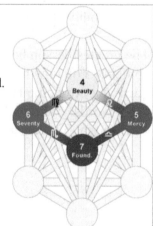

Sequence: ☋ Severity \<SCORPIO\> Found.
\<LIBRA\> Mercy \<LEO\>
Beauty \<VIRGO\> Severity

Return: ☋ Severity \<VIRGO\> Beauty
\<LEO\> Mercy \<LIBRA\>
Found. \<SCORPIO\> Severity

This Gate illustrates that the source of this whole dynamic is the Solitary Self of Tiphareth. Its root is the very highest aspect of the temporal mental body and it is with this spirit of the *very best* of Self that it is formed. This Gate outlines the second quadrangle of the Tree and as such it is the most stable form of the mental body; and it acts to anchor the nascent astral body as it develops. Consequently this Gate brings great internal stability to those who work it.

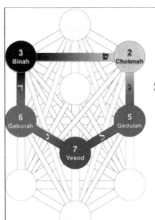

GATE #50

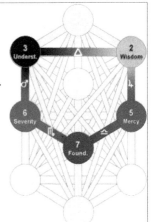

Sequence: ↻ Severity <SCORPIO> Found.
<LIBRA> Mercy <JUPITER> Wisdom
<FIRE> Underst. <MARS> Severity

Return: ↻ Severity <MARS> Underst.
<FIRE> Wisdom <JUPITER> Mercy
<LIBRA> Found. <SCORPIO> Severity

Following on the last Gate, this Gate unites that stability with a higher source of power: Shin/Fire. Working this Gate will increase one's internal stability many times over.

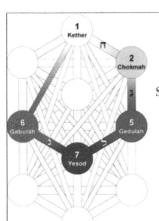

GATE #51

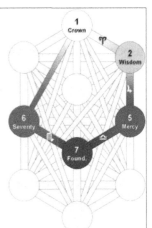

Sequence: ↻ Severity <SCORPIO> Found.
<LIBRA> Mercy <JUPITER> Wisdom
<ARIES> Crown <HP:1-6> Severity

Return: ↻ Severity <HP:6-1> Crown
<ARIES> Wisdom <JUPITER> Mercy
<LIBRA> Found. <SCORPIO> Severity

So now we introduce the reason for this dynamic. It begins here and is spread over the next three Gates; with the most important being the next Gate #52. The reason being pointed to is the process of Self-realization of The "I". With this Gate, the focus is on the creative aspects of the Kethric Brilliance and working it will inform you this and some of its implications.

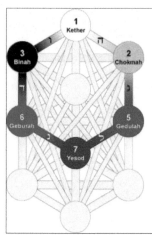

GATE #52

Sequence: ↻ Severity <SCORPIO> Found.
<LIBRA> Mercy <JUPITER> Wisdom
<ARIES> Crown <TAURUS>
Underst. <MARS> Severity

Return: ↻ Severity <MARS> Underst.
<TAURUS> Crown <ARIES> Wisdom
<JUPITER> Mercy <LIBRA>
Found. <SCORPIO> Severity

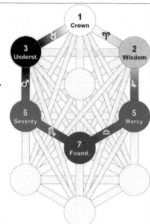

THIS IS ONE OF THE MOST IMPORTANT GATES!

Obviously, this is the upper hexagon of the Gra Tree. It is a statement of perfect balance and harmony, especially when you consider everything it encompasses. It contains the entire Supernal and Mental realms united, or rather, *integrated* as one. It rests upon the Foundation/Yesod but does not really partake in it.

This *is* the driving force behind the Self-realization process of The "I", in symbolic form. And since this is a <u>Gate of Nun/Scorpio</u>, it points to just how important the aspect of *self-determination* is in the whole scheme of things, how much of a turning point it really is.

This Gate contains within itself *all* the Paths we've dealt with thusfar and as such it infers a sense of completion and stability to the core of the incarnate Self. Working it will afford you a degree of balance and solidity heretofore unknown to you. You will come to Understand what your own core Self *is* in all its splendor and glory, as well as its commonness. Never forget that *all* selves are thus! You are both 'nothing special' and 'infinitely special' at the same moment.

You should work this Gate slowly and carefully. At all times be cognizant of what lies within the hexagon, taking special note of the two Mother Letters and Tiphareth.

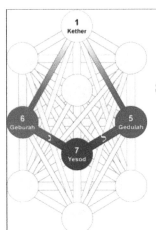 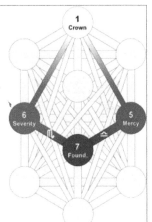

GATE #53

Sequence: ↻ Severity <SCORPIO> Found.
<LIBRA> Mercy <HP:5-1>
Crown <HP:1-6> Severity

Return: ↻ Severity <HP:6-1> Crown
<HP:1-5> Mercy <LIBRA>
Found. <SCORPIO> Severity

This Gate places that whole process of Self-realization directly in the hands of Kether and places *your* part of that process into proper perspective: you are a child of The One. It again points out how pivotal a moment the balance/self-determination dynamic is and just how important it is to what comes ahead. You will learn from this Gate how great a responsibility you inherit with each incarnation!

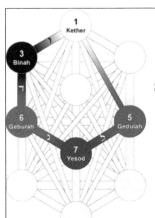 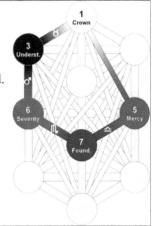

GATE #54

Sequence: ↻ Severity <SCORPIO> Found.
<LIBRA> Mercy <HP:5-1> Crown
<TAURUS> Underst. <MARS> Severity

Return: ↻ Severity <MARS> Underst.
<TAURUS> Crown <HP:1-5> Mercy
<LIBRA> Found. <SCORPIO> Severity

This Gate closes the series concerning the balance/self-determination dynamic with a final emphasis on the great personal responsibility I mentioned previously. Working this Gate will show you what that responsibility entails as well as the consequences of failing to meet the obligations that come with it.

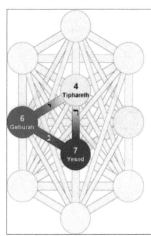

GATE #55

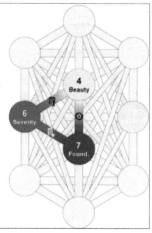

Sequence:↻ Severity <SCORPIO> Found.
<SUN> Beauty <VIRGO> Severity

Return:↻ Severity <VIRGO> Beauty
<SUN> Found. <SCORPIO> Severity

These final six Gates of Nun/Scorpio focus on Understanding your power of self-determination. With this Gate you learn specifically how it depends upon and arises out of the perfection of your own unique power. Or put another way, how it is the product of your Solitary Self's act of perfecting its Geburah self.

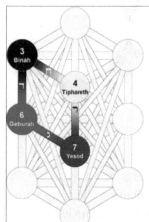

GATE #56

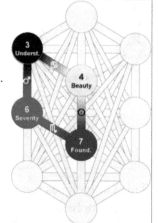

Sequence:↻ Severity <SCORPIO> Found.
<SUN> Beauty <CANCER>
Underst. <MARS> Severity

Return:↻ Severity <MARS> Underst.
<CANCER> Beauty <SUN>
Found. <SCORPIO> Severity

This Gate traces that power back to its origin in your Greater Self. From working this Gate you will learn your Greater's motivations and how your power of self-determination fits into your Greater's expression of its EM.

GATE #57

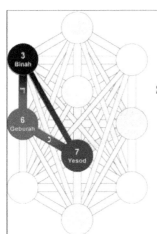

Sequence: ↻ Severity <SCORPIO> Found.
<HP:7-3> Underst. <MARS> Severity

Return: ↻ Severity <MARS> Underst.
<HP:3-7> Found. <SCORPIO> Severity

This Gate will inform you of the pivotal role that your exercising of your power of self-determination plays in your karmic path; both how it affects your karma and how your karma affects it.

GATE #58

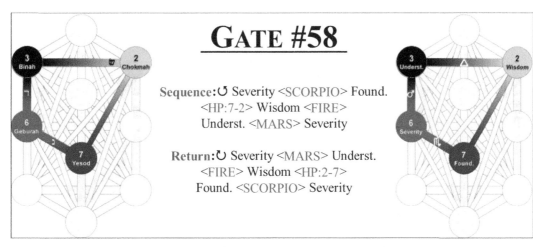

Sequence: ↻ Severity <SCORPIO> Found.
<HP:7-2> Wisdom <FIRE>
Underst. <MARS> Severity

Return: ↻ Severity <MARS> Underst.
<FIRE> Wisdom <HP:2-7>
Found. <SCORPIO> Severity

This Gate will inform you about the degree to which EM plays its role in your power of self-determination, how it is a necessary part of your manifesting your own EM. It also points to a higher origin of this power.

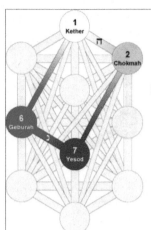

GATE #59

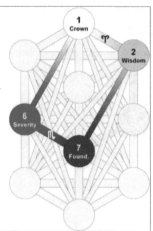

Sequence: ↻ Severity <SCORPIO> Found. <HP:7-2> Wisdom <ARIES> Crown <HP:1-6> Severity

Return: ↺ Severity <HP:6-1> Crown <ARIES> Wisdom <HP: 2-7> Found. <SCORPIO> Severity

Now we point to its true, ultimate origin in Kether. Here again you learn how important your power of self-determination is to the grand process of Self-realization. From this Gate you will learn anew to value and appreciate this power more fully.

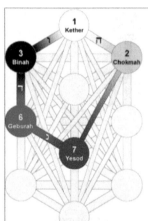

GATE #60

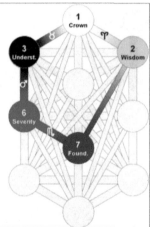

Sequence: ↻ Severity <SCORPIO> Found. <HP:7-2> Wisdom <ARIES> Crown <TAURUS> Underst. <MARS> Severity

Return: ↺ Severity <MARS> Underst. <TAURUS> Crown <ARIES> Wisdom <HP:2-7> Found. <SCORPIO> Severity

This completes the Tree's lessons about your power of self-determination with a strong instruction about the fulfillment of your personal EM. Determining for yourself is crucial to the full expression of your EM in each incarnation.

===

Special Note: After working this Gate the requisite three times, I suggest that you visit APPENDIX ONE and perform the special work described there, *before* moving on to Gate #61.

===

NETZACH / VITALITY

נצח

KEYWORD: RESONANCE

The Hebrew word 'Netzach' is usually translated as *Victory* but this seems nonsensical to me; therefore I translate it as *Vitality* since that is closer to what this Sephirot is all about. Netzach is the energy of the astral realm and that energy is interactive. In other words, it's the energy that arises due to the incessant interaction between 'self' and 'other'.

Everything in this realm of significance affects every other thing. Significance is always an energetic exchange between one thing and another. I affect you by virtue of my relative significance to you and you affect me by virtue of your relative significance to me. Thus I don't directly exert an influence over you; but rather how you feel about me, the relative significance you ascribe to me, is a *self-inflicted* influence, an influence arising from within you as a *reaction* to me. And I in turn generate a similar self-inflicted influence in response to you, etc.

This is called *resonance* and this is what Netzach represents above all else. We cannot help but resonate with 'other'; it's automatic and spontaneous and we normally have no conscious control over it. It is the astral manifestation of the primal '*urge to merge*' that we are so familiar with.

Through resonance we become more similar and our *alikeness* increases. There is an opening of the boundaries of 'self' and the barriers between 'self' and 'other' begin to blur. I begin to take on your characteristics and you mine. Our EM begins to meld and create connections of alikeness.

One important difference between resonance and past manifestations of the '*urge to merge*' that we've encountered is that, in the astral, we are not bound by the mental realm law of 'like attracts like'. In the astral realm, *opposites* may also attract instead of repelling each other. Resonance can develop between total opposites just as easily and automatically as alike things. Thus in the astral realm *every* thing affects *every* other thing through the medium of significance.

We must remember here that significance is a *self-generated*, totally subjective evaluation based upon a comparison to our past experiences. At its root, of course, is an expression of EM that we are reacting to but the relative power of the significance that we derive comes from *us* and *our* valuation, not from 'other'. In essence, all of the power of the astral realm is generated by *us*, the inhabitants, by our resonating! Not only do we generate this power; we also *feed* off this power and therefore thrive. Netzach is truly the realm of *Vitality*.

For us humans, this translates into *emotion*; which is nothing other than the impact that relative significance has upon our psyche and our bodies. It's for this reason that Netzach is described as the sphere of the emotions; technically however this is not the case. The transition or evolution from resonance to emotion actually happens with the formation of the Static Self and physical body through the Path of Tzaddi/Aquarius (which will come much later).

Nonetheless, one can encounter within Netzach all the classical archetypes of the emotions: a.k.a. the ancient gods and goddesses. Primary among them is the Venus/Aphrodite archetype which is actually an influx from Gedulah via the Path of Kaph/Venus. This most appropriate considering that Netzach forms the bottom of the Pillar of Mercy.

Of course EM is what's really behind these archetypes; what we humans define as the gods and goddesses of old are simply very powerful groupings of EM. These groupings penetrate into the astral realm as specific, universal sets of *significance*.

So Netzach is the source of all the power within the astral realm. For example, it is the source of the astral energy you feel when consciously inhabiting your astral body. It is also the essence of what we who study Franz Bardon's *IIH* know as the Vital Energy.

In Netzach one can come to know all about resonance, astral energy, Vital Energy and the emotional archetypes. Harnessing them and making use of them however, doesn't really come until Hod.

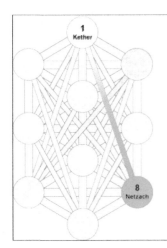

GATE #61
HIDDEN PATH: 1>8

Sequence: Crown <HP:1-8> Vitality

Return: Vitality <HP:8-1> Crown

Keyword: A blessing

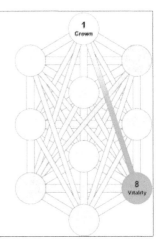

I've been struggling these past few days trying to figure out what to say about this Gate. Truth is it's actually indescribable. As is its mirror, Gate #80 HP:1>9.

In general though there are a few things worth mentioning. There are only four Gates (Hidden Paths) that cross *two* Mother Letters. This Gate and Gate #80 both cross Shin/Fire and Aleph/Air; and, Gates #110 and #111 both cross Aleph/Air and Mem/Water. Gates #61 and #80 traverse from the supernal realm (Kether), through the entire mental realm and end in the astral realm; while #110 and #111, traverse from the lower supernal realm, through the mental *and* astral realms and end all the way down in the material realm. This is deeply significant, to say the least!

All I can really say about this Gate is that it is a blessing from Kether upon Netzach. As you descend you will meet with the sensation of penetrating trough a sort of membrane between each realm and same for the ascent though it is less noticeable. From working this Gate you will learn what it means for Kether to be fully present within Netzach.

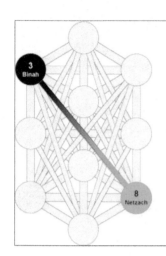

GATE #62
HIDDEN PATH: 3>8

Sequence: Underst. <HP:3-8> Vitality

Return: Vitality <HP:8-3> Underst.

Keyword: Astral karma

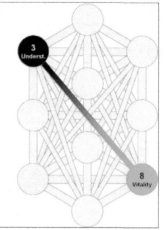

This Gate and its mirror Gate #81 HP:2>9, are both very significant. First of all they are the only Paths that cross directly over the Aleph-Resh crossing, the exact center point of the Tree. They both are also the only connections between the lower supernal realm and the lower astral realm.

Furthermore, they illustrate certain oppositions that exist in the Tree that are otherwise only apparent when the Tree is rendered in three dimensions. The oppositional relationship between Binah and Netzach, and between Chokmah and Hod, are *very* significant and turn out to be a major part of the overall balance of the Tree (illustrated by their crossing of Aleph-Resh). [The other three dimensional oppositions are Kether-Malkuth, Tiphareth-Yesod, and Gedulah-Geburah.]

They are also both the only non-Mother Letter Paths to directly connect the two side Pillars. This Gate in particular is extra special in that it is the *only* Path that connects the Pillar of Severity directly to the Pillar of Mercy: all other connections between the Pillars go in the *opposite* direction from Mercy to Severity. So they are in this way akin to the Mother Letters, especially in terms of their significance and the structural integrity they confer to the geometry of the Tree.

This Gate is about the connection between your Greater Self and that part of your astral body responsible for resonance. It is about the astral karma that dictates what you are capable of resonating with, as well as the power of that resonance.

Working this Gate on the descent, it passes first over Yod/Virgo, then over the Aleph-Resh crossing, and finally over Lamed/Libra before ending in Netzach. At each of these locations you will experience a corresponding noticeable effect: at Yod/Virgo things clarify; at Aleph-Resh things individualize; and at Lamed/Libra things attain an appropriate balance. You will learn from this journey all about how your astral karma affects your ability to resonate with 'other' and the limits of your own emotional scope. The return journey provides a profitable opportunity the analyze the makeup of this karmic influence quite closely.

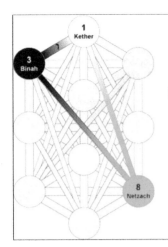

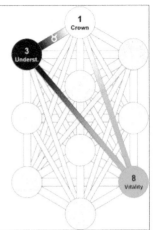

GATE #63

Sequence: ↻ Underst. \<HP:3-8> Vitality
\<HP:8-1> Crown \<TAURUS> Underst.

Return: ↺ Underst. \<TAURUS> Crown
\<HP:1-8> Vitality \<HP:8-3> Underst.

This is another blessing from Kether upon Netzach. The message here is that The "I" only and always wishes for and works for your <u>perfection</u>. By working this Gate you can consciously and intentionally *accept* this blessing.

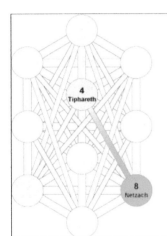

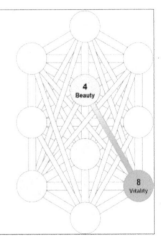

GATE #64
HIDDEN PATH: 4>8

Sequence: Beauty \<HP:4-8> Vitality

Return: Vitality \<HP:8-4> Beauty

Keywords: Balance, Limitation

This is the connection between the pure Solitary Self and the resonating Sentient Self. Its crossings over Aleph/Air and Lamed/Libra both confer a balancing effect, with an emphasis on the collectivizing nature of the Pillar of Mercy. This is aimed squarely on your ability to interact with 'other'. This is a very strong imprint from your Solitary Self onto your astral self.

By working this Gate you will understand the limitations of your Solitary Self in so far as the limits of your ability to resonate with 'other': we all have a limited spectrum of what/who we can relate to that changes and evolves with each incarnation.

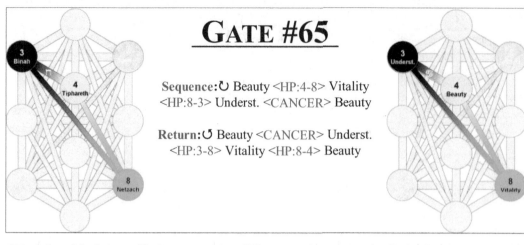

GATE #65

Sequence: ↻ Beauty <HP:4-8> Vitality
<HP:8-3> Underst. <CANCER> Beauty

Return: ↺ Beauty <CANCER> Underst.
<HP:3-8> Vitality <HP:8-4> Beauty

Working this Gate will show you the differences between the limitations upon resonance imposed by your astral karma and those imposed by your Solitary Self. These limitations diverge along the Path of Cheth/Cancer.

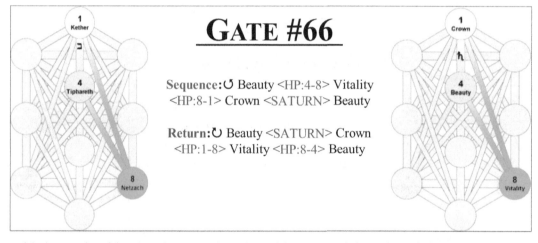

GATE #66

Sequence: ↻ Beauty <HP:4-8> Vitality
<HP:8-1> Crown <SATURN> Beauty

Return: ↺ Beauty <SATURN> Crown
<HP:1-8> Vitality <HP:8-4> Beauty

This is another blessing from Kether shared by both Tiphareth and Netzach. By working this Gate you can once again *accept* this blessing.

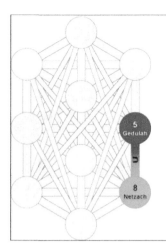

GATE #67

כ KAPH (PALM OF HAND)

VENUS ♀

Sequence: Mercy <VENUS> Vitality

Return: Vitality <VENUS> Mercy

Keyword: Power to resonate,
Emotional archetypes

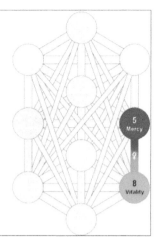

As our fifth Double Letter, Kaph is assigned to the planet Venus. The Hebrew word translates into English as *palm of hand* or, more appropriately, *cupped hand* which the Letter actually looks like. It is the caressing hand of Venus, filled with affection, reaching down from Gedulah and filling Netzach with the astral version of mental collectivity: resonance.

Kaph is the source of resonance and it drains all of the mercy within the Pillar of Mercy, into Netzach, the Pillar's terminus. This is Mercy in its lowest, densest, most personalized manifestation. But resonance is not just an astral, emotional thing; it also carries over into the physical realm. We also *physically*, electro-magnetically resonate with everything around us.

Through resonance, we quite literally astrally *and* physically connect with the world around us. This, of course, is nothing other than that primal *urge to merge* that we are, by now, so familiar with; but this time that *urge* occurs within the astral realm of *symbolic meaning*.

In the Tree, Venus (Gedulah to Netzach) is symbolically the child of Jupiter (Chokmah to Gedulah); thus it carries the archetypes we encountered in Gimel down into the astral realm where they become 'emotional archetypes' in Kaph.

Working this Gate you can learn all about this transition of archetypes into emotional archetypes: which archetypes you naturally relate to or resonate with and which you don't and why. You also learn all about resonance itself: what it is and how it works and the limits of your own power to resonate.

Also contained within this Gate is knowledge of the magic of resonance or *emulation magic* and the art of the *transference of awareness* from 'self' to 'other'. For the artists among my readers there is also much to be learned here regarding the *creation of beauty* in astra-physical form.

GATE #68

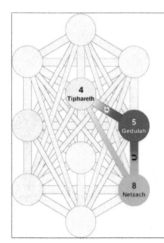

Sequence: ↻ Mercy <VENUS> Vitality
<HP:8-4> Beauty <LEO> Mercy

Return: ↻ Mercy <LEO> Beauty
<HP:4-8> Vitality <VENUS> Mercy

Here we have the Solitary Self's impact on our astral power of resonance. It demands that we always bring the *very best* of our Self to the party. Working this Gate will show you how important this is and the effect that it has, especially when it becomes conscious and intentional.

GATE #69

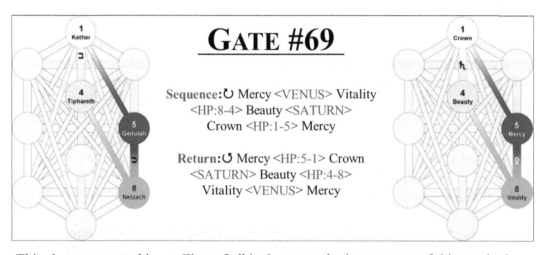

Sequence: ↻ Mercy <VENUS> Vitality
<HP:8-4> Beauty <SATURN>
Crown <HP:1-5> Mercy

Return: ↻ Mercy <HP:5-1> Crown
<SATURN> Beauty <HP:4-8>
Vitality <VENUS> Mercy

This shows us two things. First of all it shows us the importance of this particular phase (resonance) in the process of Self-realization of The "I". Without *resonance* the further evolution of our interaction between 'self' and 'other' would be impossible. Secondly it shows us the nature of the relationship between Kether and Tiphareth, between The Big "I" and the small I; how they work as one and not two.

By working this Gate you more fully *accept* the blessing of Kether upon both Gedulah and Tiphareth by integrating it into Netzach.

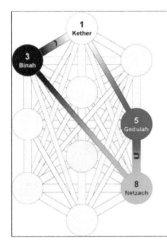

GATE #70

Sequence: ☋ Mercy <VENUS> Vitality
<HP:8-3> Underst. <TAURUS>
Crown <HP:1-5> Mercy

Return: ☋ Mercy <HP:5-1> Crown
<TAURUS> Underst. <HP:3-8>
Vitality <VENUS> Mercy

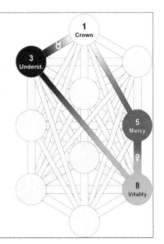

This is an interesting and highly significant unification of the zodiacal sign of Taurus (Vav) with its planetary ruler, Venus (Kaph). Especially telling is what this connection entails: Kether and Binah and two Hidden Paths.

This is, among other things, a blessing from Kether and from your Greater Self; and that blessing is upon your ability to interact with 'other'. Working this Gate *perfects* your resonating.

This is also the perfect Gate for the artist as working it will greatly increase your ability to perceive and to portray beauty.

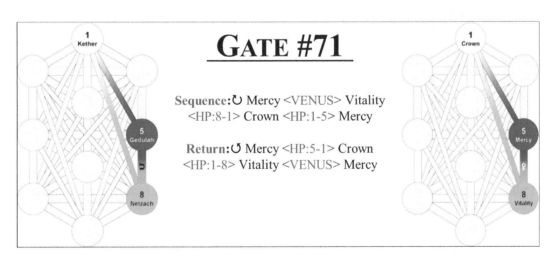

GATE #71

Sequence: ☋ Mercy <VENUS> Vitality
<HP:8-1> Crown <HP:1-5> Mercy

Return: ☋ Mercy <HP:5-1> Crown
<HP:1-8> Vitality <VENUS> Mercy

This is nothing other than a very powerful blessing by Kether upon your power of resonance and everything that Kaph represents. Working this Gate provides you with the opportunity to consciously and intentionally accept this blessing.

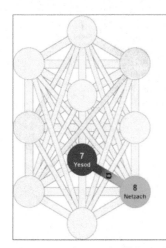

GATE #72

ס **SAMEKH** (PROP)

SAGITTARIUS ♐

Sequence: Found. <SAGIT> Vitality

Return: Vitality <SAGIT> Found.

Keywords: Vital Energy,
Responsibility

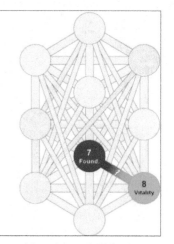

Here we have the last of our Fire sign Paths: Sagittarius, mutable Fire ruled by Jupiter. The Hebrew word 'Samekh' means *a prop* in English; something that supports or stabilizes something else, which seems an odd fit with the Sagittarius symbolism. If we look deeper however, it begins to align.

Sagittarius is a half-human, half-horse archer; in other words, a Centaur archer. A Centaur is a Greek mythological figure representing a bridge between the human and the "animal" natures, mostly considered more akin to a wild beast than a civilized man. One major exception was Chiron, the Wounded Healer and teacher of many great healers such as Asclepius. Chiron was also an archer, having been taught by his mother, Aphrodite. So Sagittarius is both of these things: wise healer and primal beast,

In regard to Samekh, he symbolizes a particular phase in the Self-realization of The "I"; namely, the flow of evolution in awareness between the initial realization of self-determination (Yesod) and the reality of the responsibilities that it imposes upon the individual (Netzach). Remember, this is a *Fire sign* Path, an echo of that original one of Heh/Aries that joined Kether with Chokmah and the "I Am". Self-realization is always a hallmark of the Fire sign Paths.

Philosophically speaking, this is both a great wounding and a great healing which *supports* the continuing evolution of awareness.

This also comes with overtones of the exacting precision of an archer; but our archer is ruled by the Great Benefic, Jupiter, so he is kind and truthful and noble by nature. There is great force and intention behind each of his arrows and they are all guided by his great insight.

The archer's energy here is the frission of 'self' interacting and resonating with 'other', an infinite number of times over. This is the astral energy of active significance that flows along the Path of Samekh from Yesod into Netzach and fills Netzach. And just as the Kethric Brilliance was the *movement* of The "I" Awareness from Kether to Chokmah, from "I" to "I Am!", so to is this astral energy the *movement* of The "I" Awareness from Yesod to the realization of personal responsibility in Netzach. It is the 'astral light' in echo of the Kethric Brilliance.

In Franz Bardon's *Initiation Into Hermetics*, we know this as the <u>Vital Energy</u> which is used primarily for healing. So the VE comes from this passage of Samekh and working this Gate will inform you of everything to know about the VE: its origins and causes, and its uses and powers.

Furthermore, working this Gate will teach you a great deal about healing; and about how *accepting responsibility* for one's own actions is at the root of most healing processes. The type of healing included here is of the intuitive, empathic and highly targeted sort (as opposed to the intellectualized, analytical sort).

By working this Gate you will receive the mark of Jupiter, of Nobility that will persist in all your interactions with 'other'. You will find that you always act with honor and truthfulness henceforth.

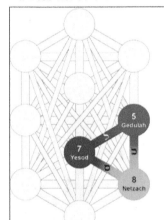 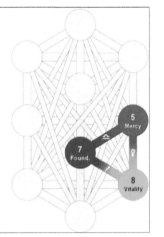

GATE #73

Sequence: ☾ Found. <SAGIT> Vitality <VENUS> Mercy <LIBRA> Found.

Return: ☾ Found. <LIBRA> Mercy <VENUS> Vitality <SAGIT> Found.

With this Gate you will learn how *balance* and *beauty* are the main ingredients that make up the Vital Energy. This will greatly enhance your mastery of the VE.

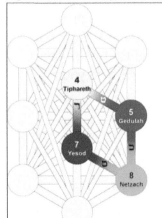 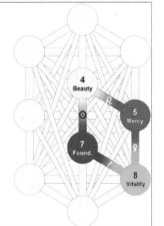

GATE #74

Sequence: ☾ Found. <SAGIT> Vitality <VENUS> Mercy <LEO> Beauty <SUN> Found.

Return: ☾ Found. <SUN> Beauty <LEO> Mercy <VENUS> Vitality <SAGIT> Found.

With this Gate you can learn the best ways, techniques and reasons for you personally to use the VE. Again, greatly enhancing your mastery.

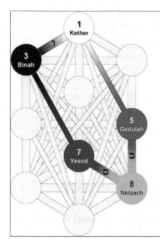

GATE #75

Sequence: ℧ Found. <SAGIT> Vitality
<VENUS> Mercy <HP:5-1> Crown
<TAURUS> Underst. <HP:3-7> Found.

Return: ℧ Found. <HP:7-3> Underst.
<TAURUS> Crown <HP:1-5> Mercy
<VENUS> Vitality <SAGIT> Found.

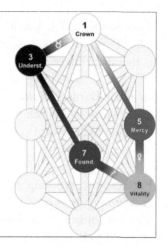

You learn from this Gate about the importance of *responsibility*, both personal and collective, and the effect that the degree to which you accept it has upon your whole astral experience. This Gate is a joint blessing of Understanding from Kether and your own Greater Self.

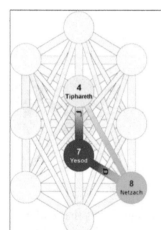

GATE #76

Sequence: ℧ Found. <SAGIT> Vitality
<HP:8-4> Beauty <SUN> Found.

Return: ℧ Found. <SUN> Beauty
<HP:4-8> Vitality <SAGIT> Found.

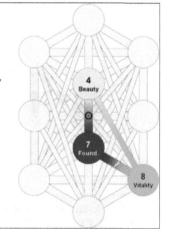

Having been blessed with Understanding in the previous Gate #75, you are now able to learn, through working this Gate, all about working with the VE _as_ your Tiphareth Solitary Self (the Air and Fire regions of your Mental Body). In other words, this Gate offers training as it were, in manipulating the VE with your 'higher Mind', taking your mastery to a still higher level.

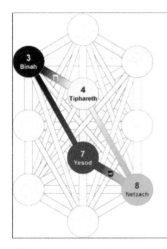

GATE #77

Sequence: ↻ Found. <SAGIT> Vitality
<HP:8-4> Beauty <CANCER>
Underst. <HP:3-7> Found.

Return: ↺ Found. <HP:7-3> Underst.
<CANCER> Beauty <HP:4-8>
Vitality <SAGIT> Found.

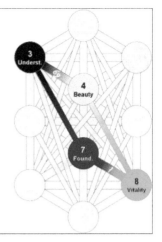

Working this Gate will put you in touch with your incarnational lineage, all the way back to your connection with your Greater Self, in regard to your history of using the VE (and similar energies) for healing and other magical acts. Here is where all of your accumulated karma in this regard is revealed. You can also learn how to rectify your karma as desired.

GATE #78

Sequence: ↻ Found. <SAGIT> Vitality
<HP:8-3> Underst. <HP:3-7> Found.

Return: ↺ Found. <HP:7-3> Underst.
<HP:3-8> Vitality <SAGIT> Found.

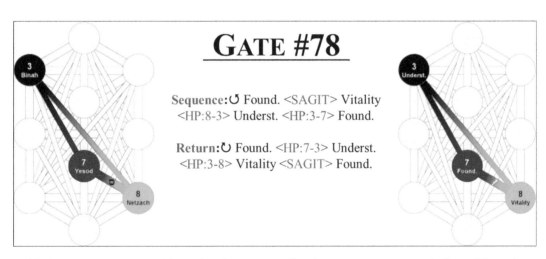

This is your Greater Self putting her stamp firmly upon your Yesod, Samekh and Netzach; upon your power to resonate and take responsibility and all that that includes. This is a very intimate and powerful blessing which you have the opportunity to *accept* by working this Gate.

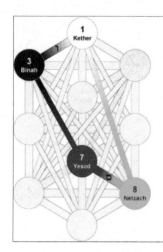

GATE #79

Sequence:↺ Found. <SAGIT> Vitality
<HP:8-1> Crown <TAURUS>
Underst. <HP:3-7> Found.

Return:↻ Found. <HP:7-3> Underst.
<TAURUS> Crown <HP:1-8>
Vitality <SAGIT> Found.

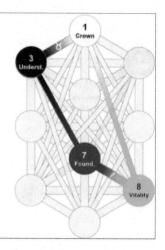

This is Kether affirming and amplifying this blessing upon your power to resonate and take responsibility. This is completes a powerful blessing which you have the opportunity to *accept* by working this Gate.

Hod / Splendor

הוד

KEYWORDS: DISSONANCE,
DURATION, RATIONAL INTELLECT,
POWER OF CHOICE

The two side Pillars are always poles of a single thing and here that one thing is the interaction between 'self' and 'other'. The merciful, forceful pole of Netzach is resonance and therefore the severe, formative pole of Hod is *dissonance*.

Taken to its logical extreme, unchecked resonance would eventually lead to a state where 'self' loses all of its uniqueness and *becomes* 'other'. Dissonance and the uniqueness of 'self' is that check and it's just as fundamental to being as resonance and the *urge to merge*. Simply put, it is a manifestation of the *self-preservation instinct* inherent to *all* life; an instinct that arises from the realization of the Solitary Self's own uniqueness in Geburah.

'Self' can only resonate with 'other' just so far before this *unconscious* instinct automatically kicks in and 'self' begins to counter with varying degrees of dissonance. However, before that point of extremis at which instinct takes over, dissonance can be a choice; and even when it has taken over, the *degree* of dissonance is a matter of choice.

Hod therefore takes the inherited factor of 'self-determination' a step forward and it becomes the *power of choice*. It is because of the introduction of this *power to choose* that this Sephirot gets its name of Hod or *Splendor* in English: this one, seemingly simple power, given to each Sentient Self, so utterly transforms the universe and multiplies its complexity by infinity that the only word that can possibly describe its appearance is indeed Splendor. The appearance is one of an infinitely faceted diamond in full sunlight; it entrances and hypnotizes and one cannot look away, such is its allure.

The consequences are literally innumerable but I will try to enumerate a few of the most pertinent for you. Probably the most important for this discussion is the effect this power of choice has on human consciousness, most specifically its structure.

The power of choice necessitates a 'chooser' and this is the *rational intellect* of Hod. Now the rational intellect is an interesting beast. Contrary to how it is treated in modern culture it is *not* objective by nature. It exists solely within the realm of subjective significance and *all* of its evaluations and choices are rooted in this self same relative significance. Objectivity is under the purview of the Higher Mind, the Air and Fire regions of the Mental Body, while the rational intellect is part of the Water region of same. It can *connect* with the Higher Mind but this takes a degree of conscious intention which the rational intellect ordinarily operates without.

So, the rational intellect of Hod is the chooser, the decider, the feeler (or rather that part of the awareness that is conscious of the perception of sensation), and the namer or identifier. It has all of these functions that operate pretty much automatically. Each one works with the medium of *significance* processed through *memory*: the significance of relevant past experiences is compared and evaluated and a result is reached, a decision made, etc.

Every astral and physical thing in existence has this same power to choose. *Every* thing! Don't let the fact that each thing's expression of this power may look different than your own fool you into thinking otherwise. One of the greatest crimes perpetrated by humanity is to treat our fellow beings as if they are incapable of choosing for themselves!

The deeper secret is that this power is *so* great that no one can actually decide for another. One can be dissuaded or forced into another course of action but the power to choose is *only* in the individual's own hands. If the decision is truly held to, *no* other power can override it, even to the point of death; for this power is stronger than even the instinct of self-preservation. Normally such strength of decision is only possible when the Higher Mind is involved but its power, all comes from here in Hod.

Because of all these byproducts coming from the power of choice and from these opposing poles of resonance and dissonance, the final component of 'time' is realized: *duration*. Since every being has some version of the 'chooser' to its awareness and the medium that each chooser works with is the memory of past significance, the recognition or realization of duration, of an accumulation of past memories and their sequence, arises; and thus the whole astral realm experiences duration along with sequence, change and continuity. In other words, Hod is the birthplace of time, where time is set into motion, thanks mostly to Mem/Water which is the final Path completing Hod.

Aside from the effect on awareness the overall effect on the astral realm as a whole is one of clarification solidification, crystallization and complexification. It really is an Infinite Splendor! Everything is *very* defined and refined here, just a short step away from physical rigidity. Each moment of time seems much shorter and yet much fuller, much more packed with activity at the same time.

Hod is often imagined as a great library, filled with books covering all of human knowledge, and to a certain symbolic extent this is true. To the trained astral eyes, each of those myriad facets of the Splendorous Diamond expresses one aspect each of Essential Meaning presented to the intellect in a form that it can comprehend; much like an open book, although there are no printed words and no reading per se. It does however, require the Higher Mind to access.

All interaction with 'other' in Hod involves resonance and dissonance and always, *always* choice. We are at every turn and in every moment *required* by 'other' to make a choice. That is what the astral demands of us in advance of physical incarnation. Each choice we make is a test of sorts that examines the quality of each one of our choices. It is a test of character that is meant to always expose what lurks in the depths. This is how we evolve and is a gift of the Divine Provider. It is what drives us ever forward along our karmic path.

I think this is why Franz Bardon's work of character transformation in *IIH* is always associated with this Sephirot. Part of the lesson or teaching if you will, of Hod is just how important personal character is to this phase in the Self-realization of The "I" and to reaching the ultimate aim through incarnation. Our character is the lead that we are in the process of transforming into gold; incarnation after incarnation, over and over we keep circulating and refining.

We must not forget that Hod is finally the mother of Malkuth, the realm of time-space and of consequence; and that the Sentient Self becomes the Static Self, or Solitary-Sentient-Static Self.

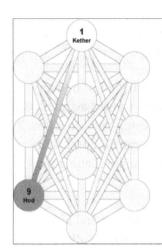
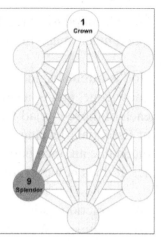

GATE #80
HIDDEN PATH: 1>9

Sequence: Crown <HP:1-9> Splendor

Return: Splendor <HP:9-1> Crown

Keyword: Blessing

This Gate is a blessing from Kether upon Hod. As you descend, you will notice each of the seven times you cross another Path and same for the ascent though it is less noticeable. From working this Gate you will learn what it means for Kether to be fully present within Hod.

[Note: There are nine instances of what I call a *double crossing* of Paths (where two Paths cross another Path with a total of three Paths converging) and one instance of a *triple crossing* (where three Paths cross another Path with four total Paths converging). You have already experienced three double crossings (Teth-HP:2>7-HP:1>8, Aleph-Resh-HP:3>8, Aleph-HP:2>7-HP:4>8) and this Gate (Yod-HP:3>7-HP:1>9) makes your fourth. Your next Gate of HP:2>9 also crosses the second double crossing you've already experienced making it into our single triple crossing <u>at the fabled Aleph-Resh crossing</u>. Each of these double and triple crossings are significant occasions which can be explored further during your working of their respective Gates.]

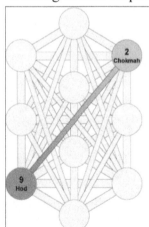
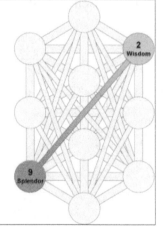

GATE #81
HIDDEN PATH: 2>9

Sequence: Wisdom <HP:2-9> Splendor

Return: Splendor <HP:9-2> Wisdom

Keyword: Information

<u>**This is a very significant Gate, especially for the hermeticist!!!**</u>

I'd like for you to look back in Gate #62 (HP:3>8) where I talked about the Aleph-Resh crossing and especially what I said about the oppositional relationships between the Sephirot. This Gate brings all of that into very sharp focus as it places the last stamp upon the exact center point of the whole Tree: the Aleph-Resh crossing.

But let me first give you a few interesting facts about these oppositions or mirrorings:

Kether has 7 powers (emanations or generative Paths) and zero creators (higher influences). That's the highest number of powers and the lowest number of creators in the Tree. Its opposite, Malkuth, has zero powers and 7 creators, the exact opposite of Kether with the highest number of creators and lowest of powers in the Tree.

Chokmah has the second highest number of powers, 6, and second lowest number of creators, 1. Hod is the exact opposite with 1 power and 6 creators. And so it continues: Binah (5p+2c) <> Netzach (2p+5c); Tiphareth (5p+3c) <> Yesod (3p+5c); Gedulah (4p+3c) <> Geburah (3p+4c).

Four of the five sets of oppositions meet at the Aleph-Resh crossing point and even the Kether-Malkuth opposition centers itself at the Aleph-/Resh crossing point. It is truly the point of ultimate balance.

So, back to Gate #81 . . .

This Gate is, quite literally, Chokmah filling each facet of that infinitude of facets to the Great Diamond that is Hod, with its Essential Meaning. That is why it serves as a sort of library of information: the information being expressed by Chokmah's EM is readily available to the rational intellect (with the help of the Higher Mind) through this Hidden Path. At the personal level, this is all of the EM that you can possibly comprehend during this particular incarnation, so working this Gate will be *very* informative.

You will notice every one of the nine times you cross another Path, most especially the Aleph-Resh triple crossing. Each feels like a binding and a completion. At the Aleph-Resh it ceases to be Universal and becomes ever more personal as you descend; with the opposite being true on the ascent.

The more you are able to engage your Higher Mind, especially the Fire region, the more you will benefit from working this Gate. As I said at the beginning, this Gate is especially significant for the Hermeticist or true Philosophist.

This special relationship between Chokmah and Hod is meant to provide an objective source of information to the otherwise subjective rational intellect and I advise that you make good use of it for it is truly a gift.

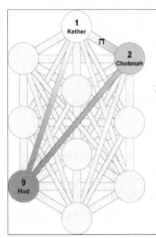

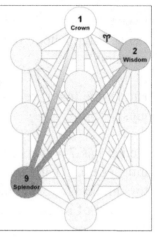

GATE #82

Sequence: ↻ Wisdom <HP:2-9> Splendor
<HP:9-1> Crown <ARIES> Wisdom

Return: ↺ Wisdom <ARIES> Crown
<HP:1-9> Splendor <HP:9-2> Wisdom

This is a joint blessing from Kether and Chokmah upon Hod, especially upon the rational intellect and the decider/namer mind. The point of working this Gate is that you *Accept* this blessing and understand it.

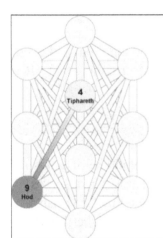

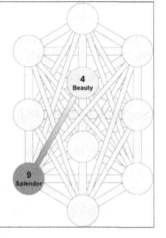

GATE #83
HIDDEN PATH: 4>9

Sequence: Beauty <HP:4-9> Splendor

Return: Splendor <HP:9-4> Beauty

Keyword: Self-awareness

This is a direct influence from your Solitary Self upon the whole structure of the Hod stage of Awareness; a sort of reaffirmation of the wholeness of who you are in this and every incarnation.

Working this Gate will clarify your sense of 'self' but in your own context; in other words, not 'self' in relation to 'other' but rather 'self' for self's sake. It will show you who *you* are, as if in a universe with no 'other'. The four Paths you cross (one double) will all make themselves felt but perhaps more significantly on the descent.

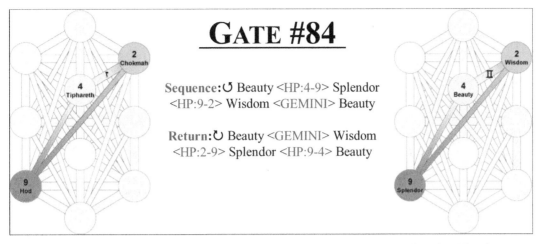

GATE #84

Sequence: ↻ Beauty <HP:4-9> Splendor <HP:9-2> Wisdom <GEMINI> Beauty

Return: ↻ Beauty <GEMINI> Wisdom <HP:2-9> Splendor <HP:9-4> Beauty

Now Chokmah, with the help of Zayin/Gemini, brings the *fact* of 'other' back to the equation and shows us who we are, but this time in relation to 'other'. Through working this Gate we get to see ourselves in these two lights, from these two perspectives *and* we get to evaluate the differences. With the Higher Mind involved, this can be extremely enlightening and have a great influence over (especially) the nobility of the rational intellect.

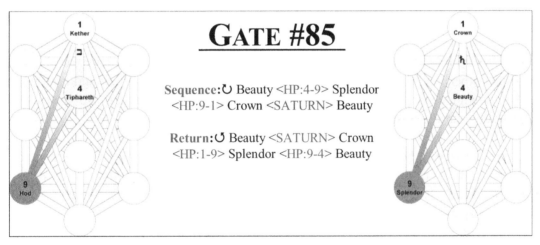

GATE #85

Sequence: ↻ Beauty <HP:4-9> Splendor <HP:9-1> Crown <SATURN> Beauty

Return: ↻ Beauty <SATURN> Crown <HP:1-9> Splendor <HP:9-4> Beauty

And now we finish with a blessing from The "I" on both Tiphareth and Hod and the energy that flows between the two. By working this Gate and *accepting* its blessing you complete a particular set of transformations that began with Gate #80.

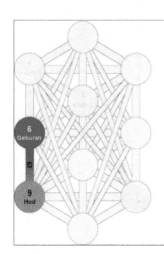
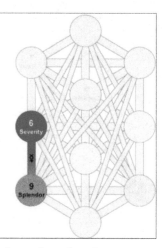

GATE #86

פ PEH (MOUTH)

MERCURY ☿

Sequence: Severity <MERC> Splendor

Return: Splendor <MERC> Severity

Keywords: Communication, Discernment

The Double Letter 'Peh' means *mouth* in English and is attributed to the planet Mercury. What do we do with our mouth? We speak, we communicate; and we also eat and taste but that's less relevant here.

So Peh is about our power to communicate. This of course, is a bit different than *expressing* ourselves which is a natural function of *all* Essential Meaning. Co-mmunicating takes *two*, whereas expressing takes only one; thus communication is expression in the realm of 'self' and 'other'.

We express to 'other' in hope that and with aim of, the 'other' understanding what we have expressed. In communication, we must modify and adapt our expression to suit 'other' and that's where Peh comes in: the situational adapting and crafting of our own meaning's expression. The ability to communicate greatly advances, facilitates and eases our interactions with 'other'!

In speaking the Hebrew language *and especially in uttering the Hebrew Letters qabbalistically*, the mouth and the placement of the tongue within the mouth, plays an important role. Each Letter is to be pronounced with a specific placement of the tongue thusly:

GROUPS	LETTERS
Dentals	Z, S, Sh, R, Tz
Palatals	G, I, K, Q
Gutturals	A, Ch, H, O
Linguals	D, T, L, N, Th
Labials	B, V, M, P

So Peh is the stage upon which the adaptation of EM is enacted and as any actor knows, the stage and its scenery play as big a role as the dialogue.

This Path then, is our ability to communicate with 'other'. Its source is Geburah, the place of our greatest and most powerful uniqueness and as a consequence, the quality of our ability to communicate is equally unique. No 'other' communicates exactly *as* we do, nor exactly *what* we do.

Of course to be able to communicate, certain changes in, and evolution of, consciousness must occur. First and foremost, the power of *discernment* must arise. One must be able to discern the nature and requirements of any given situation and then *decide* the best course to take and which adaptation will work best in the situation. Bound up within Peh then is a thinking, expressive awareness with discernment and the power to decide.

The mouth also holds our sense of taste which itself is a power of discernment as we evaluate a specific flavor based on our past experiences of flavor, both similar and dissimilar. Also we receive physical nourishment through our mouths; much as we receive interpersonal, social nourishment through communication.

By working this Gate you will come to know your own unique ability to communicate; not only to know it but to *improve* it. Through this Gate you can directly increase the influence of your Greater Self over your power of communication by grounding yourself in your Geburah. And by engaging your Higher Mind in this Gate you can greatly improve your intuitive abilities in regard to communicating with 'other' and thus tailor your expression precisely to another's understanding. The possibilities are limited only by your imagination.

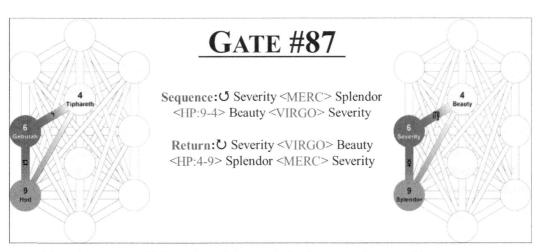

GATE #87

Sequence: ↺ Severity <MERC> Splendor
<HP:9-4> Beauty <VIRGO> Severity

Return: ↻ Severity <VIRGO> Beauty
<HP:4-9> Splendor <MERC> Severity

Working this Gate will bind the Higher Mind of your Solitary Self to your communication and discernment abilities; thus empowering and refining them. This Gate may also be used in the perfecting of the accuracy of your pronunciation of the Hebrew Letters when learning qabbalistic utterance.

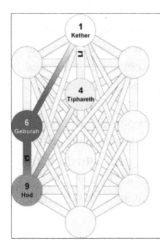

GATE #88

Sequence: ↻ Severity \<MERC> Splendor
\<HP:9-4> Beauty \<SATURN>
Crown \<HP:1-6> Severity

Return: ↻ Severity \<HP:6-1> Crown
\<SATURN> Beauty \<HP:4-9>
Splendor \<MERC> Severity

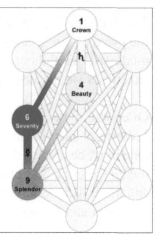

This Gate integrates your power of communication and discernment with the Fire region of your temporal Mental Body and its direct connection to the Supernal Mental Body. This can take both of these powers to surprising heights of intuitiveness! Your ability to communicate extremely arcane and complex concepts to another's understanding will vastly improve.

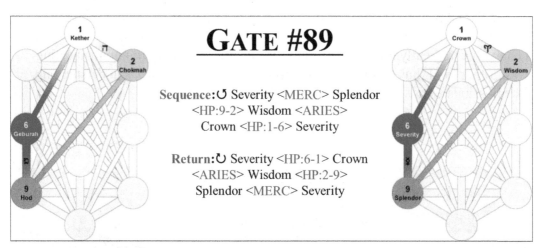

GATE #89

Sequence: ↻ Severity \<MERC> Splendor
\<HP:9-2> Wisdom \<ARIES>
Crown \<HP:1-6> Severity

Return: ↻ Severity \<HP:6-1> Crown
\<ARIES> Wisdom \<HP:2-9>
Splendor \<MERC> Severity

Working this Gate *thoroughly* will enable you to communicate any aspect of EM to another with clarity and precision. It has an extremely creative impact on your ability to communicate. Also, qabbalistic utterance will be able to contain and express a greater quantity of EM and will become markedly more creative.

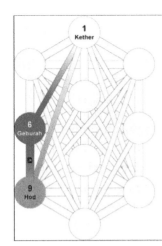

GATE #90

Sequence: ℧ Severity <MERC> Splendor <HP:9-1> Crown <HP:1-6> Severity

Return: ℧ Severity <HP:6-1> Crown <HP:1-9> Splendor <MERC> Severity

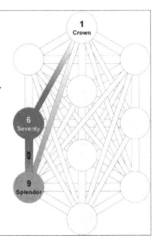

Through working this Gate you can, if you wish, become a Master Communicator. At the very least it is a Kethric Blessing upon your powers of communication and discernment which you can *accept* here. This is *the most* beneficial Gate for anybody studying qabbalistic utterance!

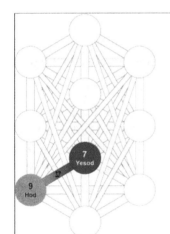

GATE #91

ע AYIN

(EYE, SPRING, NAUGHT)

CAPRICORN ♑

Sequence: Found. <CAPRI> Splendor

Return: Splendor <CAPRI> Found.

Keyword: Choice

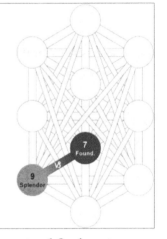

The Hebrew 'Ayin' has three meanings in English: an *eye*, a natural fresh water *spring*, or nothing / *naught*. As disparate as these three may seem at fist glance, they do still all relate to this Path.

Its zodiacal correspondence is the cardinal Earth sign of Capricorn, ruled by Saturn. It marks both the longest night and the very beginning of the Sun's increase or return; it is both an ending and a beginning, both a cold wet season of decay and the igniting of the spark of life within the rot.

The symbol for Capricorn is a sea-goat: top half goat and bottom half a fish's tail. This is said to represent the god Pan who in trying to escape the onslaught of Typhon, jumped into the Nile to disguise himself as a fish but was only half successful, ending up with only the bottom part of his body transformed. It is interesting to note that the other zodiacal Path coming from Yesod, Samekh/Sagittarius, is also represented by a dual bodied creature. This is a reminder that the astral realm is an *intermediary* between the mental and the physical.

Furthermore, in kabbalah, Ayin and Capricorn are said to manifest the universal quality of *laughter*. So it is also expresses shades of the universal jokester!

What Ayin represents in the Tree, and what ties all of these symbols together, is the *power to choose*. This is what is really meant by the often touted "free will": it is the essence of free will. In reality, one can will anything one desires and the universe will take no notice but when one *chooses*, the universe suddenly changes. Choosing is the ultimate creative act for when one chooses, the universe adjusts itself to that choice and consequences will *automatically* follow.

Every choice generates its own consequences. The two are inseparable and to my mind, this is where the association with the universal jokester enters in! Don't the consequences of our choices often seem like some sort of joke being played on us by a humorous universe? And sometimes, our choices can lead to *naught*!

In fact, each choice creates *unpredictable* changes in the structure of the universe. Normally these are only small changes that effect just us and our immediate environment but sometimes (very, very rarely) they can change the whole world. This of course relates to the natural spring symbolism of Ayin; the best image of which is a desert oasis, bustling with life amid arid desolation.

Choosing is a *creative* act that is usually done in the wild, so to speak, meaning with unpredictable consequences; but it *can* be done with foresight and tailored to create only predicted and intended reactions. Ayin's *eye* points us to the foresight and vision necessary to use the power of choice in a truly constructive, magical way. In fact, using the power to choose *intentionally* is the primary method for resolving negative karma.

While the power of choice is related to self-determination, they are not truly the same thing. The former is the child of the latter: only a self-determined being can make a choice. You must remember here, that I am speaking of *all* things and not only humans. We are *all* constantly changing the universe with our choices! (Thus Hod is the Infinite Splendor.)

An action is a choice, a spoken word is a choice, an inner resolution is a choice; truly choice is at the heart of so much of our reality.

By working this Gate you can learn all about the nature of choice and its connection to consequence. With added effort you can learn how to use this power to advantage and consciously shape outcomes.

It is significant that this marks the halfway point in the 182 Gates. This should give you a clear indication of how complex the remaining transition from astral to physical is.

GATE #92

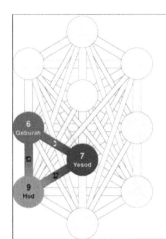

Sequence:☋ Found. <CAPRI> Splendor <MERC> Severity <SCORPIO> Found.

Return:☊ Found. <SCORPIO> Severity <MERC> Splendor <CAPRI> Found.

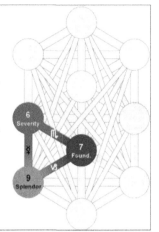

This Gate aligns our power of choice with our powers of communication and self-determination. Working it will increase the force behind our choices as well as our ability to clearly communicate them to others.

GATE #93

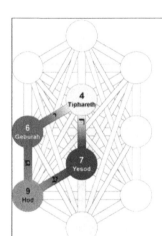

Sequence:☋ Found. <CAPRI> Splendor <MERC> Severity <VIRGO> Beauty <SUN> Found.

Return:☊ Found. <SUN> Beauty <VIRGO> Severity <MERC> Splendor <CAPRI> Found.

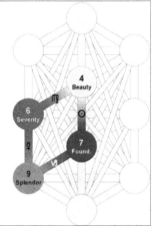

This Gate unites our powers of choice and communication with the Higher Mind of our Solitary Self. Working this Gate will inform you of the differences *intention* will make to your choosing. A great deal can be learned about the art of choosing here.

GATE #94

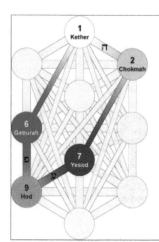

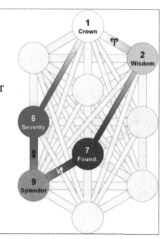

Sequence: ☊ Found. <CAPRI> Splendor <MERC> Severity <HP:6-1> Crown <ARIES> Wisdom <HP:2-7> Found.

Return: ☋ Found. <HP:7-2> Wisdom <ARIES> Crown <HP:1-6> Severity <MERC> Splendor <CAPRI> Found.

Working this Gate brings with it a supernal blessing of creativity to your united powers of communication and choosing. It will greatly increase your ability to communicate your choices to others and thus shape any consequences resulting therefrom.

GATE #95

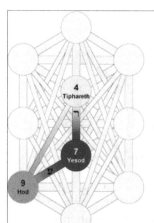

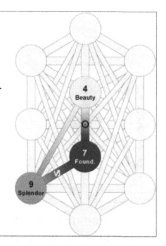

Sequence: ☊ Found. <CAPRI> Splendor <HP:9-4> Beauty <SUN> Found.

Return: ☋ Found. <SUN> Beauty <HP:4-9> Splendor <CAPRI> Found.

Working this Gate will teach you all about the making of intentional choices with the Higher Mind of Tiphareth: how it is done, what is required and what are the possible results.

GATE #96

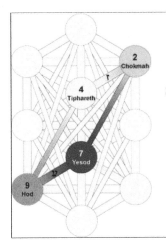
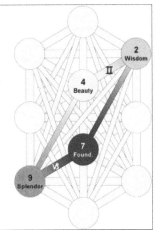

Sequence: ↺ Found. <CAPRI> Splendor <HP:9-4> Beauty <GEMINI> Wisdom <HP:2-7> Found.

Return: ↺ Found. <HP:7-2> Wisdom <GEMINI> Beauty <HP:4-9> Splendor <CAPRI> Found.

Working this Gate brings the Fire region of your Mental Body into play and reaffirms that the relationship with 'other' is the reason that choice even exists in the first place. Our choices reveal us to 'other' and their choices reveal their selves to us within the astral realm, especially to eyes that perceive EM. Through this Gate we can learn how to read choices, as it were.

GATE #97

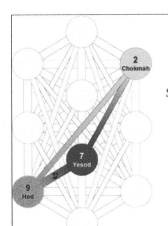
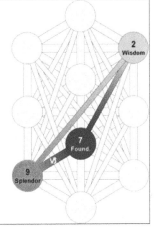

Sequence: ↺ Found. <CAPRI> Splendor <HP:9-2> Wisdom <HP:2-7> Found.

Return: ↺ Found. <HP:7-2> Wisdom <HP:2-9> Splendor <CAPRI> Found.

Here we learn about the relationship between choice and EM. You *must* work this Gate with the Fire region of your Mental Body to truly benefit from it!

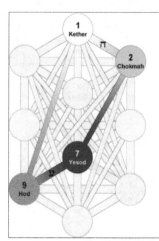

GATE #98

Sequence: ℧ Found. <CAPRI> Splendor
<HP:9-1> Crown <ARIES>
Wisdom <HP:2-7> Found.

Return: ℧ Found. <HP:7-2> Wisdom
<ARIES> Crown <HP:1-9>
Splendor <CAPRI> Found.

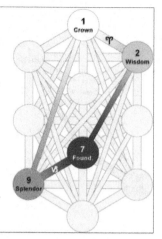

First of all, there is a creative blessing from Kether and Chokmah upon your power to choose and upon your choosing which you can accept by working this Gate.

Additionally, you can learn from this Gate an aspect of the Magic of EM having to do with making choices in a specific way (that I won't elaborate here). To gain this knowledge, you must work this Gate with the Fire region of your Mental Body and then immediately integrate the experience into the Air region. To *work* this particular magic (as opposed to just learning about it) you must then *become* this Gate with your *whole* being: mental, astral and physical.

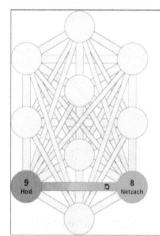

GATE #99

מ MEM (WATER)

ARCHETYPAL WATER

Sequence: Vitality <WATER> Splendor

Return: Splendor <WATER> Vitality

Keywords: Resonance/Dissonance,

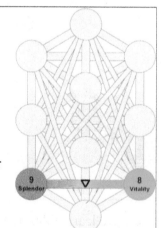

The Hebrew 'Mem' means *water* or *the waters* (ocean) in English and is the Mother Letter of Water. As with the two Mother Letters before it, Mem represents the continuum between two poles and defines a realm, in this case the Astral Realm of significance. It is the astral polarity of resonance and dissonance, of opening and closing: the Netzach and Hod ends of the continuum respectively.

These waters are the Primal Waters from which all physical life has sprung. This is a metaphorical way to say, it's the astral realm which precedes and serves as template for, the physical. The astral realm is "watery" in that it is fluid and insubstantial, always changing before one's eyes. Furthermore, it is a constant exchange of energy between 'self' and 'other', back and forth, opening and closing, giving and taking.

To the ancients, this Path was known as the "Gan Eden" or *Garden of Earthly Delights* in English; which is a very apt description of the astral realm. It has an emotional charge that excites and entrances. It lures you in ever deeper and grabs hold of your imagination. This is due to the fact that it is a realm made up entirely out of significance and also the energy exchange between 'self' and 'other' which is addictive by nature.

Hand in hand with the endless resonant and dissonant, opening and closing of 'self' to 'other' comes the realization of the final component of time: *duration*. This perception of duration comes about because we are constantly opening and closing to 'other' (in fact our whole existence if one of opening and closing, opening and closing, without end) and we *remember* the sequence of openings and closings and in that memory, we realize that time has elapsed between the last instance of having closed and the current instance. And, even more has elapsed between the time before last and this, etc., etc.

And so we have duration, the final ingredient of time: Change and Continuity from Shin/Fire, Sequence from Aleph/Air and now, Duration from Mem/Water. 'Time' is defined (by me) as an infinitely enduring sequence of events that take place within the context of infinite change woven together by infinite continuity.

So, to be clear, the astral realm exists within time. However, astral time is not like the physical clock time we're used to; in the astral, time is all wonky and fluid. You know the *feeling* (i.e., an astral perception) of time compressing or expanding already: an hour can seem like a minute and vise versa. But while there *is* time in the astral, the realm and its inhabitants are not *bound* by time per se. Time becomes binding only in the physical realm when it is joined with space to become space-time.

The ancients held that there was a sequential hierarchy to the Elements with Fire at the top, Air next, then Water, all sitting atop the Earth. Fire is ephemeral and volatile and always reaching upwards like a flame. Air is also ephemeral but not particularly volatile and partakes somewhat of the Water being turned to vapor by the Fire above; it seems to move neither up nor down of its own accord. The Water always flows downward into the Earth, always a slave to Earth's force of gravity. And the Earth is solid, unmoving and heavy, even brittle at times. So Mem *flows* downward, ever toward physical manifestation or Earth: it is always a *moving* exchange of energy from Netzach/resonance toward Hod/dissonance and back again; from opening to closing to opening to closing to . . . ad infinitum.

When working this Gate you will definitely feel the directional flow of Mem. At first it will be straight towards Hod and dissonance (closing of 'self'); but once you reach Hod, you will understand that it is within your *power to choose* to reverse the flow and return to a state of resonance. In any event, the nature of this continuum (as is the case with all three of the Mother Letters) is that the default is always the pole of Mercy which, in this case, is resonance; so you will eventually be drawn back to Netzach. In this sense it's sort of like the waves washing up on the shore and then retreating; back and forth, back and forth, never really stopping.

Through working this Gate of Mem, you will learn about resonance and dissonance: how they interact and how one flows into the other; how to consciously manipulate either or both, and how to negate or engender either or both. You will also learn from this how intrinsic your Power to Choose is to this relationship and how you are *continuously* choosing.

You also have the opportunity to learn about the astral substance (significance) itself and how to master its manipulation. Furthermore, you can learn ever so much about time: what it is and is not; how to manipulate its perception (at least); and, how it interacts with space.

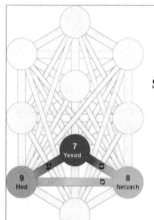

GATE #100

Sequence: ↻ Vitality <WATER> Splendor <CAPRI> Found. <SAGIT> Vitality

Return: ↺ Vitality <SAGIT> Found. <CAPRI> Splendor <WATER> Vitality

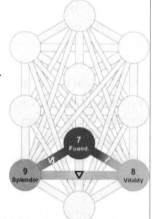

Working this Gate will balance your Power to Choose with your Will to Resonate and will solidify the astral realm for you. It will also help you understand your incarnational placement in this specific moment and period of time.

GATE #101

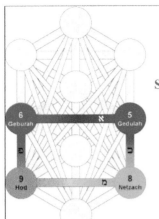

Sequence: ↻ Vitality <WATER> Splendor
<MERC> Severity <AIR>
Mercy <VENUS> Vitality

Return: ↺ Vitality <VENUS> Mercy
<AIR> Severity <MERC>
Splendor <WATER> Vitality

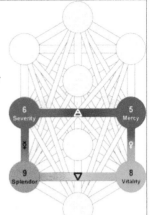

This Gate will unite your astral powers of resonance and dissonance with their higher, mental corollaries of alikeness and uniqueness. You will learn from this experience that it is the same essential nature of Self driving both of these continuums, the same necessity of Self-realization that causes them to manifest in this way. This unification of the Air and Water is done with an emphasis on both responsibility and communication.

GATE #102

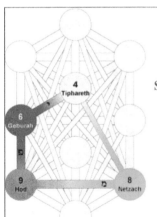

Sequence: ↻ Vitality <WATER> Splendor
<MERC> Severity <VIRGO>
Beauty <HP:4-8> Vitality

Return: ↺ Vitality <HP:8-4> Beauty
<VIRGO> Severity <MERC>
Splendor <WATER> Vitality

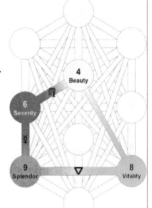

Working this Gate will begin to process of integrating your Higher Mind (specifically the Air region of your mental body) into your astral awareness. This Gate provides you with a better ability to communicate astrally, as well as a sharper sense of discernment.

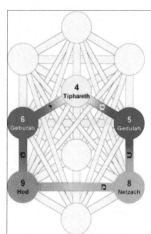

GATE #103

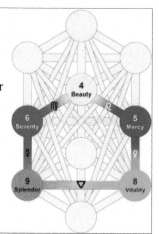

Sequence: ↺ Vitality <WATER> Splendor
<MERC> Severity <VIRGO> Beauty
<LEO> Mercy <VENUS> Vitality

Return: ↻ Vitality <VENUS> Mercy
<LEO> Beauty <VIRGO> Severity
<MERC> Splendor <WATER> Vitality

Working this Gate will complete the integration of your Tiphareth Solitary Self with your astral Sentient Self to the extent that your astral awareness will be seated or focused within the Air region of your mental body at all times. This is a very balanced and balancing experience.

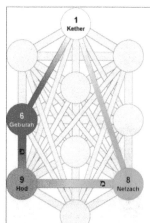

GATE #104

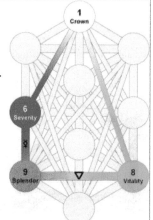

Sequence: ↺ Vitality <WATER> Splendor
<MERC> Severity <HP:6-1>
Crown <HP:1-8> Vitality

Return: ↻ Vitality <HP:8-1> Crown
<HP:1-6> Severity <MERC>
Splendor <WATER> Vitality

This Gate begins the integration of the Fire region of your mental body into your astral awareness. This process begins with a blessing and inspiration from Kether, primarily upon your abilities of communication in your interactions with 'other'. It is up to you to *accept* both.

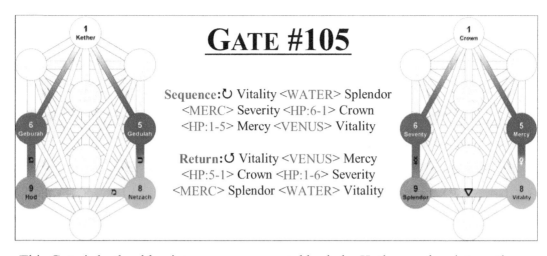

GATE #105

Sequence: ↻ Vitality <WATER> Splendor
<MERC> Severity <HP:6-1> Crown
<HP:1-5> Mercy <VENUS> Vitality

Return: ↺ Vitality <VENUS> Mercy
<HP:5-1> Crown <HP:1-6> Severity
<MERC> Splendor <WATER> Vitality

This Gate is both a blessing upon your mental body by Kether, and an integration of the Fire region of your mental body with your astral awareness, *via the Air region of your mental body* (in other words, not a *direct* integration). You must *accept* the blessing for the integration to occur.

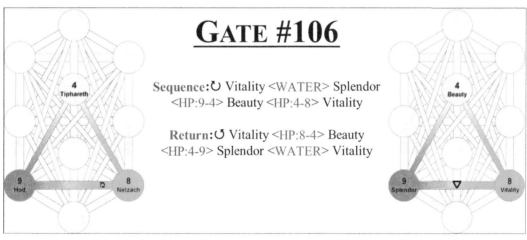

GATE #106

Sequence: ↻ Vitality <WATER> Splendor
<HP:9-4> Beauty <HP:4-8> Vitality

Return: ↺ Vitality <HP:8-4> Beauty
<HP:4-9> Splendor <WATER> Vitality

This Gate is a *direct* firming up or solidifying reaffirmation of the seating of your astral awareness in your higher Solitary Self. You identify consciously as your Solitary Self within your Sentient Self or as a mental body inhabiting an astral body. [This solidification is a *necessary* step in advance of Gate #108.]

GATE #107

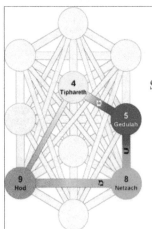

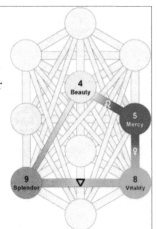

Sequence: ↻ Vitality <WATER> Splendor
<HP:9-4> Beauty <LEO>
Mercy <VENUS> Vitality

Return: ↺ Vitality <VENUS> Mercy
<LEO> Beauty <HP:4-9>
Splendor <WATER> Vitality

This Gate is a compliment to Gate #102 and completes what was begun there. Working this Gate formally completes the integration of the Air region of your mental body into your astral awareness by making certain you *always* remember your responsibilities in, and bring the *very best* of yourself to, all your astral interactions. You *must* complete the work of this Gate to benefit from the next Gate #108.

GATE #108

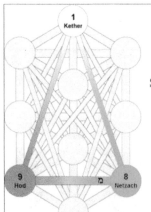

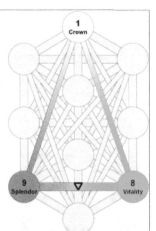

Sequence: ↻ Vitality <WATER> Splendor
<HP:9-1> Crown <HP:1-8> Vitality

Return: ↺ Vitality <HP:8-1> Crown
<HP:1-9> Splendor <WATER> Vitality

This is a blessing that transforms your astral awareness. If *accepted* in its fullness, it can change your entire astral experience. This blessing can unite the Fire region of your temporal mental body with your astral body, to the extent that you will *always* have immediate, unfettered access any time you wish.

The acceptance of this blessing and its subsequent integration of your Fire region with your Water region is *essential* for a true understanding of what is yet to come with Malkuth.

GATE #109

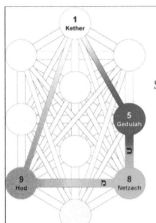

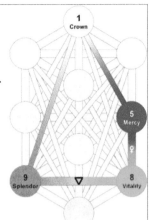

Sequence: ↺ Vitality \<WATER\> Splendor
\<HP:9-1\> Crown \<HP:1-5\>
Mercy \<VENUS\> Vitality

Return: ↻ Vitality \<VENUS\> Mercy
\<HP:5-1\> Crown \<HP:1-9\>
Splendor \<WATER\> Vitality

With this Gate, The "I" reminds us of the default state of Mercy to which Aware-ness always returns, and of the responsibilities that we must always remember. If you truly take this reminder to heart, you will *receive* Kether's blessing upon you and add the final touch to the integration of Fire, Air and Water.

It is only as beings of Fire, Air and Water that we can enter the Earth of Malkuth and become the Masters of *our* Domain!

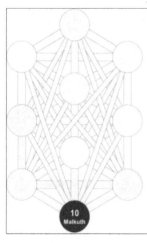
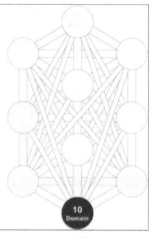

MALKUTH / DOMAIN

מלכות

KEYWORDS: STATIC SELF,
PHYSICALITY, CONSEQUENCE

So . . . Malkuth . . . How to explain? That's always been the question: how do I wrap my words around such a complex thing so that anybody can understand what I'm saying? It could easily descend into gibberish! Fortunately for you, my Understanding has improved over the years and I think that now, finally, I can succeed. So, here goes . . .

It all comes down to time. Or at least how we perceive and experience time. At the Supernal Level of Kether, Chokmah and Binah, time is a singular, enclosed event of infinite proportions. The _whole_ of infinite time exists as a _singular_ Now Moment. That Now Moment is filled with infinite change, woven through by infinite continuity. In other words, the Now Moment of the Supernal Realm contains the whole of infinite time, <u>all at once</u>.

Now a Supernal Awareness can cope with that infinite amount of Meaning all at once; _but no other level of Awareness can_. When in the process of Self-Realization, The "I" descends through the Akasha and splits into an infinite number of particles and becomes the sequential realm of Tiphareth, each one of those particles of awareness can only integrate but a small portion of the Supernal Now. Consequently the perception and experience of time changes: that infinite flow becomes sequentialized and there is a defined or experienced separation between events and things that does not exist in the Supernal experience.

The Solitary Self then, comprehends and experiences a much, much smaller portion of the infinite flow of time and so its Now moment contains far less, far fewer events and things. And what it does perceive is all happening in sequence and this has the effect of making the threads of continuity which tie each part of the sequence together, much more apparent.

This splitting of the One Awareness into an infinite number of parts occurs for a reason: it's part of Its process of Self-Realization. Its path to Self-Realization requires that in order to truly know ItSelf, It must see and experience ItSelf from *every* perspective. So The One becomes the many so it can understand and know ItSelf. And once it began, nothing can stop It reaching Its goal. In other words, it *must* reach the most finite experience of time possible: physical incarnation.

And that is really the question of Malkuth: How does a Solitary Self become a physical self? This is what the Tree is trying to tell us; or rather, it tells us how The "I" becomes physical, step by step. But it is as Solitary Selves that The "I" makes this descent into physicality.

In order for Mind to manifest itself physically it needs a medium between mind and matter, a type of body or covering that will enable it to connect directly with matter. We call this the *astral* (or "of the stars"). [Qabbalistically, this is a reference to Venus and Mercury.]

The glue as it were, that binds mind to matter is *significance*, primarily because of its emotional (personal opinion) content. Significance lets mind hard-wire into matter because matter *is* <u>concentrated, crystallized significance</u>.

The introduction of significance to the equation, plus the fact that we must constantly interact with an infinite number 'other', means that the contents of the Now moment again shrinks. This is in order for the Sentient Self to integrate and consciously experience it.

Since significance demands of us so much associating of past experiences with each other and the present, we begin to perceive and experience the *duration* inherent to time, and the fact that it stretches out before us to infinity. This places us firmly *in* time, in *this* present moment, *this* Now, defined by *these* parameters. Every 'other' around us exists in their own personal 'bubble of Nowness' containing as much of the Now as they can integrate at any given moment. The Sentient Self is capable of handling a greater portion of Now than the average *physical* person (Static Self), but no where near as much as the Solitary Self.

Every moment of the astral existence is absolutely full of emotional significance and personal importance, all of which generates immense energy (from the interaction/exchange). This energy, which *unites* mind with matter, is what *causes* matter to exist.

Quantum Physics (as of 2024) is getting painfully close to understanding how this part works. Unfortunately I am not equipped to give you a dissertation in such things so I will have to give you the layman's edition with sprinklings of the symbolic thrown in!

It has to do with vibration, frequency and the transition between wave-form and particle-form. Because the energy of the astral realm is *so* intense and so dense, it starts to evolve from 'energy wave-form' with specific frequencies, into 'particulate form' such as quarks, photons, electrons, gravitons, etc. There is in fact, a 'zone of transition', much like the Akasha above, which is where astral matter becomes physical matter.

Essentially, physical matter is *organized* into the forms we see <u>by</u> Mind; symbolically speaking, matter "adheres" to Mind. In other words, every physical form organized by Mind, is the direct expression of Essential Meaning. This is why we can directly perceive EM by merely looking at the objects or beings around us.

There's a sort of New Age saying that goes "we are not our bodies". That's not exactly true. More properly, "our bodies are *us*". Yes, "we are *more than* just our physical body" (which is really what the saying meant), but while we're here saying these things, we are always *in* this physical body! It is the direct expression of who we are. And it tells those with eyes to see, *exactly* who we are.

So, in this way, roughly speaking, Mind is bound to matter, hard-wired into it; or from another angle, matter is magnetically attracted to each astra-mental sinew and vein until the form is complete. The astra-mental wave-form crystallizes into a particle-form. Nothing is really added or taken away; instead the whole is *transformed* or transmuted in an essentially Alchemical way.

For us humans, the result is our humanoid bodies, with our five senses, two arms and legs, etc. We are a physio-astra-mental expression of our specific package of Essential Meaning. Never forget: *every* physical thing has this same three-in-one structure. <u>*Every*</u>!

So, what this does to time is rather remarkable. With the crystallization of the astral matter, time crystallizes too. It is transformed into a present moment or Now Moment that has an infinitely-finite duration, within which there is no sequential change. Change has just stopped; or rather, the moment is so brief that we are between changes, and having stopped, there is no sequence. The only thing that remains to any degree is continuity which brings a static solidity to the present moment. Here in Malkuth the infinitely-*finite* Now is the exact opposite to the infinitely-*infinite* Now of Kether.

And yes . . . here's the real Mystery of Malkuth . . . by the nature of infinities, <u>the infinitely-finite is the same as the infinitely-infinite</u>. The former leads to the latter. In other words, if you pursue the ever smaller, ever decreasing Malkuth present moment down that rabbit hole toward infinity, you come out in Kether.

Remember way back near the beginning of this long bunch of words when I said that the image on the left is the same as the middle? Well the one on the far right is the same as both: it *contains* both and is the product of both. The left *leads* to the right and the right *leads* to the left.

So Malkuth contains the whole Tree, it receives it and provides it with temporal form as Static Selves, stuck in the infinitely-finite present. This present moment is the only point at which anything exists. *All* of our perceptions and experiences and actions and expressions take place in the awareness of an immediate nowness. Even when we remember, it is with the awareness that we are remembering *now*.

Modern humans express a broad range in how far down that rabbit hole of the infinitely-finite they can be conscious of. Generally speaking it's not very far at all and that's why we manifest our *brains* and root our five senses in it. We develop, during that transmutation of the astral into the physical, what I call the 'brain-bound awareness', ruled mainly by the un- and sub-conscious layers of awareness.

This common day level of consciousness is limited entirely by the brain: by its electronics and its mechanics. The brain is normally capable of processing just a snap shot of the present moment that contains a few nanoseconds of information. And it subsequently takes an additional few nanoseconds to process that perception before taking the next snap shot, and so on. All of which is normally done by the brain-bound, un- and sub-conscious mind. In other words, it's usually relegated to our auto-pilot.

In this way, bit by bit, the awareness of the Static Self is able to make sense of the world; otherwise, it would be overwhelmed by the amount of information and meaning contained within each moment. And, it ordinarily does not possess the powers of focus to reach down into the rabbit hole to the end. [That's all it takes by the way: intention and focus. Many, in fact most of our ancestors, have found their way to The "I" *through* the Earth!]

The Malkuth Awareness is the <u>Earth Region</u> of the temporal Mental Body. This is your everyday awareness as you go about your daily business. It is for the most part un- and sub-conscious by nature but that is always up to the individual. Higher Mind is always close to hand.

Malkuth is the realm of consequence. Every choice produces consequences and in this realm they are realized in solid form. Karma becomes a very real and immediate force here.

Malkuth is formed by the influx of 7 Paths: from Chokmah, Binah, Gedulah, Geburah, Yesod, Netzach and Hod. Each of these can be said to be one of the seven ways that we are bound to our incarnation; so I call them the 'seven bindings':

From Chokmah: EM which becomes DNA or atomic structure.
"   Binah: Karma
"   Gedulah: Connection to the collective / Adaptability.
"   Geburah: Relationship to Power / Steadfastness.
"   Yesod: Descent of Solitary Self / Continuity.
"   Netzach: Emotion / Significance.
"   Hod: Rational Intellect / Brain-bound mind.

The Hebrew 'Malkuth' is usually translated as "dominion" but this is incorrect. For that reason I use simple *Domain* instead. The reason that I have begun this journey with you in Kether, top-down, instead of the more normal bottom-up approach is because in order for one to truly understand, and take one's place of command in, Malkuth, you have to fill it with the Meaning of everything that comes above it. Otherwise you are lost in Malkuth without Understanding and it is all a struggle to make any progress. In effect, you have to bring your Crown (Kether) with you for Malkuth to truly be your Domain.

Here in Malkuth you can learn so many things! Too many for me to name. Besides, that's better left for you to discover on your own.

So, did any of that make sense? Have I succeeded at all? I hope that you can at least see enough of the Essential Meaning of my words to get the general idea!

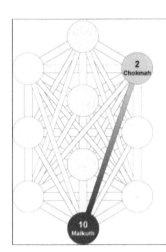

GATE #110
HIDDEN PATH: 2>10

Sequence: Wisdom <HP:2-10> Domain

Return: Domain <HP:10-2> Wisdom

Keywords: EM / DNA

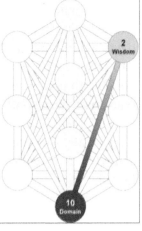

This Path represents the full evolution from the great infinite ocean of undifferentiated Essential Meaning, through the layers of differentiation and individuation, all the way down to the very, very specific set of EM that you are manifesting through your current incarnation. At the level of Malkuth, your EM manifests as your DNA, that utterly unique code that translates as your physical body and yours alone. If you were a chunk of lead or a bright star shining in the night, it would be your specific atomic structure instead of your DNA; but in (almost) all organic life, this manifests as DNA.

As you work this Gate from Chokmah 'down', you follow along and witness the descent and specification of EM through your Greater Self, to your Solitary Self, and then watch as it gains an even more uniqueness as it enters the astral realm and your Sentient Self, until it finally comes to rest in its most specific and final iteration as the physical body of your Static Self. With each incarnation it changes ever so slightly but still remains greatly the same and it is for this reason that we often look remarkably like past incarnations. It also points out that most families share large quantities of their EM with other family members.

Working this Gate teaches you that your body and its DNA *is* you. You may be more than just your body but your body is all *you*, it is the immediate and utterly truthful manifestation of who *you* are in this moment. No other Mind can express itself through *your* body: it simply won't fit or be able to function and interact in the material realm.

You will learn what aspects of your appearance originate with your Greater Self (we often look similar to other Individuals projected by our Greater), which originate with your Solitary Self (there are always great similarities between each incarnation), and which are new or unique to your present incarnation, *and why*. You can also learn that as you change during your incarnation you will have a great degree of control over how those changes manifest in your body. In other words, your body is your own creation and responsibility and you can, to a great degree, determine the appearance and especially the health of your body.

You will notice that this Hidden Path crosses over numerous other Paths in its journey: nine in fact, with two double-crossings, one of which includes Aleph. It is the final crossing of Mem (on the descent) when EM wave-form finally crystallizes into DNA. With time (many decades?) and very deep study/practice it becomes possible to take *conscious* control of this process and transform your DNA; thus rejuvenate or in some other way transform your physical body.

There really is no better Gate than this for getting to know exactly who you are and why. Nor really any better "fulcrum point" from which to affect change therein.

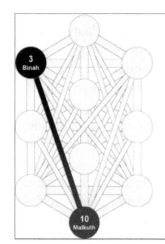

GATE #111
HIDDEN PATH: 3>10

Sequence: Underst. <HP:3-10> Domain

Return: Domain <HP:10-3> Underst.

Keywords: Karma / The Path

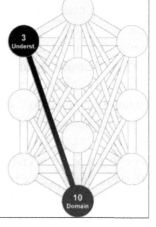

This Gate shows you the sources and the rationale for every stage of your karma right down to this very moment in your current incarnation: the karma you inherit from your Greater Self and from your Solitary Self and the karma specific to this lifetime and even that arising from this instant of time-space. You will find the *why?* to be just as important and informative as the *what*! You can learn from working this Gate *exactly* what is the nature and the specifics of your unique path (that you follow whether you want or not). As with the last, this hidden Path also crosses nine other Paths during its descent: with two doubles, one of which includes Aleph. At the descending crossing of Mem near the end, *all* of the consequences inherent to your karma are realized and become 'manifest in stone', as it were.

If you work this Gate sufficiently it becomes possible to *consciously* resolve various karmic issues: first those generated during your current incarnation; then those inherited from past incarnations via the Solitary Self; and finally even some of those inherited from your Greater Self. There is no better Gate than this one for understanding and correcting one's own karma! Here we are given ample opportunities to repay old debts!

GATE #112

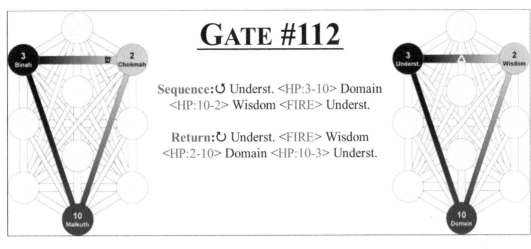

Sequence: ↻ Underst. <HP:3-10> Domain
<HP:10-2> Wisdom <FIRE> Underst.

Return: ↻ Underst. <FIRE> Wisdom
<HP:2-10> Domain <HP:10-3> Underst.

From working this Gate you will learn all about the ways in which karma and EM influence each other, especially one's expression of them both during incarnation.

Excuse me; I need to digress for a moment. I keep using "karma" as the descriptor of HP:3>10 but this isn't exactly accurate. What this Path is, is **The Path** that we are here to follow, that we are destined to follow if you will, that we have no choice but to follow: our own unique role in the Cosmos. Karma though, is how we most easily recognize our Path because it is the cosmic corrective force that always redirects us back to our Path whenever we go astray. Karma arises *only* when we stray from our Path. It is always a gift from Divine Providence. Karma is always a *positive* thing even if we happen to categorize it as 'good' or 'bad' depending upon how much we benefit from it or not as the case may be.

Within this Gate and the next in particular, the Hidden Path of 3>10 has more to do with our *Path* than with our karma. So from this Gate you learn still more about your Path and the effect it has on both the composition of your bundle of EM and your quality and quantity of its expression. Also, you will learn about the converse affect that your EM has upon the formation and execution of your Path. The deep working of this Gate (and the next) and the Understanding that it will generate, is the foundation for achieving the higher works I mentioned in the previous two linear Gates: namely the prolongation of life and the resolution of the Greater Self's karma. Without it (and the next), neither are possible.

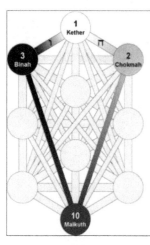

GATE #113

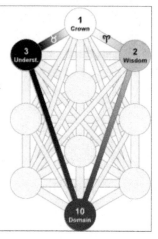

Sequence: ↺ Underst. <HP:3-10> Domain
<HP:10-2> Wisdom <ARIES>
Crown <TAURUS> Underst.

Return: ↺ Underst. <TAURUS> Crown
<ARIES> Wisdom <HP:2-10>
Domain <HP:10-3> Underst.

This is one of three very special Gates of Malkuth that afford a method of not only connecting the incarnational awareness directly with The "I" and Kether, but also of bringing The "I" down, *directly into* the infinitely-finite temporal present moment and one's own incarnational awareness (physio-astra-mental body). When one *becomes* all three of these special Gates *simultaneously*, Kether *automatically* fills Malkuth *through or as you*. These three Gates are:

Gate #113 **Gate #125** **Gate #165**

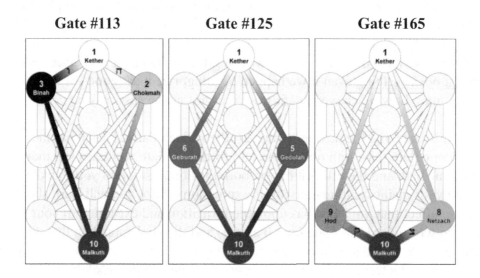

This Gate is a blessing from Kether upon both your Path and your EM which, if you fully *accept*, can transform both. If nothing else, it *will* transform your relationship with both! It is a very creative and purifying blessing that readily enables the higher workings from the two linear Paths I've mentioned previously. Mastery of this Gate endows one with the 'cosmic permission' so to speak, for such 'high magic'.

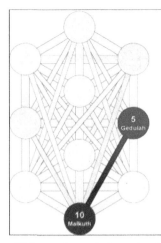

GATE #114
HIDDEN PATH: 5>10

Sequence: Mercy <HP:5-10> Domain

Return: Domain <HP:10-5> Mercy

Keywords: Adaptability,
Connection to collectives

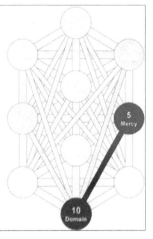

This Path and Gate is all about the quality and quantity of your connection to the various collectives of awareness that you are naturally a part of. It also indicates the nature, range and limitations of your adaptability. Working this Gate you will learn about the importance of adaptability in navigating though life, how to increase your own adaptability and how it is related to the quality and quantity of your connections to collectivism. The more support from collectives you experience, the greater your adaptability to circumstance and therefore, the greater your ability to stick to your Path.

The decent along this Hidden Path crosses three hidden Paths and two Lettered Paths, the last of which is Mem. The first three crossings sort of 'pluck the strings', so to speak, of higher influences upon Netzach, your ability to resonate with 'other'; and the final crossing of Mem, 'plucks the string' of, and releases the effects of, the consequences of how you manage your interactions. So working this Gate gives you an opportunity to make alterations and improvements in how you adapt to the ever-changing moment.

GATE #115

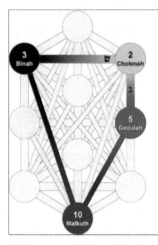
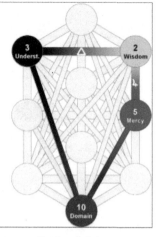

Sequence: ↻ Mercy <HP:5-10> Domain
<HP:10-3> Underst. <FIRE>
Wisdom <JUPITER> Mercy

Return: ↻ Mercy <JUPITER> Wisdom
<FIRE> Underst. <HP:3-10>
Domain <HP:10-5> Mercy

These next three Gates illuminate the ways and reasons that your Path and its related karma, impact and determine both the collectives that you connect with, and the range of your abilities to adapt to circumstance. This particular Gate shows you how EM influences this dynamic connection between Binah and Gedulah and is fundamentally responsible for the origin of your Path and your collectives.

Working this Gate begins to bring greater balance and communication between the two poles of Binah and Chokmah in so far as they are the source of your Path and collectivization. This Gate also initiates a process that doesn't finish until immediately before the Linear Gate of Tav.

GATE #116

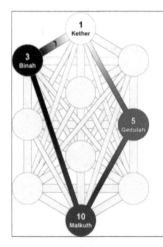
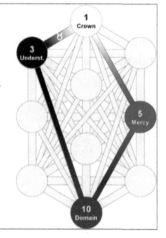

Sequence: ↻ Mercy <HP:5-10> Domain
<HP:10-3> Underst. <TAURUS>
Crown <HP:1-5> Mercy

Return: ↻ Mercy <HP:5-1> Crown
<TAURUS> Underst. <HP:3-10>
Domain <HP:10-5> Mercy

This Gate is a very direct blessing from Kether upon your ability to adapt to the challenges of your Path. It is as usual, advised that you fully *accept* this blessing as it will play a big role in the work yet to come.

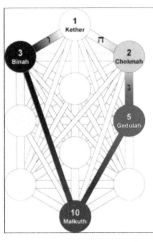

GATE #117

Sequence: ☉ Mercy <HP:5-10> Domain <HP:10-3> Underst. <TAURUS> Crown <ARIES> Wisdom <JUPITER> Mercy

Return: ☉ Mercy <JUPITER> Wisdom <ARIES> Crown <TAURUS> Underst. <HP:3-10> Domain <HP:10-5> Mercy

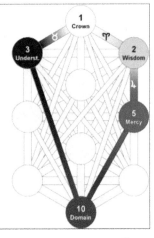

This Gate is a gift of an extra added bit of creative inspiration to your powers of adaptability and shows how important adaptability truly is in regard to your fulfilling your Path. With this extra bit of creative inspiration you will be able to increase the range of collective awarenesses that you are able to draw upon during your present incarnation. In effect, your allies as you travel along your Way will increase in number and significance.

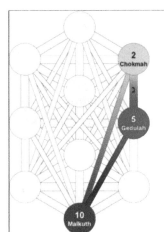

GATE #118

Sequence: ☉ Mercy <HP:5-10> Domain <HP:10-2> Wisdom <JUPITER> Mercy

Return: ☉ Mercy <JUPITER> Wisdom <HP:2-10> Domain <HP:10-5> Mercy

This Gate is all about those aforementioned allies, as well as all of the collectives that aid your passage through incarnation. The Universe really *is* on your side and this Gate illustrates that fact in no uncertain terms, as you will discover from its working. You will come to understand here what and who benefits you, and how and why they do.

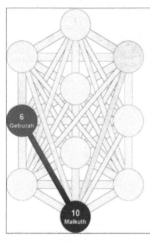

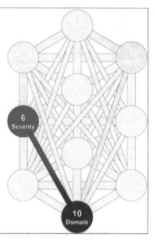

GATE #119
HIDDEN PATH: 6>10

Sequence: Severity <HP:6-10> Domain

Return: Domain <HP:10-6> Severity

Keywords: Connection to power,
Steadfastness, Ego

This Hidden Path is about your relationship with power, both your personal power and power in general.

Working this Gate will clarify the quality and quantity of your connection to your own unique power (your Geburah) and allow you to make changes in the nature of this connection. Most especially, this Gate will expose any lack or excess in your steadfastness of character. A strong sense of self or ego is important so long as it doesn't become egotism and braggadocio; this Gate will show you where it does and how to prevent it from happening. It will also show where your character is weakest and how to repair this lack.

As with HP:5>10, this Path makes five crossings. The first three show you the influences beyond your control that determine certain aspects of your inherent attitude towards power; and the last two are either where egotism and braggartliness arise or where nobility is found.

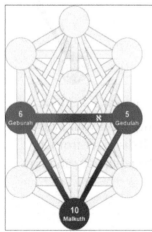

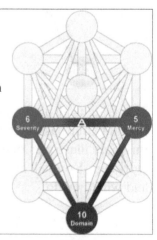

GATE #120

Sequence: ↻ Severity <HP:6-10> Domain
<HP:10-5> Mercy <AIR> Severity

Return: ↻ Severity <AIR> Mercy
<HP:5-10> Domain <HP:10-6> Severity

This Gate is meant to remind you that power is only positive and constructive when it is in service to the collective awareness. Working this Gate will balance these two forces through Aleph and leave you more at peace with your experiences of power.

GATE #121

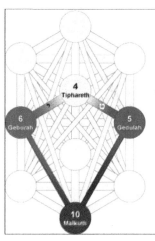

Sequence: ↺ Severity <HP:6-10> Domain
<HP:10-5> Mercy <LEO>
Beauty <VIRGO> Severity

Return: ↻ Severity <VIRGO> Beauty
<LEO> Mercy <HP:5-10>
Domain <HP:10-6> Severity

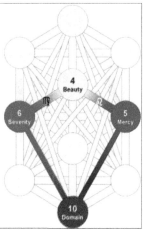

Working this Gate will truly unite your access to power with your commitment to your collectives through your higher Mind or Solitary Self awareness. It will thus become a permanent union and any propensity for egotism will be quickly taken care of. A greater sense of humility arises within one.

GATE #122

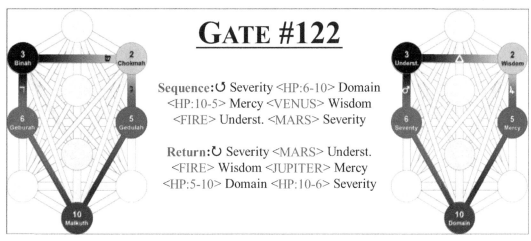

Sequence: ↺ Severity <HP:6-10> Domain
<HP:10-5> Mercy <VENUS> Wisdom
<FIRE> Underst. <MARS> Severity

Return: ↻ Severity <MARS> Underst.
<FIRE> Wisdom <JUPITER> Mercy
<HP:5-10> Domain <HP:10-6> Severity

Working this Gate results in a greater understanding of the Universal significance of the astra-physical dedication of power to service of the collective. This is meant to transform you to such a degree that it will become impossible for you to even consider using your own power in any other way.

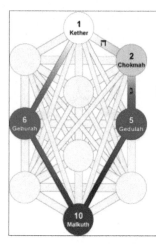

GATE #123

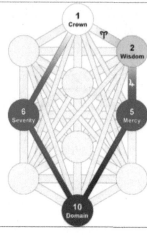

Sequence: ↻ Severity <HP:6-10> Domain <HP:10-5> Mercy <JUPITER> Wisdom <ARIES> Crown <HP:1-6> Severity

Return: ↺ Severity <HP:6-1> Crown <ARIES> Wisdom <JUPITER> Mercy <HP:5-10> Domain <HP:10-6> Severity

This Gate will instruct you as to the true nature of power as a *creative* force and it will clearly show you your own role in the cosmic play of power.

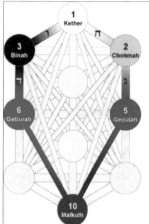

GATE #124

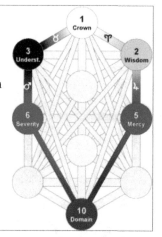

Sequence: ↻ Severity <HP:6-10> Domain <HP:10-5> Mercy <JUPITER> Wisdom <ARIES> Crown <TAURUS> Underst. <MARS> Severity

Return: ↺ Severity <MARS> Underst. <TAURUS> Crown <ARIES> Wisdom <JUPITER> Mercy <HP:5-10> Domain <HP:10-6> Severity

Working this Gate will teach you about the universal forces at play in every exercising of your own power and in power at large. It will also make it crystal clear how and why power is completely dependant upon collectivized awareness and how the *urge to merge* is its very root cause. This is very balancing overall and brings a sense of peace.

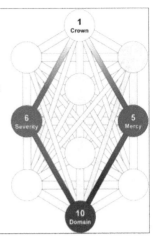

GATE #125

Sequence: ☾ Severity <HP:6-10> Domain
<HP:10-5> Mercy <HP:5-1>
Crown <HP:1-6> Severity

Return: ☾ Severity <HP:6-1> Crown
<HP:1-5> Mercy <HP:5-10>
Domain <HP:10-6> Severity

I call this "the Gate of Humility" because that is the overriding effect of its working. Once *accepted*, this direct blessing from Kether upon the unified state of your power and your collectivity, *permanently* unites the two in such a way that all egotism and braggadocio is permanently eliminated from your character. Plus, it will totally realign your relationship to and execution of, your own unique power and transform it into a great blessing to all your collectives. Furthermore, your relationship to external powers will ease and no external power will be able to stand against you.

This is the second of the special Gates I mentioned in Gate #113 and once worked and the blessing is *accepted*, it affords a method of direct connection between the Static Self and Kether.

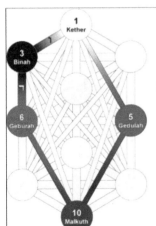

GATE #126

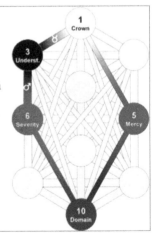

Sequence: ☾ Severity <HP:6-10> Domain
<HP:10-5> Mercy <HP:5-1> Crown
<TAURUS> Underst. <MARS> Severity

Return: ☾ Severity <MARS> Underst.
<TAURUS> Crown <HP:1-5> Mercy
<HP:5-10> Domain <HP:10-6> Severity

This Gate puts the final touch to the transformation and regeneration of the relationship between your personal power and collectivism in general. It places your Greater Self in the role of guardian of this important relationship. From here forward, these changes are permanent and will last throughout all your future incarnations.

GATE #127

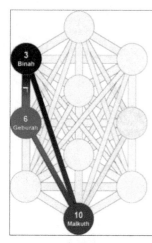

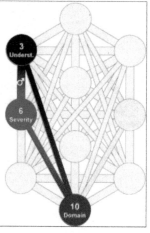

Sequence: ↻ Severity <HP:6-10> Domain <HP:10-3> Underst. <MARS> Severity

Return: ↻ Severity <MARS> Underst. <HP:3-10> Domain <HP:10-6> Severity

Working this Gate provides you with the opportunity to purge and rectify any and all karma related to past abuses of your personal power. It also helps you to see the importance of exercising your power appropriately according to your Path in life. This will inevitably align your ego expression with your Path.

GATE #128

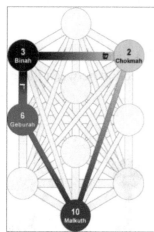

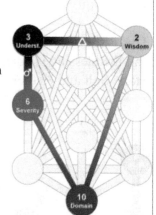

Sequence: ↻ Severity <HP:6-10> Domain <HP:10-2> Wisdom <FIRE> Underst. <MARS> Severity

Return: ↻ Severity <MARS> Underst. <FIRE> Wisdom <HP:2-10> Domain <HP:10-6> Severity

The nature of your personal power and the limitations you will experience in exercising it come, to a great extent, from the specific array of EM you ultimately express or manifest. This Gate will show you exactly what those peculiarities and limitations are and from whence they arise.

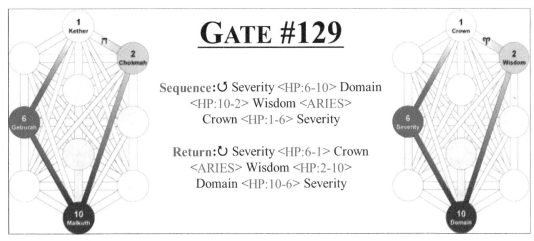

GATE #129

Sequence: ↻ Severity <HP:6-10> Domain
<HP:10-2> Wisdom <ARIES>
Crown <HP:1-6> Severity

Return: ↺ Severity <HP:6-1> Crown
<ARIES> Wisdom <HP:2-10>
Domain <HP:10-6> Severity

Here Kether gives a blessing upon your EM and your individual power as they unite to manifest in Malkuth and the present moment of time-space. Once *accepted*, this blessing walks with you, so to speak, throughout the remaining years of your current incarnation.

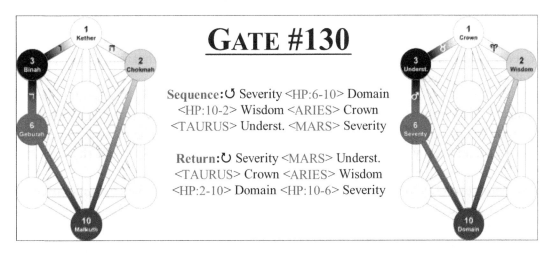

GATE #130

Sequence: ↻ Severity <HP:6-10> Domain
<HP:10-2> Wisdom <ARIES> Crown
<TAURUS> Underst. <MARS> Severity

Return: ↺ Severity <MARS> Underst.
<TAURUS> Crown <ARIES> Wisdom
<HP:2-10> Domain <HP:10-6> Severity

This Gate represents the last stage in preparing the ground of Malkuth in readiness for Gate #131 and the descent of the core consciousness in the form of your Solitary Self wrapped in its cloak of Sentience. By working this Gate you solidify certain necessary changes to the astra-mental foundation of Malkuth which allow Mind to finally bind with matter. The whole dynamic between your EM/DNA, your Path/Karma, your attachment to collectivity and adaptability, and your connection to your personal power and solidity of character, hereby achieve the required balance and integration.

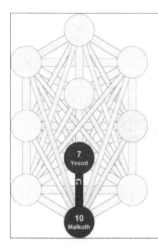

GATE #131

ת TAV (CROSS, MARK, SIGN)

MOON ☽

Sequence: Found. <MOON> Domain

Return: Domain <MOON> Found.

Keywords: Rhythm, Crystallization, Descent of Self

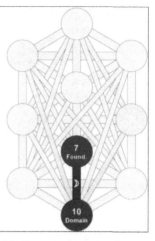

'Tav' is the last letter of the Hebrew alphabet and it is a Double Letter assigned to the Moon. The word 'Tav' means a *cross or mark*: a symbol which happens to be an oft used Alchemical symbol for Elemental Earth. In fact, Tav is considered by some to be the Mother Letter of Earth, even though it is definitely not a traditional Mother Letter (it is a vertical Path and a Double Letter, both of which violate the requirements of a Mother Letter). Where this idea comes from is Tav's sequence in the "32 Paths of Wisdom" (which are derived from the 32 times the name Elohim is mentioned in Genesis One of the Torah). Aleph is the 8th Path of this sequence; Mem is the 16th; Shin is the 24th; and Tav is the 32nd, meaning that every 8th Path in the sequence represents an Element.

Thus 'Tav'=Earth which does happen to fit, in an off-hand way, with the symbolism of the Gra Tree. In a more literal sense, the Moon is also the closest planet to our Earth and really rules all life on the planet through her ever-present rhythm.

We could even say 'Tav'=Moon=rhythm of life for it is indeed the rhythmic force exerted by the Moon that actually binds Mind to matter. <u>It is the Moon's rhythmic influence that physically transforms the wave-form of consciousness into the particle-form of the brain's workings, and the wave-form of astral matter into the particle-form of physical matter</u>. In the Tree, the Path of 'Tav' is the conduit through which the whole of the Solitary Self's consciousness, with its connection to the Greater Self and The "I", descends into the physical body of the Static Self.

In working this Gate you will cross only one Path: Mem, the Mother Letter of Water and the barrier between the astral and the physical realms. This is an Akasha-like barrier known to physics and metaphysics of the past as the *ether* or *aethyr*, a proto-physical energetic substance that is the basis of all physical matter. What it is in fact is that area or region of transition from wave-form to particle-form; caused by the magnetic effect that the Moon has upon the incredibly dynamic body of vibrating significance of the "lower" astral (the "Gan Eden" or "Garden of Earthly Delights").

The Moon/Tav has a crystallizing effect upon the astral *and* the mental, upon Form *and* Force. In other words, *both* are bound together in matter and given a *final* form. One of the main messages of the Tree is that it's *ALL* present here in Malkuth: Kether, Tiphareth, Yesod and Malkuth *simultaneously*. The body is not a separate thing . . .

In working this Gate you will be crossing back and forth through this ether-zone and you will therefore learn all about this transition between wave-form and particle-form. You will learn *exactly* what is happening; the how and the why of it, and you may even grow to control it over time. Remember, it's not only astral matter that changes here but also consciousness itself takes on a new form; you will also learn all about this and how to manipulate it as well.

You will experience an irresistibly strong downward pull toward Tav. This is a manifestation of the Cosmic Will to incarnate within the infinitely-finite present moment for Its own Self-realization; it is to experience the essence of Cosmic Magnetic Force. Not only is Awareness *pulled* into Malkuth with a black-hole like attraction, it also *rushes* into it with an urgent eagerness the likes of which you will never have experienced before! I advise that you do *not* fight this pull; but rather, joyfully follow along. *Go with the flow*, as they say!

Once you have reached Malkuth *without resistance*, you will find that you are at liberty to move against the flow and can easily take your time returning to Yesod. In this way you will learn much, much more from this Gate than you would otherwise.

If you wish, this Gate can teach you everything there is to know about Moon magic and working with the rhythms of Nature.

GATE #132

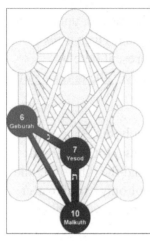
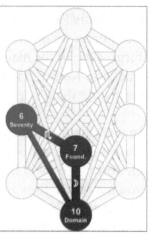

Sequence: ☽ Found. <MOON> Domain <HP:10-6> Severity <SCORPIO> Found.

Return: ☾ Found. <SCORPIO> Severity <HP:6-10> Domain <MOON> Found.

This Gate and the next connect the descending awareness to the Pillar of Severity or Form which in turn, influences the quality of the descending awareness. Here the connection is with the Severe aspect of the Solitary Self and in working this Gate the Solitary Self sees to it that its uniqueness is fully expressed by the descending awareness. This has a supportive, reinforcing and clarifying effect.

GATE #133

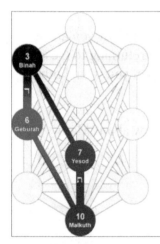
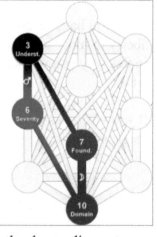

Sequence: ☽ Found. <MOON> Domain <HP:10-6> Severity <MARS> Underst. <HP:3-7> Found.

Return: ☾ Found. <HP:7-3> Underst. <MARS> Severity <HP:6-10> Domain <MOON> Found.

Here the Supernal Severity, Binah, exerts its influence upon the descending astramental awareness and makes certain that the expression of its own essence, along with that of the Solitary Self, is made crystal clear. There is a profound and unexpected effect upon one's karma to be gained from working this Gate! Please notice that this Gate encircles the Gate of Karma and HP:3>10 and encompasses our entire Path of Life. Working this Gate and completing the circuit in *both* directions, transmits some sort of harmonic, magnetic effect upon HP:3>10, which in turn has a clarifying and purifying impact upon our material karma.

GATE #134

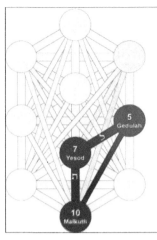

Sequence: ↺ Found. \<MOON> Domain
\<HP:10-5> Mercy \<LIBRA> Found.

Return: ↻ Found. \<LIBRA> Mercy
\<HP:5-10> Domain \<MOON> Found.

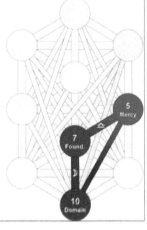

This Gate and the next connect the descending awareness to the Pillar of Mercy or Force which in turn, influences the quality of the descending awareness. Here the connection is with the Merciful aspect of the Solitary Self and in working this Gate the Solitary Self sees to it that its adaptability and its power to resonate are fully expressed by the descending awareness. This has a supportive, reinforcing and balancing effect.

GATE #135

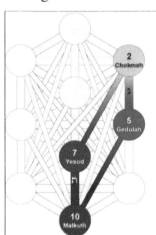

Sequence: ↺ Found. \<MOON> Domain
\<HP:10-5> Mercy \<JUPITER>
Wisdom \<HP:2-7> Found.

Return: ↻ Found. \<HP:7-2> Wisdom
\<JUPITER> Mercy \<HP:5-10>
Domain \<MOON> Found.

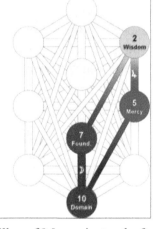

This Gate is the mirror of Gate #133, just concerning the Pillar of Mercy instead of Severity. Here the Supernal Mercy, Chokmah, exerts its influence upon the descending astra-mental awareness and makes certain that the expression of its own essence, along with that of the Solitary Self, is made crystal clear.

Please notice that this Gate encircles the Gate of EM/DNA and HP:2>10, within which all of the circumstances of one's incarnate existence are included. Working this Gate reinforces the fact that adaptability, compromise and unity of purpose are Universal factors and are especially important in the dense material realm of consequence. Nobility of character throughout all of one's interactions with 'other' is the message and lesson here. By working this Gate (in both directions), a harmonic electrical effect is exerted upon it that enables a power of adaptability which has the ability transform all difficult circumstances in instant.

GATE #136

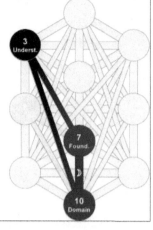

Sequence: ↻ Found. <MOON> Domain <HP:10-3> Underst. <HP:3-7> Found.

Return: ↺ Found. <HP:7-3> Underst. <HP:3-10> Domain <MOON> Found.

This Gate and the next, Gate #137, are really both parts of a single blessing whose genuine origin is Kether. Kether can only connect to Malkuth *directly* in one way: through the joining of the infinitely-finite present moment with the infinitely-infinite Now Moment at the heart of Malkuth. Otherwise, Kether connects *indirectly* and its main connection is through the Pillar of Equilibrium or Self whose final step is the Path of Tav.

The first half of this blessing involves Binah but this is the very highest Supernal aspect of Binah, not the Greater Self level. It is *all* of Infinite Form Itself blessing you; blessing your Path, the walking of your Path, your karma and your descent into *this* incarnation. All you have to do in return is *accept* it.

GATE #137

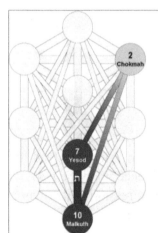
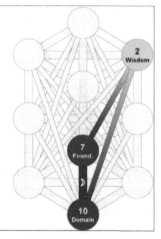

Sequence: ↻ Found. <MOON> Domain <HP:10-2> Wisdom <HP:2-7> Found.

Return: ↺ Found. <HP:7-2> Wisdom <HP:2-10> Domain <MOON> Found.

This half of the blessing comes from Chokmah, the very "highest" level; that moment in which The "I" first says "I Am" to ItSelf . . . what It *Is*, is **_you_**! This is really a blessing of grace, of gracefulness, of acceptance and appreciation in every moment of your incarnation. If you *accept* it, it will complete the blessing of Kether and grant you a rather serene peacefulness.

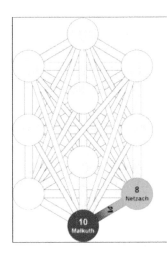
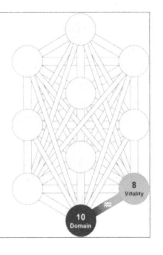

GATE #138

צ TZADDI (FISH-HOOK)

AQUARIUS ♒

Sequence: Vitality \<AQUAR\> Domain

Return: Domain \<AQUAR\> Vitality

Keyword: Emotions

The Hebrew 'Tzaddi' means *fish-hook* in English and actually sort of looks like something worth tying to the end of your fishing line. This is an interesting allusion to the next and final Path of Qooph/Pisces, the Fishes; and seems to indicate that Tzaddi plays a role in how Qooph also binds our awareness to our bodies.

Since Tzaddi is a Simple Letter it is assigned the zodiacal sign of fixed Air, Aquarius, ruled by Saturn. Both zodiacal signs here at the bottom of the Tree (Aquarius/Tzaddi and Pisces/Qooph) are ruled by Saturn; signifying a limit or outer reach or, in this case, the nadir or ending.

The image of Aquarius is the "Water Bearer" and this is a very important indication of Tzaddi's function! Tzaddi is the transmutation or translation of *significance and resonance* into astra-physical *emotion*. Emotion is a force that takes over our astral feeling *and* our physical bodies, eliciting an *automatic* hormonal and electrical response. The *initial* response to emotion is instinctive, unconscious and totally beyond our control; only after this initial response does the ability to take conscious control over our emotions arise.

So it's with the fish-hook of Tzaddi that *emotions* are caught and thus they bind our awareness to our physical body. In other words, *emotion* binds us to physical incarnation. This is a *Watery* process: magnetic, fluid, and tending downward toward physical manifestation; thus the image of 'Water *Bearer'*.

The sign for Aquarius ♒ is indicative of the fact that we're here in the region of transformation from wave-forms into particle-forms. In this case it's the significance-resonance wave-form that is transforming into hormonal-electrical particle-form of emotion. In effect, Tzaddi "catches" the astral wave-form and "lands" it as a physical particle-form.

When working this Gate, you will be able to learn how and why this transmutation happens, and how and why it binds you to your body. You may even learn how to intercede to an extent in the initial automatic reaction. You will certainly learn all about *consciously* controlling your secondary reactions to emotion that are normally driven by the subconscious mind.

Additionally, the Path of Tzaddi is where the *astral* Elements, Fluids and VE become *physical* things in the magician's hands; so if you (as a magician) are having difficulty with the *material* manifestation of any of the above, then this Gate can be of help in terms of your understanding of the mechanics of this transition.

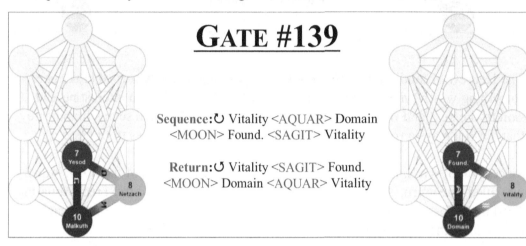

GATE #139

Sequence:↻ Vitality <AQUAR> Domain <MOON> Found. <SAGIT> Vitality

Return:↻ Vitality <SAGIT> Found. <MOON> Domain <AQUAR> Vitality

This Gate is primarily about the relationship between Vital Energy and emotion: how emotional energy is basically the VE; the way in which the two mix and why. It is also about mastery of the VE in the *material* realm, which can be learned from working this Gate.

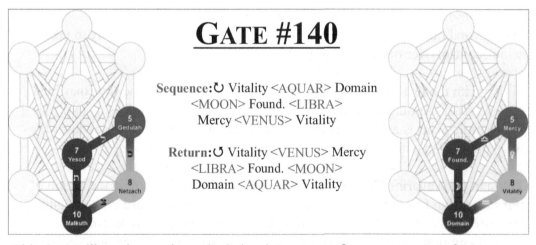

GATE #140

Sequence:↻ Vitality <AQUAR> Domain <MOON> Found. <LIBRA> Mercy <VENUS> Vitality

Return:↻ Vitality <VENUS> Mercy <LIBRA> Found. <MOON> Domain <AQUAR> Vitality

This Gate will teach you about the balancing nature of resonance upon the emotions and how resonance is the goal of emotion, as well as being the basis of emotion. Additionally, this Gate is also about mastery of the Elements in the *material* ream and much can be learned to that end.

GATE #141

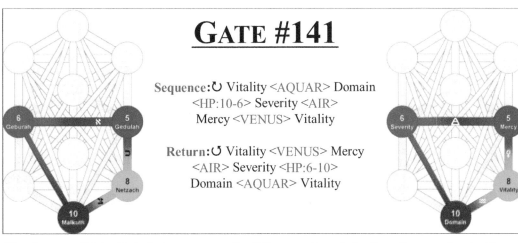

Sequence: ↻ Vitality <AQUAR> Domain
<HP:10-6> Severity <AIR>
Mercy <VENUS> Vitality

Return: ↺ Vitality <VENUS> Mercy
<AIR> Severity <HP:6-10>
Domain <AQUAR> Vitality

The intent of this Gate is to expose all of the emotional dysfunction you've built up over your many incarnations regarding power in general as well as your own unique power: in coping with them and with exercising them. It is also meant to help heal those wounds and repair any dysfunctions with the aid of your collectives and through resonance. This can be quite cathartic and healing and it is a process that is *necessary* for continuing.

GATE #142

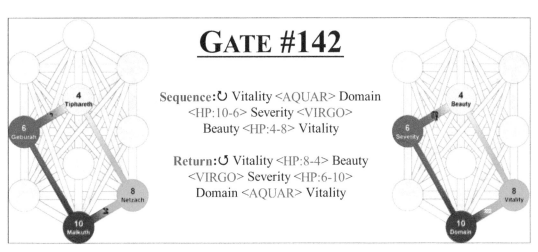

Sequence: ↻ Vitality <AQUAR> Domain
<HP:10-6> Severity <VIRGO>
Beauty <HP:4-8> Vitality

Return: ↺ Vitality <HP:8-4> Beauty
<VIRGO> Severity <HP:6-10>
Domain <AQUAR> Vitality

If you let it, this Gate has the power to realign or reset your emotional relationship with power, both general and personal. The old wounds from past lives are to a great extent healed and the power of attention (quantity of awareness) that was formerly focused on the pain of those wounds, is released and freed to be put to better use.

GATE #143

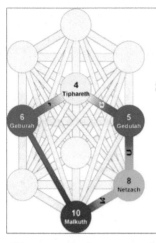

Sequence: ↻ Vitality <AQUAR> Domain <HP:10-6> Severity <VIRGO> Beauty <LEO> Mercy <VENUS> Vitality

Return: ↺ Vitality <VENUS> Mercy <LEO> Beauty <VIRGO> Severity <HP:6-10> Domain <AQUAR> Vitality

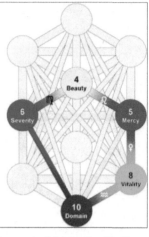

The renewed energy released by the last Gate is now fully integrated into the Solitary Self and the Higher Mind directs it along the Teth/Leo channel and devotes it to bringing *the best* of oneself to the forefront. This renewal manifests as a change in the relationship between your power to resonate and your instinctual emotional responses. In other words, you will now experience greater control.

GATE #144

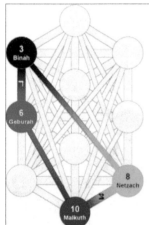

Sequence: ↻ Vitality <AQUAR> Domain <HP:10-6> Severity <MARS> Underst. <HP:3-8> Vitality

Return: ↺ Vitality <HP:8-3> Underst. <MARS> Severity <HP:6-10> Domain <AQUAR> Vitality

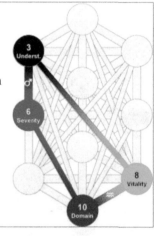

This Gate and the five that follow are all about various aspects of the *higher* function of the dynamic relationship between emotion and power. This Gate and the next three have to do with the influence of our Greater Self and the way that it directs the energies generated by the emotion-power interaction. Working this Gate opens the lines of communication, so to speak, and your Greater Self is empowered to directly influence your resonation and thus shape your emotional reality.

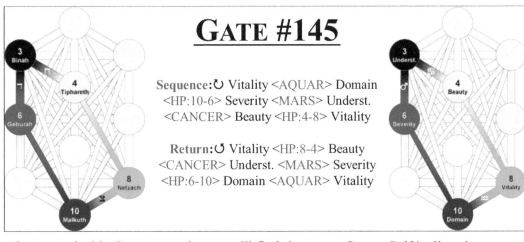

GATE #145

Sequence: ☉ Vitality <AQUAR> Domain <HP:10-6> Severity <MARS> Underst. <CANCER> Beauty <HP:4-8> Vitality

Return: ☉ Vitality <HP:8-4> Beauty <CANCER> Underst. <MARS> Severity <HP:6-10> Domain <AQUAR> Vitality

If you work this Gate properly you will find that your Grater Self is directing a regenerative energy through two channels simultaneously: through HP:4>8 and H:6>10. This transforms your stance in regards your experience of emotions; you see them from a new perspective that is a bit more detached, less involved and less prone to being swept away by them. Emotions loosen their grip on the unconscious.

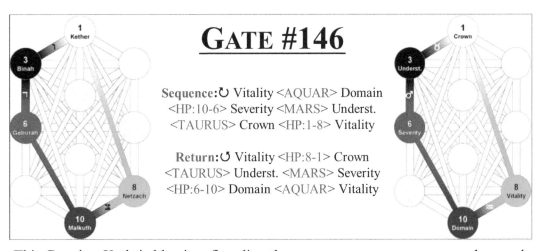

GATE #146

Sequence: ☉ Vitality <AQUAR> Domain <HP:10-6> Severity <MARS> Underst. <TAURUS> Crown <HP:1-8> Vitality

Return: ☉ Vitality <HP:8-1> Crown <TAURUS> Underst. <MARS> Severity <HP:6-10> Domain <AQUAR> Vitality

This Gate is a Kethric blessing, first directly on your power to resonate and second, an indirect blessing upon your personal power that greatly reinforces the imprint of your Greater Self. You will notice a distinct difference in either direction of travel when working this Gate.

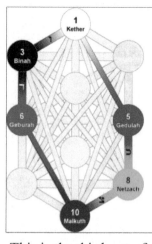

GATE #147

Sequence: ↻ Vitality <AQUAR> Domain
<HP:10-6> Severity <MARS> Underst.
<TAURUS> Crown <HP:1-5>
Mercy <VENUS> Vitality

Return: ↻ Vitality <VENUS> Mercy
<HP:5-1> Crown <TAURUS> Underst.
<MARS> Severity <HP:6-10>
Domain <AQUAR> Vitality

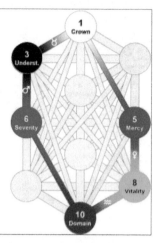

This is the third out of six hexagonal Gates and like all the hexagons, it's significant. It's a perfectly balanced Gate: the three Sephirot in the upper left are the mirror opposites (remember back a ways when I talked about to ten oppositions?) of those in the lower right; furthermore, I would classify the Paths as mirror opposites as well. Basically, this Gate is a powerful blessing from Kether reminding us that at all times the *urge to merge* is paramount along with the urge to perfection in every moment.

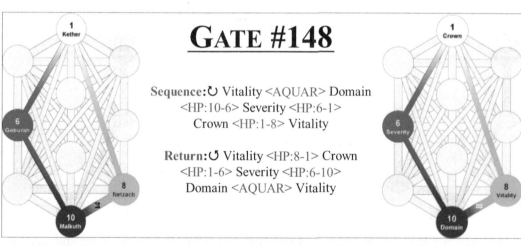

GATE #148

Sequence: ↻ Vitality <AQUAR> Domain
<HP:10-6> Severity <HP:6-1>
Crown <HP:1-8> Vitality

Return: ↻ Vitality <HP:8-1> Crown
<HP:1-6> Severity <HP:6-10>
Domain <AQUAR> Vitality

This is a direct Kethric blessing upon your ability to transmute resonant significance into emotion and express it clearly in the material ream. Since you have so thoroughly cleared and healed your relationship to power, the HP:1>6 and HP:6>10 side of the Gate acts as a *direct* influx from Kether upon Malkuth. As with all blessings, they need to be *accepted* for them to have any real value.

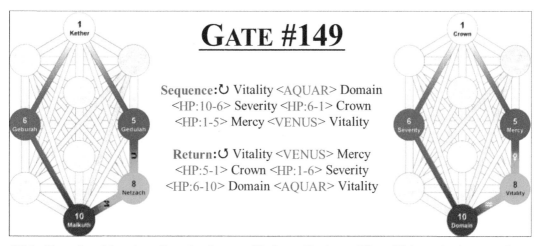

GATE #149

Sequence: ↻ Vitality <AQUAR> Domain
<HP:10-6> Severity <HP:6-1> Crown
<HP:1-5> Mercy <VENUS> Vitality

Return: ↺ Vitality <VENUS> Mercy
<HP:5-1> Crown <HP:1-6> Severity
<HP:6-10> Domain <AQUAR> Vitality

This Gate is a blessing disguised as a gift from Kether. The gift here is that working this Gate will enable you to begin to consciously control your resonance to such a degree that you are able directly shape your emotional reality. The finalizing of this gift occurs with the next Gate.

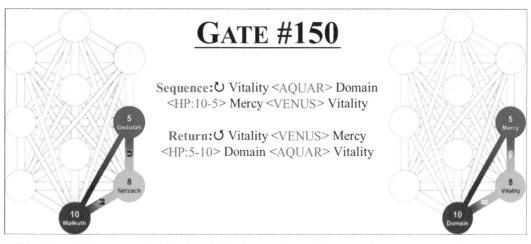

GATE #150

Sequence: ↻ Vitality <AQUAR> Domain
<HP:10-5> Mercy <VENUS> Vitality

Return: ↺ Vitality <VENUS> Mercy
<HP:5-10> Domain <AQUAR> Vitality

This Gate follows on the heels of the last and teaches you how to control your resonance so that it shapes your emotions at their root instead of their tail. This ability is <u>only enabled with the close assistance of your collectives</u>: without this aid, such control is prohibited.

GATE #151

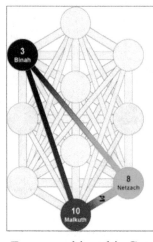
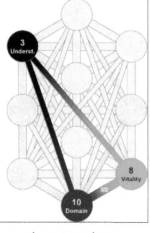

Sequence: ↻ Vitality <AQUAR> Domain <HP:10-3> Underst. <HP:3-8> Vitality

Return: ↻ Vitality <HP:8-3> Underst. <HP:3-10> Domain <AQUAR> Vitality

From working this Gate you will become able to view all of your karma as it relates to your emotional constitution and reality; and you will be able to rectify parts of it that you were unable to touch before now. Eventually, your Greater Self will be able to assume direct control.

GATE #152

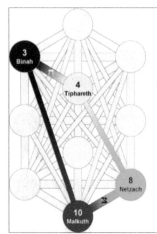
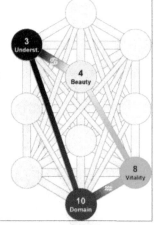

Sequence: ↻ Vitality <AQUAR> Domain <HP:10-3> Underst. <CANCER> Beauty <HP:4-8> Vitality

Return: ↻ Vitality <HP:8-4> Beauty <CANCER> Underst. <HP:3-10> Domain <AQUAR> Vitality

With this Gate the Solitary Self is engaged in the Greater Self's control over the incarnational emotional reality. This expands the degree to which the Malkuth awareness can *consciously* participate in the Greater's work.

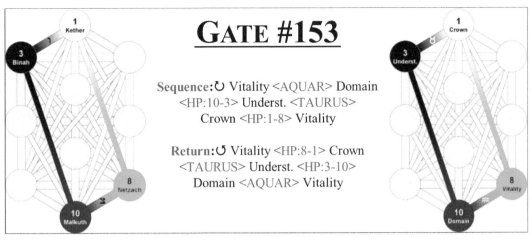

GATE #153

Sequence: ☋ Vitality <AQUAR> Domain
<HP:10-3> Underst. <TAURUS>
Crown <HP:1-8> Vitality

Return: ☊ Vitality <HP:8-1> Crown
<TAURUS> Underst. <HP:3-10>
Domain <AQUAR> Vitality

This Gate is a very powerful blessing from the Supernal Realm (Kether *and* Binah) upon everything that Netzach-Tzaddi-Malkuth represents. By *accepting* this blessing and the blessing of the next gate, you will be readied for the final step in the Gates: the Path of Qooph and the final 28 Gates.

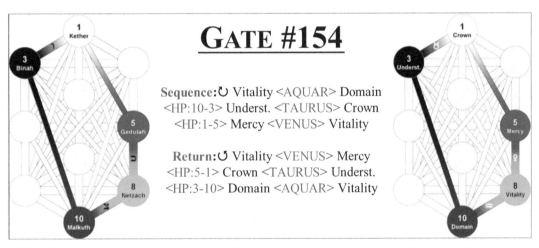

GATE #154

Sequence: ☋ Vitality <AQUAR> Domain
<HP:10-3> Underst. <TAURUS> Crown
<HP:1-5> Mercy <VENUS> Vitality

Return: ☊ Vitality <VENUS> Mercy
<HP:5-1> Crown <TAURUS> Underst.
<HP:3-10> Domain <AQUAR> Vitality

This Gate completes the blessing of the last by once again invoking the all-pervasive *urge to merge*. You can only continue with the Gates once you have *accepted* these blessings.

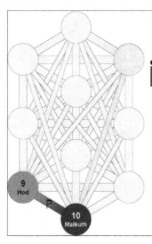

GATE #155

ק QOOPH (BACK OF HEAD, APE)

PISCES ♓

Sequence: Splendor <PISCES> Domain

Return: Domain <PISCES> Splendor

Keywords: Brain-bound awareness,
Final binding of Mind to matter

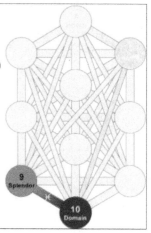

'Qooph' means *ape* or *back of head*; the latter being a reference to 'Resh" / *face*, and the former indicating a more primitive type of awareness. It is also a Simple Letter assigned to the Mutable Water sign of Pisces, ruled again by Saturn, as was Tzaddi. As with all the Water Paths, Qooph serves as the 'birth canal' for what comes next along the Pillar of Self: Malkuth and the realm of the Static Selves.

The mythology behind the symbol of Pisces (two fishes tied together) is a very clear description of Qooph's function in the Tree. When Typhon decided to attack Olympus, all the Gods and Goddesses took to hiding themselves. Aphrodite opted for the ocean and turned into a fish for camouflage and at the same time, she grabbed hold of her son Eros, turned him into a fish also, and tied him to her by the tail so they would not get separated. It's a tale of a mother's protective love for her child in a time of emergency and threat.

In our case here and now, Aphrodite is *Netzach/Tzaddi* and she binds herself to her son, *Hod/Qooph*, dives into the astral Waters and enters the material realm. Hod is truly the child of Netzach, most especially in this form as a *Power* of Hod: Qooph, representing the *brain-bound awareness* of the subconscious based solely upon emotion/Tzaddi.

As the Higher Mind of the Solitary Self entered into the astral medium, it transformed into the rational intellect of the Sentient Self, an intermediate state preceding physical manifestation. This transformation had to do with significance replacing subjective meaning as the basis upon which awareness is based: the rational intellect is totally subjectivized and rooted only in relative significance.

As mind continues its downward journey into physical manifestation, it must undergo yet another transformation and this time, the driver is the physical manifestation of significance – *emotion*. When emotion replaces significance as the currency of the realm, so to speak, awareness is distanced from the immediacy of the present moment and one's focus switches to one's emotional *response* to the present moment; or rather one's emotional response to a *snap-shot* of the most recent present moment. The materialization of awareness requires a drastic change in the nature and mechanics of perception.

This change in the nature of how awareness perceives in the material realm with the material body is what I'm calling the *brain-bound awareness*. The only way that *human* awareness can bind with matter is through a brain, which is a highly specialized organ of a specific type of flesh that transmits electrical impulses with hormonal messages. [Sorry if my oversimplification offends!]

The brain is fairly mechanical in its workings: it's predictable, routine and habitual. Therefore, mind must mutate part of itself into sub- and un-conscious modes of operation to fit into the brain. The subconscious and unconscious minds are both habitual and work automatically. The subconsciousness is normally only barely controllable by the conscious awareness; and in the case of the unconsciousness, totally beyond our control. So these phases of awareness are ideal for connecting to the brain and they sort of hard-wire themselves into its material substance so that there is no temporal lag between the experience of the flesh and of the awareness.

Even though their focus is technically speaking on the past and making comparisons to the past, they nonetheless *exist* in the Now moment: it's *Now* that they are making those comparisons and judgments and coming to those conclusions, etc. Importantly, while this phase of awareness is capable living *in* the Now, it is not normally capable of perceiving and experiencing the *fullness* of the Now. A good modern analogy would be a starving person glued to their mobile phone whilst standing in a great forest teaming with life and activity all around. The normal awareness of the Static Self (i.e., without any participation of the Higher Mind) is oblivious to the infinitely-finite present moment of Malkuth, yet all the while it stands right next to it feeling its effects on the material universe.

This binding to the brain is the *final* binding of Awareness, of the Solitary Self *and* The "I", to physical matter and the incarnate self. It ties it all together just like the tails of the two fish (caught by the hook of Tzaddi).

But the tale does not end there! This connection between Mind and matter, meager though it may be in comparison to the infinite grandeur of Mind itself, serves as a connector between matter and *ALL* of The "I". We must remember that Mind has descended the Middle Pillar of Self through Beth to Tiphareth, through Resh to Yesod, and then through Tav to Malkuth; which means that The "I" descends into Malkuth, the Solitary Self descends and the Sentient Self descends and <u>each can at any time be consciously active within the material realm *through* the Static Self</u>.

Okay, now here's a really important face of Qooph. <u>Only the Higher Mind is capable of perceiving the infinitely-finite present moment of Malkuth</u>. And the Higher

Mind must be operating with full conscious awareness *within* the Static Self in order to achieve that perception; which belies the fact that <u>the infinitely-finite present moment exists *only* in Malkuth</u>. In other words, the completion of the process of Self-realization started by The "I" way back in the beginning, all hinges upon the bridge of awareness established by Qooph here at the end.

The "ape mind" is the final and absolutely necessary ingredient! Ha!

Thus it is nothing to be denigrated and put down as one's enemy or nemesis or as inferior! The human sub- and un-consciousness is meant to be an *ally* and *friend* that works *with* the conscious awareness of the Higher Mind. If we but try, we can quite easily transform them into a *conscious* assent. [This of course is what the early Mirror work of Bardon's *IIH* is all about.]

Since the medium of the Qooph awareness is that of ever-changing emotional significance, it is quite captivating to the astral awareness; we must always see what comes next and whether or not it will be still more significant, etc. In the end, it's addictive much like mobile phones are addictive. And as we know from our experience of this and other common place addictions, they bind us in so many ways and essentially enslave us into a self-perpetuating codependent loop: a *final* binding indeed! One which is very difficult to overcome.

From working this Gate you can learn all about how and why Mind merges with matter through your brain; and how it does the same through other media in other types of beings. Because you are engaging your Higher Mind in this work, you will naturally be able to perceive much more than the Static Self awareness alone, so you will need to pay close attention and distinguish between perceptions in order to truly learn about the sub- and un-conscious parts.

At any rate, you can learn all about the nature and workings of these things and also about how to transform them from their virginal state into *conscious* allies. You will of course, discover many facts about how and why Higher Mind connects with the material realm. One could say that '*why*' is so we are able to perceive the infinitely-finite present moment and thus reconnect to source . . .

The 27 Gates that follow connect *ALL* of the higher levels of awareness to the material realm of your Static Self and physical body. All these levels of Self *must* be connected to Malkuth, through Qooph, and to your brain in order for you to be able to truly Work the infinity Gate. Obviously all of these aspects of Higher Mind have other avenues of access to Malkuth but, *for them to be consciously active through your being, they must all connect through Qooph.*

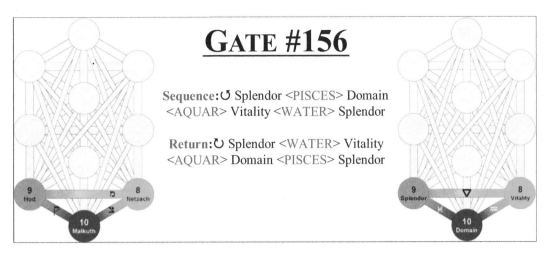

GATE #156

Sequence: ↻ Splendor <PISCES> Domain
<AQUAR> Vitality <WATER> Splendor

Return: ↺ Splendor <WATER> Vitality
<AQUAR> Domain <PISCES> Splendor

These next 11 Gates unify Qooph/Pisces and Tzaddi/Aquarius: without Tzaddi, there can be no Qooph; and without Qooph there can be no Tzaddi. Both function as a unit and in these Gates the nature of their unification is revealed.

By working this Gate you will learn how the Water is at the heart of the transmutation from astral to physical. You will learn the way and the why of it and even learn how to intercede in the process.

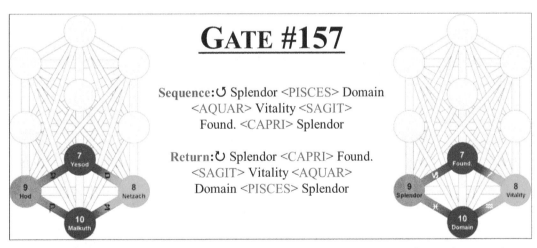

GATE #157

Sequence: ↻ Splendor <PISCES> Domain
<AQUAR> Vitality <SAGIT>
Found. <CAPRI> Splendor

Return: ↺ Splendor <CAPRI> Found.
<SAGIT> Vitality <AQUAR>
Domain <PISCES> Splendor

This Gate is the lower quadrangle of the Tree and encompasses the entire astral realm as it leads into physicality. All the archetypes are repeated here and that is the main lesson of this Gate: how the archetypes exist at every level. You can learn their exact functions at every level by studying them here at their lowest level of manifestation. This is also how the entire astral awareness integrates with the Static Self *through* Qooph.

GATE #158

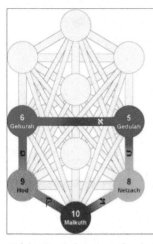

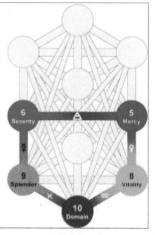

Sequence:↺ Splendor <PISCES> Domain
<AQUAR> Vitality <VENUS> Mercy
<AIR> Severity <MERC> Splendor

Return:↻ Splendor <MERC> Severity
<AIR> Mercy <VENUS> Vitality
<AQUAR> Domain <PISCES> Splendor

This Gate begins the integration of the Air region of the temporal Mental Body into the Static Self via the Qooph/Tzaddi pairing. This is the only integration of Aleph/Air and as such, it provides a balancing, centering influence that is a necessary preparation for what is to come.

GATE #159

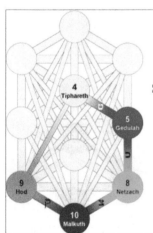

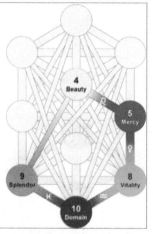

Sequence:↺ Splendor <PISCES> Domain
<AQUAR> Vitality <VENUS> Mercy
<LEO> Beauty <HP:4-9> Splendor

Return:↻ Splendor <HP:9-4> Beauty
<LEO> Mercy <VENUS> Vitality
<AQUAR> Domain <PISCES> Splendor

With the working of this Gate you begin to integrate the Fire region of the temporal Mental body. This step forward is required in preparation for the next Gate.

GATE #160

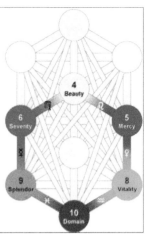

Sequence: ♄ Splendor <PISCES> Domain
<AQUAR> Vitality <VENUS> Mercy
<LEO> Beauty <VIRGO>
Severity <MERC> Splendor

Return: ♄ Splendor <MERC> Severity
<VIRGO> Beauty <LEO> Mercy
<VENUS> Vitality <AQUAR>
Domain <PISCES> Splendor

This Gate is obviously the lower hexagon on the Tree and an echo of Gate #52.
With the working of this Gate you will be integrating your Higher Mind, Air and
Fire regions, into your Static Self awareness via Qooph/Tzaddi. Additionally, you
are integrating all three of your temporal bodies with your *conscious* awareness.
This marks the reaching of a very powerful and integrating stage in your work with
the Gates!

**Immediately after working this Gate the requisite three times and before you
move on to Gate #161, you must go to APPENDIX TWO and perform the special working there. It is the same as you executed after Gate #60 with the upper hexagon, only translated for the lower.**

GATE #161

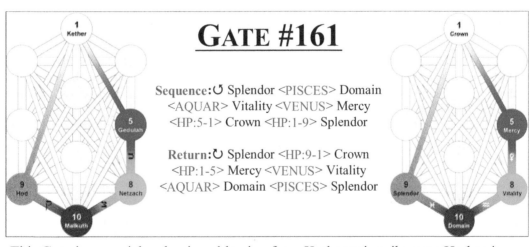

Sequence: ♄ Splendor <PISCES> Domain
<AQUAR> Vitality <VENUS> Mercy
<HP:5-1> Crown <HP:1-9> Splendor

Return: ♄ Splendor <HP:9-1> Crown
<HP:1-5> Mercy <VENUS> Vitality
<AQUAR> Domain <PISCES> Splendor

This Gate is a special and unique blessing from Kether primarily upon Hod as it
gives birth to the Static Self through Qooph. When working this Gate, you should
pay close attention to the descent from Kether; and always bring that blessing with
you the second and third times around as you descend along Qooph. Let the blessing accumulate and build with each circuit.

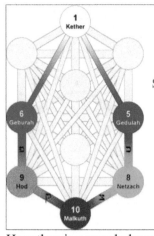

GATE #162

Sequence: ↻ Splendor <PISCES> Domain
<AQUAR> Vitality <VENUS> Mercy
<HP:5-1> Crown <HP:1-6>
Severity <MERC> Splendor

Return: ↺ Splendor <MERC> Severity
<HP:6-1> Crown <HP:1-5> Mercy
<VENUS> Vitality <AQUAR>
Domain <PISCES> Splendor

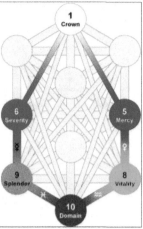

Here then is a very balanced blessing from Kether upon your Gedulah and Geburah awarenesses as they connect with your Static Self. This is an important precursor to what is to
come.

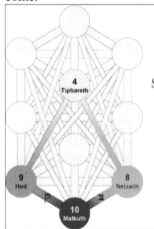

GATE #163

Sequence: ↻ Splendor <PISCES> Domain
<AQUAR> Vitality <HP:8-4>
Beauty <HP:4-9> Splendor

Return: ↺ Splendor <HP:9-4> Beauty
<HP:4-8> Vitality <AQUAR>
Domain <PISCES> Splendor

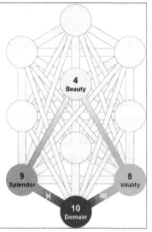

By working this Gate you will begin the final integration of the Fire region of your temporal Mental body. At this juncture the Fire region has not been set free and is not penetrating the Supernal
realm (i.e., it is limited to the temporal). Your Solitary Self integrates and acts consciously within,
or _as_, your Static Self.

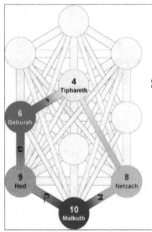

GATE #164

Sequence: ↻ Splendor <PISCES> Domain
<AQUAR> Vitality <HP:8-4> Beauty
<VIRGO> Severity <MERC> Splendor

Return: ↺ Splendor <MERC> Severity
<VIRGO> Beauty <HP:4-8> Vitality
<AQUAR> Domain <PISCES> Splendor

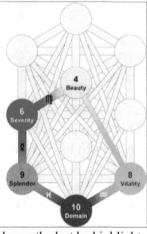

This Gate is in preparation for the next and is meant to bolster or supercharge the last by highlight-
ing your own uniqueness and power. Focus especially upon the perfecting influence of Yod/Virgo.

GATE #165

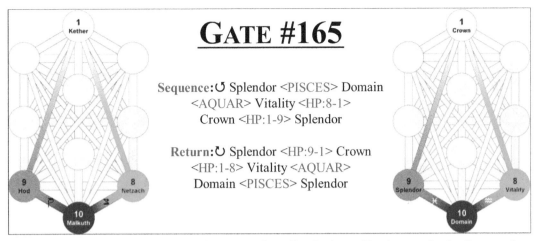

Sequence:↺ Splendor <PISCES> Domain
<AQUAR> Vitality <HP:8-1>
Crown <HP:1-9> Splendor

Return:↻ Splendor <HP:9-1> Crown
<HP:1-8> Vitality <AQUAR>
Domain <PISCES> Splendor

This is one of three very special Gates of Malkuth that afford a method of not only connecting the incarnational awareness directly with The "I" and Kether, but also of bringing The "I" down, *directly into* the infinitely-finite temporal present moment and one's own incarnational awareness (physio-astra-mental body). When one *becomes* all three of these special Gates *simultaneously*, Kether *automatically* fills Malkuth *through or as you*. These three Gates are:

Gate #113   Gate #125   Gate #165

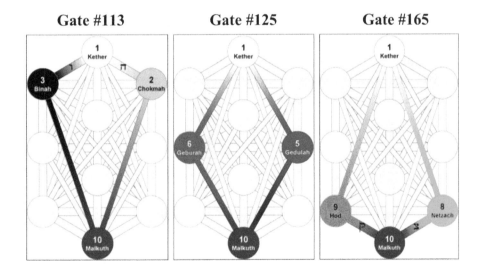

I call this "the Gate of Bliss" because that is what the working of this Gate can achieve. Here your Fire region is let loose to soar up to Kether, and becomes one with The "I" _and_ it is connected to your Static Self awareness or *conscious* mind, your brain plus emotion. This leads to ecstasy. This greatly purifies the Qooph/ Tzaddi unification, bringing it ever closer to its highest intended or archetypal standard.

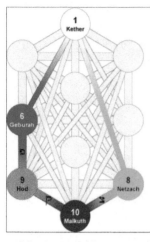

GATE #166

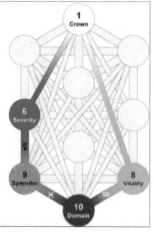

Sequence: ↺ Splendor <PISCES> Domain <AQUAR> Vitality <HP:8-1> Crown <HP:1-6> Severity <MERC> Splendor

Return: ↻ Splendor <MERC> Severity <HP:6-1> Crown <HP:1-8> Vitality <AQUAR> Domain <PISCES> Splendor

This Gate makes a necessary adjustment and reinforcement to the previous Gate. What happens here is that higher perception is grounded more fully in the uniqueness of your own specific perspective. This counters any possible inclination to an imbalance of emotion inherent in the previous Gate. Complicated I know, but please try your best to understand my words here.

This rectification is achieved through a blessing from Kether; first upon your Netzach and it's generation of physical emotion through Tzaddi, and second upon your own unique nature and perspective through Geburah and Peh. When working this Gate, you should pay close attention to both descents from Kether; and always bring that blessing with you the second and third times around. Let the blessing accumulate and build with each circuit.

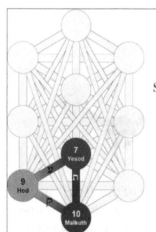

GATE #167

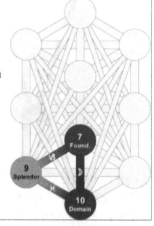

Sequence: ↺ Splendor <PISCES> Domain <MOON> Found. <CAPRI> Splendor

Return: ↻ Splendor <CAPRI> Found. <MOON> Domain <PISCES> Splendor

Now we turn away from the Qooph/Tzaddi dynamic and look to the connection of the descending awareness (Solitary Self plus Sentient Self) of Tav/Moon and the all important power to choose (Ayin/Capricorn). Working this Gate strengthens and accentuates the fruits of one's powers to *self*-determine. This is especially helpful in the process of transforming the sub-conscious into a conscious asset and character transformation.

GATE #168

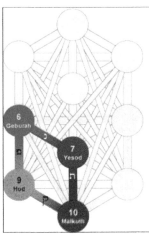

Sequence: ↺ Splendor <PISCES> Domain
<MOON> Found. <SCORPIO>
Severity <MERC> Splendor

Return: ↻ Splendor <MERC> Severity
<SCORPIO> Found. <MOON>
Domain <PISCES> Splendor

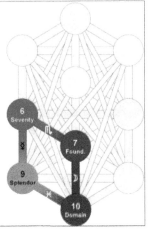

Here again it is about integrating the descending awareness with Qooph but this time, the emphasis is upon the personal uniqueness expressed by Geburah. Working this Gate matures one's power of self-determination at the level of physical interaction or expression.

GATE #169

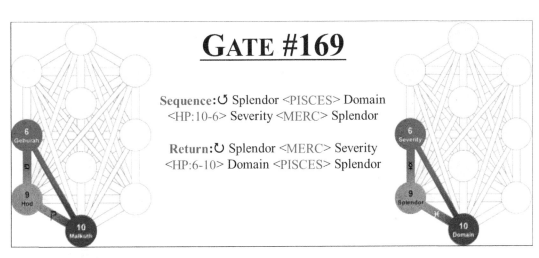

Sequence: ↺ Splendor <PISCES> Domain
<HP:10-6> Severity <MERC> Splendor

Return: ↻ Splendor <MERC> Severity
<HP:6-10> Domain <PISCES> Splendor

This is an important Gate in that it is the *only* Gate that seeks to integrate Qooph solely with your relationship to power (HP:6>10). This Gate and this connection between Qooph and your relationship to both your own power and power in general is so significant that it takes the next 9 Gates to balance and purify!

You must work this Gate very slowly and carefully and learn as much as you can from it. I recommend many more repetitions than the usual three. This is a crucial juncture! How you fare here, determines how you will fare in what's to come.

GATE #170

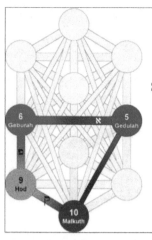

Sequence: ↻ Splendor <PISCES> Domain
<HP:10-5> Mercy <AIR>
Severity <MERC> Splendor

Return: ↺ Splendor <MERC> Severity
<AIR> Mercy <HP:5-10>
Domain <PISCES> Splendor

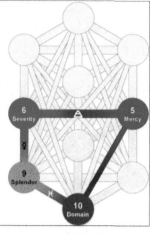

Here Gate #169 opens and places #169 in its proper, healing context of Gedulah, one's *connection* to 'other' and the *urge to merge*. We start the process of rectification with a strong reminder of the source of our power and how we must always treat power as we integrate further with Qooph. Working this Gate must shift your relationship to power as Qooph integrates your awareness into your Static Self. This is a work of the Air region of your Mental body so Aleph/Air eases the way . . .

GATE #171

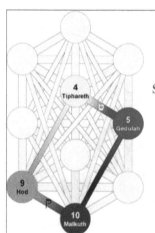

Sequence: ↻ Splendor <PISCES> Domain
<HP:10-5> Mercy <LEO>
Beauty <HP:4-9> Splendor

Return: ↺ Splendor <HP:9-4> Beauty
<LEO> Mercy <HP:5-10>
Domain <PISCES> Splendor

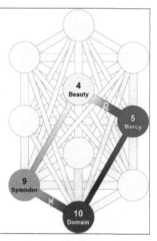

Now we take a brief shift away from focus upon your relationship to power and move to a focus on your relationship to your collective connections and its impact upon Qooph. Tiphareth becomes involved in this integration. From working this Gate you will learn valuable information regarding self-transformation.

GATE #172

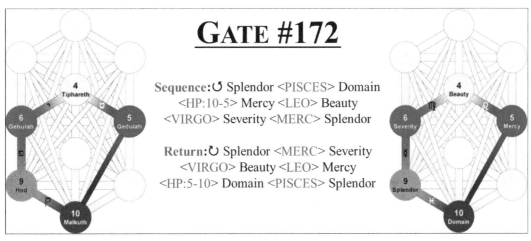

Sequence: ↺ Splendor <PISCES> Domain <HP:10-5> Mercy <LEO> Beauty <VIRGO> Severity <MERC> Splendor

Return: ↻ Splendor <MERC> Severity <VIRGO> Beauty <LEO> Mercy <HP:5-10> Domain <PISCES> Splendor

Now the whole of the Solitary Self, Air and Fire regions, becomes involved in the integration of your unique power with Qooph _and_ it is anchored to the side of Mercy and collectivism through Gedulah and HP:5>10. Working this Gate purifies the connection with Qooph.

GATE #173

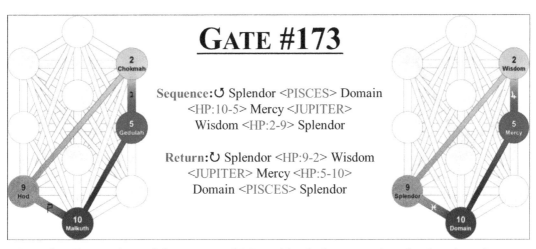

Sequence: ↺ Splendor <PISCES> Domain <HP:10-5> Mercy <JUPITER> Wisdom <HP:2-9> Splendor

Return: ↻ Splendor <HP:9-2> Wisdom <JUPITER> Mercy <HP:5-10> Domain <PISCES> Splendor

Now the Fire region of the temporal Mental body becomes involved and again we move our focus away from power and devote it fully to Mercy and collectivism. The Fire region is released and flies up to Chokmah, the region of the "I Am" awareness and infinite Essential Meaning. By working this Gate you can connect your Hod power to _know_ (its direct connection to Chokmah) with Qooph and your conscious awareness in Malkuth. The involvement of Gimel, Gedulah and HP:5>10 stabilizes this connection.

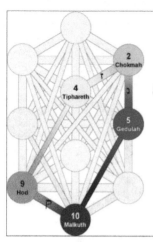

GATE #174

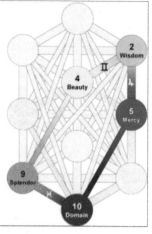

Sequence: ↻ Splendor \<PISCES> Domain \<HP:10-5> Mercy \<JUPITER> Wisdom \<GEMINI> Beauty \<HP:4-9> Splendor

Return: ↻ Splendor \<HP:9-4> Beauty \<GEMINI> Wisdom \<JUPITER> Mercy \<HP:5-10> Domain \<PISCES> Splendor

This Gate softens and contextualizes the *knowing* of Chokmah and includes the Air region of your temporal Mental body in its integration. This makes the integration more complete and practical.

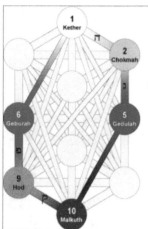

GATE #175

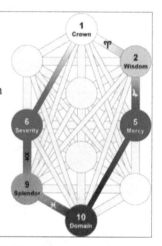

Sequence: ↻ Splendor \<PISCES> Domain \<HP:10-5> Mercy \<JUPITER> Wisdom \<ARIES> Crown \<HP:1-6> Severity \<MERC> Splendor

Return: ↻ Splendor \<MERC> Severity \<HP:6-1> Crown \<ARIES> Wisdom \<JUPITER> Mercy \<HP:5-10> Domain \<PISCES> Splendor

These next four Gates involve Kether and *require* that you *fully* release the Fire region of your temporal Mental body so that it truly reaches The "I". Although they <u>will</u> affect you profoundly, you might find it difficult to retain a conscious memory of the experience. Just go slow and savor each one *while* it's happening. You might want to start out with the intention of remembering but don't get caught up in the *need* to remember; or rather, don't let the need to remember distract from the experience itself. As I said, you *will* be affected whether you remember or not.

This Gate is a mirror or Gate #147 with the same sort of opposition of Sephirot and Paths. It is also the last of the hexagons, the sixth of six to be exact. With it we turn back to our relationship with power and its integration into the lowest level of our awareness in Malkuth via Qooph. By working this Gate with your Fire region, you will be invoking a highly creative influence into your Qooph and the integration of awareness that it represents. Forevermore, all of your power and dealings with the power of 'other', will be subservient to your *urge to merge*.

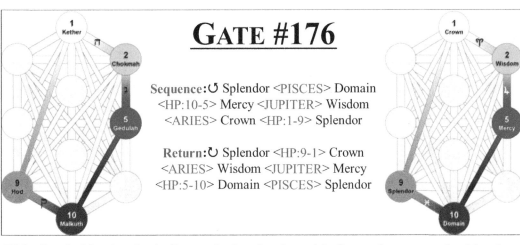

GATE #176

Sequence: ↺ Splendor <PISCES> Domain <HP:10-5> Mercy <JUPITER> Wisdom <ARIES> Crown <HP:1-9> Splendor

Return: ↺ Splendor <HP:9-1> Crown <ARIES> Wisdom <JUPITER> Mercy <HP:5-10> Domain <PISCES> Splendor

This Gate's blessing is similar to the last but here it's focused as a creative blessing upon Qooph itself.

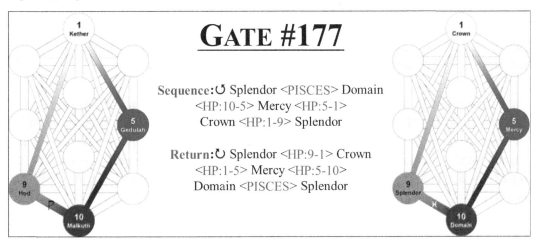

GATE #177

Sequence: ↺ Splendor <PISCES> Domain <HP:10-5> Mercy <HP:5-1> Crown <HP:1-9> Splendor

Return: ↺ Splendor <HP:9-1> Crown <HP:1-5> Mercy <HP:5-10> Domain <PISCES> Splendor

This is a direct blessing upon Qooph from Kether that veritably shouts out to the universe: "The *urge to merge* rules everything, always!"

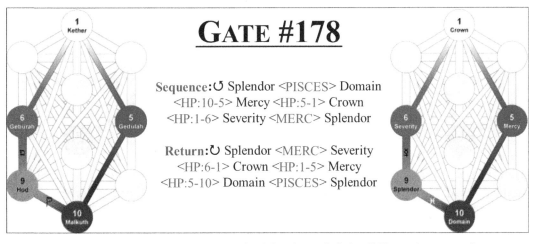

GATE #178

Sequence: ↺ Splendor <PISCES> Domain <HP:10-5> Mercy <HP:5-1> Crown <HP:1-6> Severity <MERC> Splendor

Return: ↺ Splendor <MERC> Severity <HP:6-1> Crown <HP:1-5> Mercy <HP:5-10> Domain <PISCES> Splendor

This Gate is much the same but puts the blessing slightly differently as: "All power is subservient to the collective good of All!"

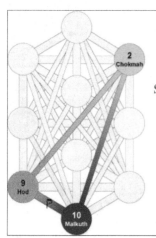

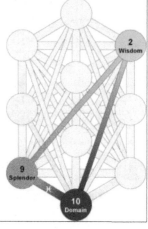

GATE #179

Sequence: ↺ Splendor <PISCES> Domain <HP:10-2> Wisdom <HP:2-9> Splendor

Return: ↻ Splendor <HP:9-2> Wisdom <HP:2-10> Domain <PISCES> Splendor

Now, with these last four Gates before the Infinity Gate, our attention turns away from considerations of power and collectivity and we focus entirely upon our expression of Essential Meaning in the physical realm which is completed and fully realized *through* Qooph. Again, all must be worked *as* your Fire region. The main player in all these Gates is HP:2>10, the Path of our own specific bundle of EM manifesting in Malkuth as our own unique DNA.

By working this particular Gate you will learn exactly how and why EM is related to your Malkuth self; what role your Qooph plays in the formation and execution of your DNA; as well as the role your EM plays in how your express your DNA in this lifetime. This knowing from Chokmah and the Understanding it generates, are necessary for successfully working the remaining Gates, so close attention should be paid.

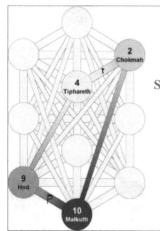

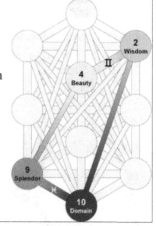

GATE #180

Sequence: ↺ Splendor <PISCES> Domain <HP:10-2> Wisdom <GEMINI> Beauty <HP:4-9> Splendor

Return: ↻ Splendor <HP:9-4> Beauty <GEMINI> Wisdom <HP:2-10> Domain <PISCES> Splendor

Here is a potent reminder and assertion of the fact that the whole point is the Self-realization of The "I"; and that process _must_ involve 'self' *and* 'other' to reach its conclusion. With the working of this Gate you will learn how and why this is so and you will learn it with the assistance of the Air region of your temporal Mental body, making it easier for you to integrate at the level of your physical awareness.

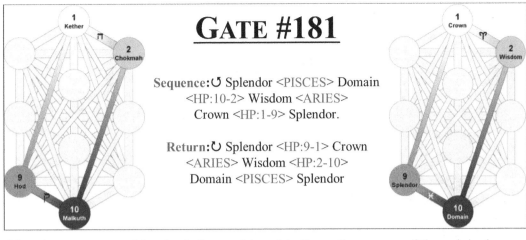

GATE #181

Sequence: ℧ Splendor <PISCES> Domain
<HP:10-2> Wisdom <ARIES>
Crown <HP:1-9> Splendor.

Return: ℧ Splendor <HP:9-1> Crown
<ARIES> Wisdom <HP:2-10>
Domain <PISCES> Splendor

Here is a very great blessing! By working this Gate, the power of the original creative movement of the One Awareness from "I" to "I AM", is handed over to Qooph directly. It is imprinted directly onto your Static Self by Qooph. If fully *accepted*, this blessing becomes permanent.

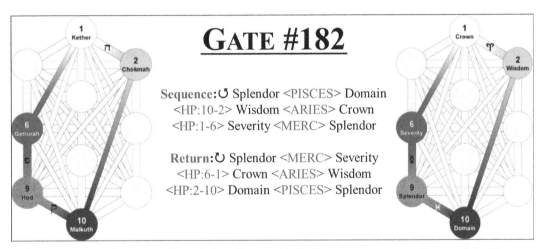

GATE #182

Sequence: ℧ Splendor <PISCES> Domain
<HP:10-2> Wisdom <ARIES> Crown
<HP:1-6> Severity <MERC> Splendor

Return: ℧ Splendor <MERC> Severity
<HP:6-1> Crown <ARIES> Wisdom
<HP:2-10> Domain <PISCES> Splendor

The Blessing of the last Gate is hereby multiplied, empowered and completed by working this final Gate. Your use of your own power and your relationship to the power of 'other' is forever transformed. The consequences are nearly infinite in number, the discovery of which I leave entirely in your capable hands!

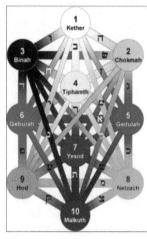

GATE ∞

THE WHOLE

Sequence: ↺↻ Simultaneous

Return: ↺↻ Simultaneous

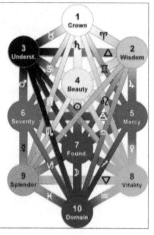

You've finally made it to the end, to the Ultimate Goal! If you've managed it by simple reading then good for you! I admire your dedication and curiosity! I hope I have inspired you to take up this work with the Gates or at least work with the Magic of Essential Form.

If by chance you are of the very few who have reached this point by actually *working* all these many Gates . . . well then, my heartiest Congratulations!!!! I thank you! The Cosmos thanks you! You have truly gone where few have trod or even knew to go.

But you mustn't stop there! There's yet one more step to take with the Tree in order to fulfill the true goal of the Magic of Essential Form: *The Infinity Gate*.

You are by now well versed in the *art* of MEF but have not yet reached its Mastery. The *art* is in <u>reaching an Understanding of the Essence of any Form through a process of *becoming* that form</u>. You have clearly honed your skill at this art by working with the *Forms* of the 182 Gates and the two hexagons. MEF is about this *becoming* an Understanding of the Essence of whatever form you are working with and here we have applied it to the Tree *but only to its parts*.

As a Form, the Essential Meaning expressed by the Gra Tree of Life is the *whole* of the *Cosmos*, so now we must become the *whole* Tree to truly fulfill MEF. By becoming the *whole* of the Tree you truly become the *whole* of The "I", with or through *every* level of your being. <u>Thus The "I" *consciously* experiences the infinitely-finite present moment of time-space *through you*: *that*</u> is the ultimate goal of MEF and the true goal of applying MEF to the Gra Tree of Life.

There are several ways to approach working the Infinity Gate, all but one involves building the Tree, piece by piece, of various sizes and in various sequences. The most straight forward and direct way is to simply *become* the whole Tree but that is generally way more easily said than done! Ha! This 'instant becoming' ability is to be *aimed* for but ordinarily proves impossible at first (not to preclude it from happening!).

The longest method by far is to work all 182 Gates consecutively and in a single session; all the while becoming each Gate and adding it to your cumulative awareness until you reach the last, at which point you <u>are</u> the whole Tree. This is certainly doable but only if you have the stamina to endure *at least* 8 hours of intensive work (without a break). I don't exactly recommend this method; although, it is a valuable experience.

What I *do* recommend for your first time however, is the method I lay out for you in **APPENDIX THREE**. It involves the full upper and lower hexagons that you have already worked with if you performed the two special workings I laid out earlier (**APPENDIX ONE** and **TWO**). First you invoke both hexagons, one on top of the other; and then, you work a special Gate called the Unicursal Hexagram, formed by the six Hidden Paths not involved in either hexagon. The Unicursal Gate ties the two hexagons together and sets the whole in motion.

A second method I can recommend involves working each Linear Gate in sequence and building the whole Tree within oneself. I always include the Sephirot as well, either by virtue of their inclusion within the Gates or separately. In **APPENDIX FOUR** I provide you with the Creative Sequence of the Linear Gates, derived from their sequence within the 182 Gates.

The next method I use frequently. It's especially suited for magical operations in which one wishes to achieve an end through MEF. For example, I use this method or aspect of MEF to create my Crystal Golems. This method involves directly following the instructions of the Sepher Yetzirah and working in a specific sequence (which in turn creates a specific effect). This sequence is displayed in **APPENDIX FIVE**. I have added the 14 Hidden Paths at the end of the S.Y. sequence (even though they are not mentioned therein) because adding them after the S.Y. sequence sets the whole Tree alive.

The final method to mention is the *Genesis Sequence*, taken directly from the 32 times the Name Elohim is mentioned is Genesis One. This is the source of the so called *32 Paths of Wisdom*. I urge caution here: it can be a surprisingly *creative* working! I have outlined this sequence for you in **APPENDIX SIX**.

APPENDIX ONE

Special work to follow Gate #60

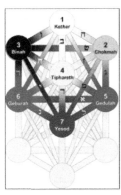

With Gate #60 you have come about a third of the way through the 182 Gates; although visually, it looks as though we've come a bit more than half way. Either way, you have completed the upper hexagon and this should give you some clue as to how complex the remainder of the Tree really is. It will be another 100 Gates before we truly complete the lower hexagon!

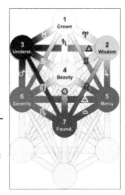

Now is the moment for me to introduce you to a deeper aspect of working the Gates: _becoming_ the Gates.

After you have worked a Gate as usual, you then prolong the working by holding all the Sephirot and connecting Paths together in your awareness. You hold onto them all simultaneously until you _become_ the Gate. You must resonate with the totality of the Gate and all its relationships until such time that you feel as though you are manifesting the Gate itself and as if you are radiating the Gate into the universe. This is what I mean by '_becoming_ the Gate'.

This is the point at which working the Gates becomes truly transformational and initiatory. It will likely be rather challenging at first but this, as always, eases with practice. In future, I advise that you work each Gate in the usual way for the requisite three times and follow this up by _becoming_ the Gate at <u>least</u> once.

The work I'm going to set out for you here is very complex and I've chosen it for this reason as your introduction to _becoming_ a Gate. It will be so unusual to you and will thus impress upon your awareness to such a greater degree that _becoming_ these Gates will actually be easier. (At least that is my hope!)

What we are going to do is explore and eventually _become_, the upper hexagon. I suggest you set aside an hour or so for this work.

The hexagon pictured above can be resolved into three six-pointed figures:

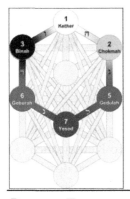
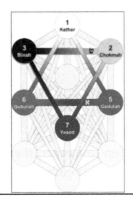
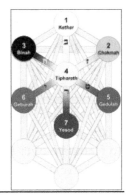

The first of these you will recognize as the hexagonal Gate #52 which was recently worked. The second figure is a combination of two triangular Gates: Gate #31 is the upward pointing triangle and Gate #35 is the downward pointing triangle. Each of these figures is composed of six Sephirot and six Paths.

The third figure on the other hand, is composed of six Gates comprised of *seven* Sephirot and six Paths, with Tiphareth being the constant throughout. The Gates in this figure are #5, #6, #8, #15, #22 and #37.

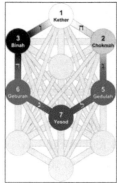 So we start with the first figure which you know as Gate #52, but we will be working it in a different sequence than we're used to. For these purposes we will start in Kether and go in a clockwise direction to Chokmah, then Gedulah, etc., till we return to where we started in Kether. Then we go back around in the opposite direction of Kether to Binah to Geburah, etc., till we return once again to Kether. That's one circuit.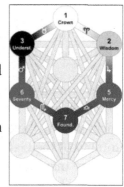

The second circuit begins in Chokmah and we progress clockwise around the circle once more and then back to Chokmah. The third circuit begins in Gedulah; clockwise around and back. The fourth circuit begins in Yesod; clockwise around and back. The fifth begins in Geburah; clockwise around and back. And finally, the sixth circuit begins in Binah; clockwise around and back to end in Binah.

Okay, so now all six Sephirot and all six Path are firmly in your awareness from every angle several times over. Now you must gather them all together and hold onto them all at once. Make them *one* thing not twelve things. Feel them as an integral whole. Stay in this state for a couple of minutes or so and then let it go.

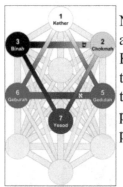 Now we turn to our second form, the two triangles of Gates #31 and #35. We will start in Kether and work our way clockwise around the six Sephirot; however, we will work each triangle in opposite directions: the upward pointing triangle clockwise and the downward pointing triangle counterclockwise.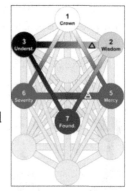

The sequence is as follows: Start in Kether and go clockwise around the triangle to Gedulah, over to Geburah and up to Kether, then back around to Kether once again. Next we go the Chokmah and go counterclockwise to Binah, then down the

Yesod and up to Chokmah once again, and then back around. Next we go to Gedulah and progress clockwise over to Geburah, up to Kether and back to Gedulah, and then back around. Next we go to Yesod and progress counterclockwise up to Chokmah, over to Binah and back to Yesod, and back around. Next we go to Geburah and progress clockwise up to Kether, down to Gedulah and over to Geburah, and back around. And finally we go to Binah and progress counterclockwise to Yesod, up the Chokmah and over to Binah, and back around.

So, having gone around both triangles from every direction possible and touched upon each Sephirot and all six Paths many times over, you must now hold all twelve factors simultaneously in your awareness as a *one* thing. You must *become* this joining of Gates and radiate its essence out into the universe. When you are ready, move on to the final figure.

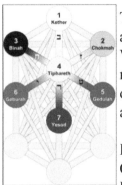

The sequence for this form is very complicated at first so I suggest you study it beforehand. We will be progressing through the Sephirot in numerical order twice; first in descending order from Kether through Yesod and then in ascending order from Yesod to Kether.

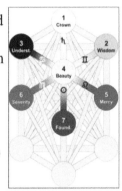

First circuit: Kether to Tiphareth; Tiphareth to Chokmah and back to Tiphareth; Tiphareth to Binah and back to Tiphareth; Tiphareth to Gedulah and back to Tiphareth; Tiphareth to Geburah and back to Tiphareth; Tiphareth to Yesod and back to Tiphareth <u>and then back up to Kether</u>.

Second circuit: Yesod to Tiphareth; Tiphareth to Geburah and back to Tiphareth; Tiphareth to Gedulah and back to Tiphareth; Tiphareth to Binah and back to Tiphareth; Tiphareth to Chokmah and back to Tiphareth; Tiphareth to Kether and back to Tiphareth <u>and then back down the Yesod</u>.

You must now *become* this six-pointed star of Tiphareth. Feel yourself radiating its essence into the universe. Hold onto this awareness with all your might.

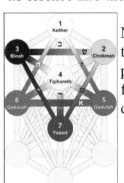

Now overlay the previous form composed of the two interlocking triangles on top of the Tiphareth Star. *Become* this new expanded form. The radiant star is now constrained to a degree. Hold onto this awareness.

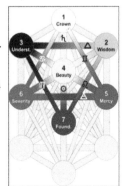

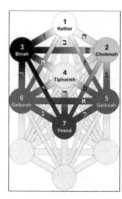

Now add the hexagonal Gate #52 to the form you are amassing and feel how it confines and encircles the Tiphareth Star, giving it definite form. *Become* the upper hexagon of the Tree! *Feel* its power!

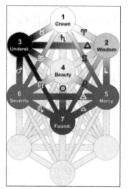

Remain in this exalted state of awareness for as long as you can or wish.

APPENDIX TWO

Special work to follow Gate #160

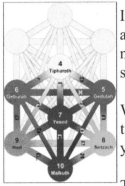 Immediately after Gate #60 I had you perform a special working of the upper hexagon and now, after Gate #160, it's time to do the same sort of working of the lower hexagon.

What we are going to do is explore and eventually *become*, the lower hexagon. I suggest you set aside an hour or so for this work.

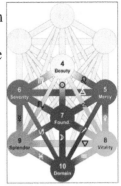

The hexagon pictured above can be resolved into three six-pointed figures:

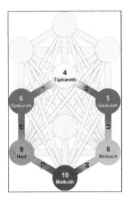 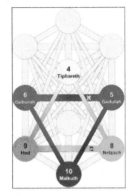 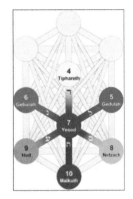

The first of these you will recognize as the hexagonal Gate #160 which was recently worked. The second figure is a combination of two triangular Gates: Gate #106 is the upward pointing triangle and Gate #120 is the downward pointing triangle. Each of these figures is composed of six Sephirot and six Paths.

The third figure on the other hand, is composed of six Gates comprised of *seven* Sephirot and six Paths, with Yesod being the constant throughout. The Gates in this figure are #37, #40, #47, #72, #91 and #131.

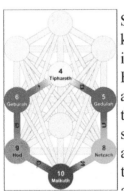 So we start with the first figure which you know as Gate #160, but we will be working it in a different sequence than we're used to. For these purposes we will start in Tiphareth and go in a clockwise direction to Gedulah, then Netzach, etc., till we return to where we started in Tiphareth. Then we go back around in the opposite direction of Tiphareth to Geburah to Hod, etc., till we return once again to Tiphareth. That's one circuit.

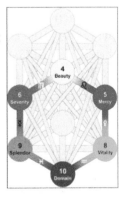

The second circuit begins in Gedulah and we progress clockwise around the circle once more and then back to Gedulah. The third circuit begins in Netzach; clockwise around and back. The fourth circuit begins in Malkuth; clockwise around and back. The fifth begins in Hod; clockwise around and back. And finally, the sixth circuit begins in Geburah; clockwise around and back to end in Geburah.

Okay, so now all six Sephirot and all six Path are firmly in your awareness from every angle several times over. Now you must gather them all together and hold onto them all at once. Make them *one* thing not twelve things. Feel them as an integral whole. Stay in this state for a couple of minutes or so and then let it go.

Now we turn to our second form, the two triangles of Gates #106 and #120. We will start in Tiphareth and work our way clockwise around the six Sephirot; however, we will work each triangle in opposite directions: the upward pointing triangle clockwise and the downward pointing triangle counterclockwise.

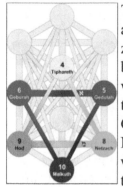 The sequence is as follows: Start in Tiphareth and go clockwise around the triangle to Netzach, over to Hod and up to Tiphareth, then back around to Tiphareth once again. Next we go the Gedulah and go counterclockwise to Geburah, then down the Malkuth and up to Gedulah once again, and then back around. Next we go to Netzach and progress clockwise over to Hod, up to Tiphareth and back to Netzach, and then back around. Next we 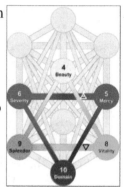 go to Malkuth and progress counterclockwise up to Gedulah, over to Geburah and back to Malkuth, and back around. Next we go to Hod and progress clockwise up to Tiphareth, down to Netzach and over to Hod, and back around. And finally we go to Geburah and progress counterclockwise to Malkuth, up the Gedulah and over to Geburah, and back around.

So, having gone around both triangles from every direction possible and touched upon each Sephirot and all six Paths many times over, you must now hold all twelve factors simultaneously in your awareness as a *one* thing. You must *become* this joining of Gates and radiate its essence out into the universe. When you are ready, move on to the final figure.

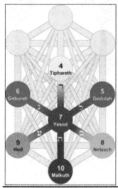 The sequence for this form is very complicated at first so I suggest you study it beforehand. We will be progressing through the Sephirot in numerical order twice; first in descending order from Tiphareth through Malkuth and then in ascending order from Malkuth to Tiphareth.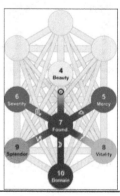

First circuit: Tiphareth to Yesod; Yesod to Gedulah and back to Yesod; Yesod to Geburah and back to Yesod; Yesod to Netzach and back to Yesod ; Yesod to Hod and back to Yesod ; Yesod to Malkuth and back to Yesod <u>and then back up to Tiphareth</u>.

Second circuit: Malkuth to Yesod; Yesod to Hod and back to Yesod; Yesod to Netzach and back to Yesod; Yesod to Geburah and back to Yesod; Yesod to Gedulah and back to Yesod; Yesod to Tiphareth and back to Yesod <u>and then back down the Malkuth</u>.

You must now *become* this six-pointed star of Yesod. Feel yourself radiating its essence into the universe. Hold onto this awareness with all your might.

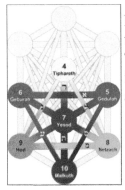

Now overlay the previous form composed of the two interlocking triangles on top of the Tiphareth Star. *Become* this new expanded form. The radiant star is now constrained to a degree. Hold onto this awareness.

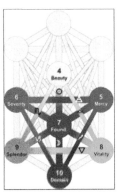

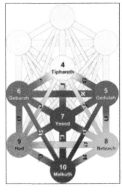

Now add the hexagonal Gate #160 to the form you are amassing and feel how it confines and encircles the Yesod Star, giving it definite form. *Become* the lower hexagon of the Tree! *Feel* its power!

Remain in this exalted state of awareness for as long as you can or wish.

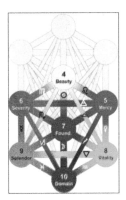

At the end of the 182 Gates I have illustrated an Infinity Gate which is the Tree, as a whole, with all of the Paths and Sephirot all at once. The object of this Gate is to *become* the <u>whole</u> Tree simultaneously. In APPENDIX THREE you will find a method for doing this that builds upon our work with the upper and lower hexagons by adding the six special Hidden Paths that bind the two hexagons together.

APPENDIX THREE
Special Work to follow Gate #182

THE INFINITY GATE

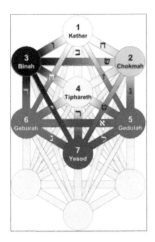 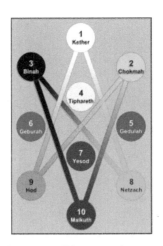 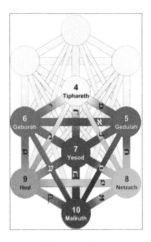

The figures on the left and right you will recognize as the upper and lower hexagons respectively; but the figure in the center will be new to you. The hexagram formed by these six special Hidden Paths is the one and only _Unicursal_ Hexagram Gate in the Gra Tree and it is what binds the two hexagons together.

Here is the method:

First you must invoke the upper hexagon and _become_ it; then _become_ the lower hexagon and overlay it upon the upper so that you hold both simultaneously. Finally you must work the Unicursal Hexagram Gate and _become_ it along with the upper and lower hexagons.

The sequence for working the Unicursal Gate is simple. First pass starts in Kether and proceeds to Netzach, then Binah, then Malkuth, then Chokmah, then Hod, then Kether, and back around. Second (and final) pass starts in Malkuth and proceeds to Binah, then to Netzach, then to Kether, then to Hod, then to Chokmah, then to Malkuth, and back around.

Here is the result:

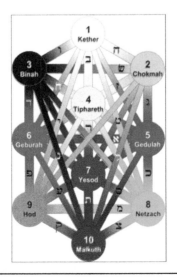

APPENDIX FOUR

THE CREATIVE SEQUENCE OF PATHS

[Left-to-right and top-to-bottom.]

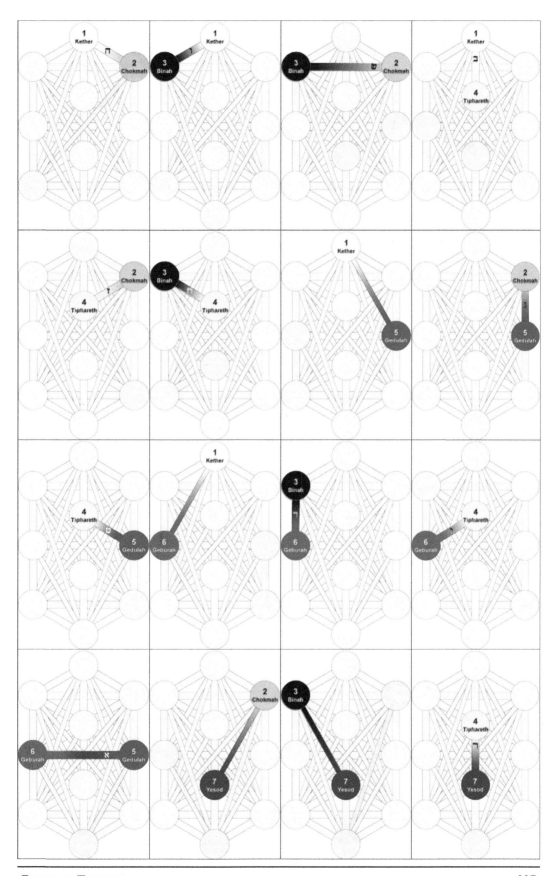

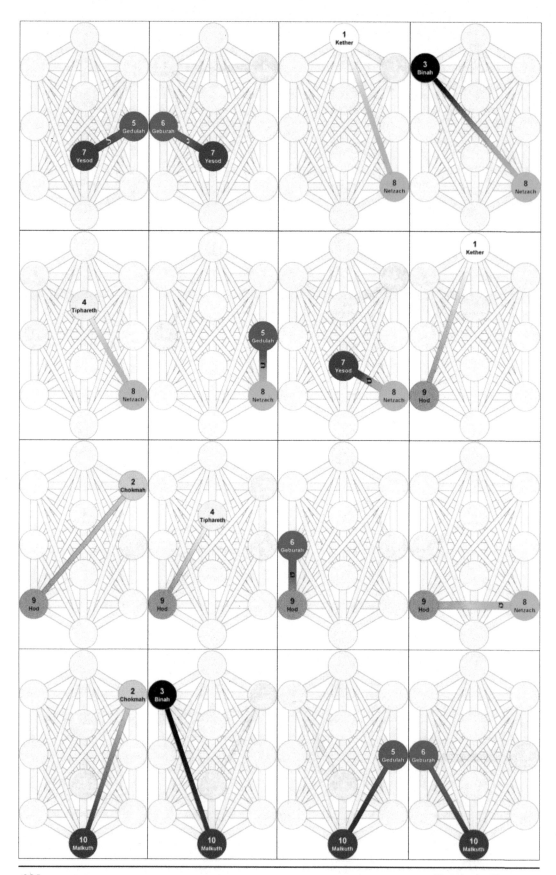

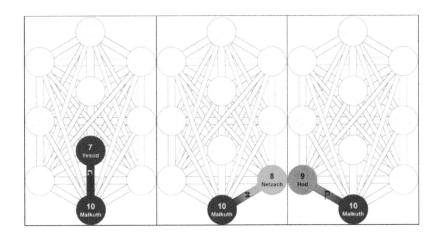

APPENDIX FIVE

THE SEPHER YETZIRAH'S
CREATIVE SEQUENCE OF SEPHIROT AND PATHS
[Left-to-right and top-to-bottom.]

The 10 Sephirot —

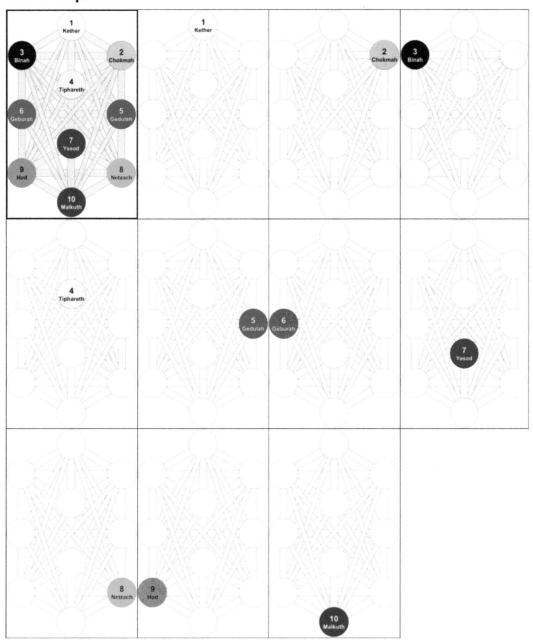

The 3 Mother Letters —

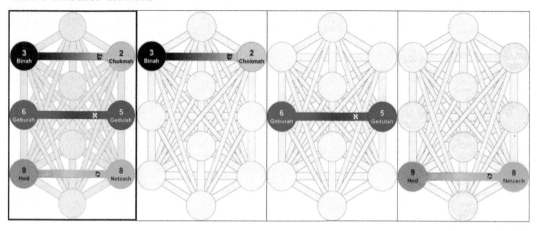

The 7 Planetary Letters —

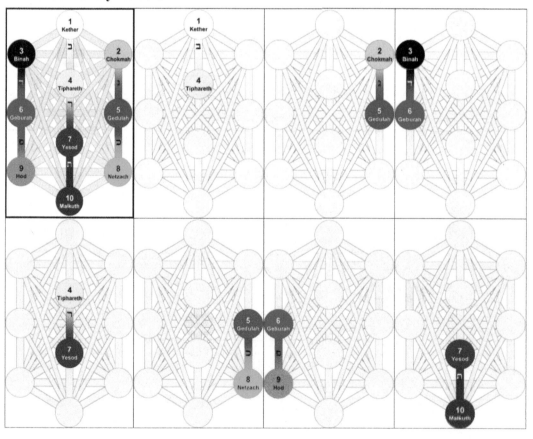

The 12 Zodiacal Letters —

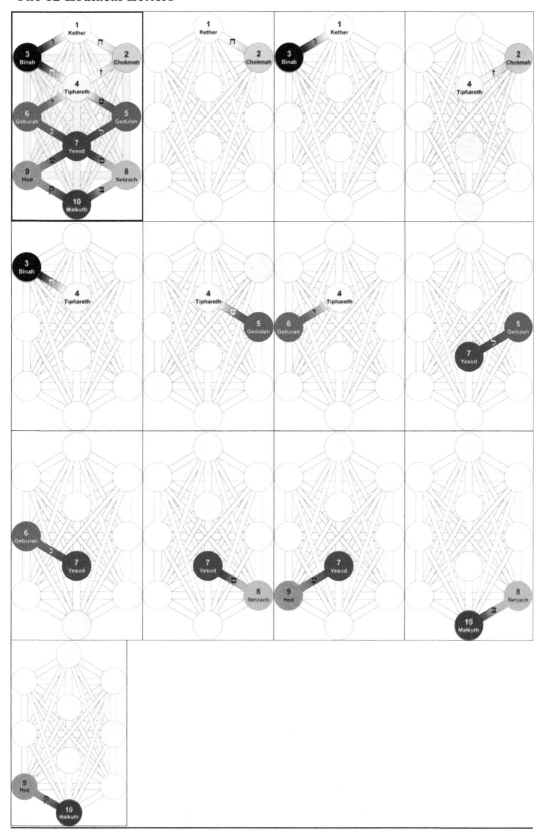

The 14 Hidden Paths (not in S.Y.) —

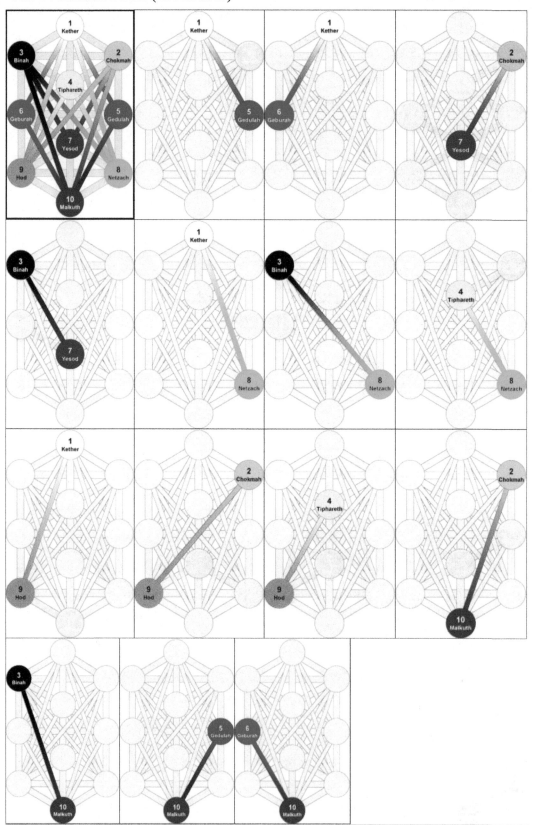

APPENDIX SIX

THE GENESIS ONE
CREATIVE SEQUENCE OF SEPHIROT AND PATHS

THE 32 PATHS OF WISDOM
[Left-to-right and top-to-bottom.]

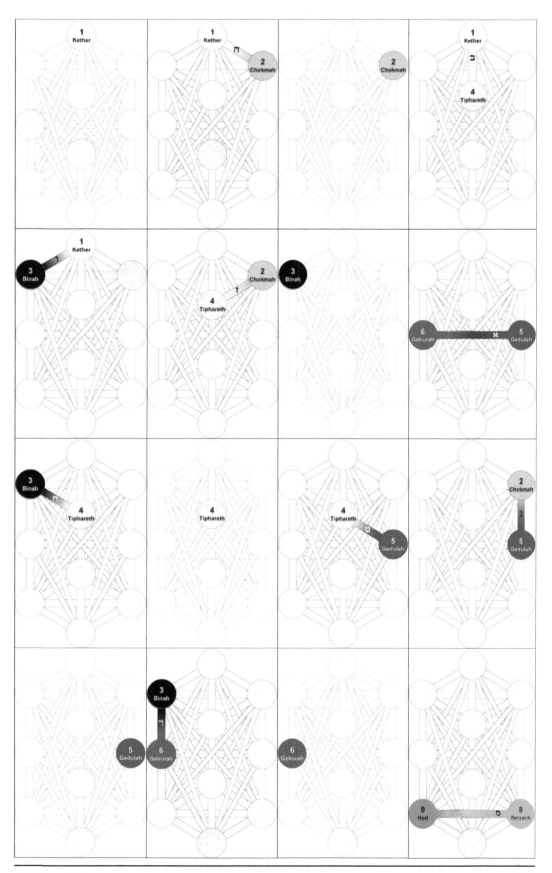

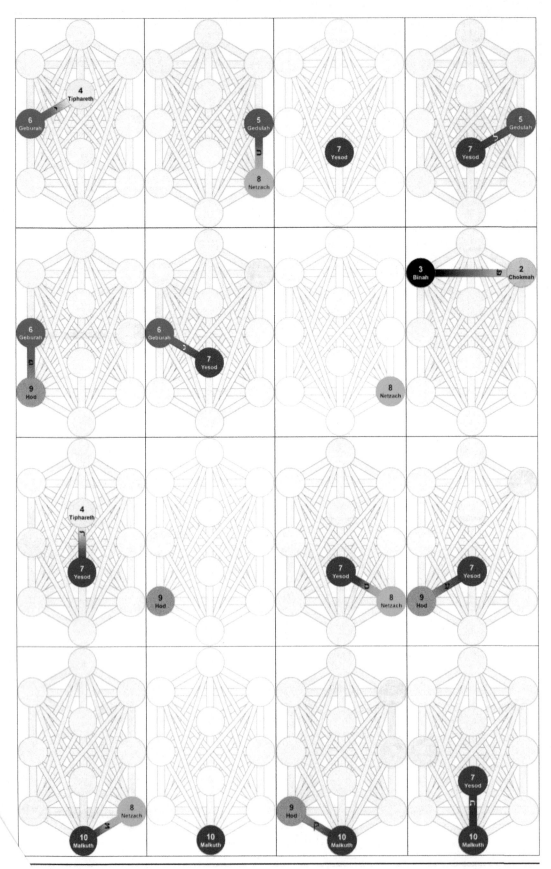

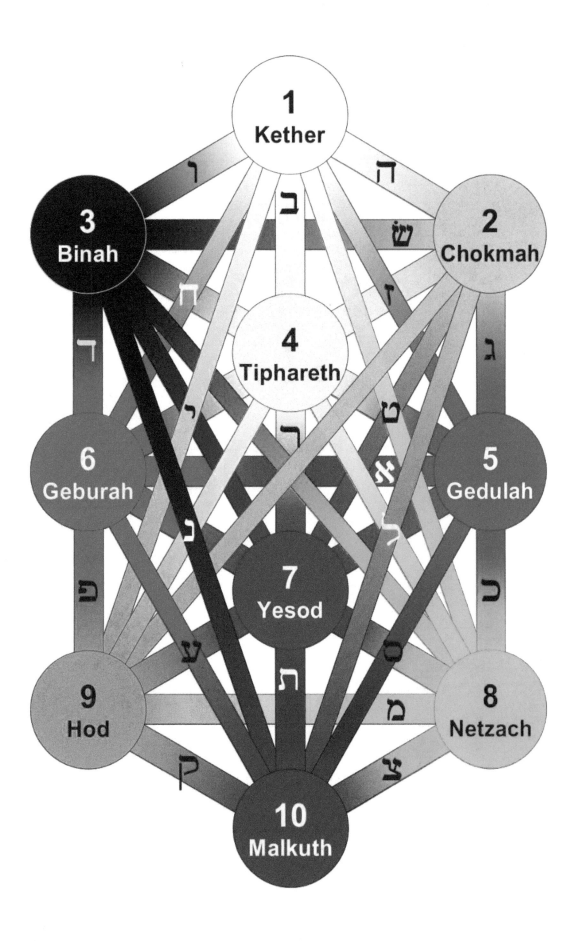

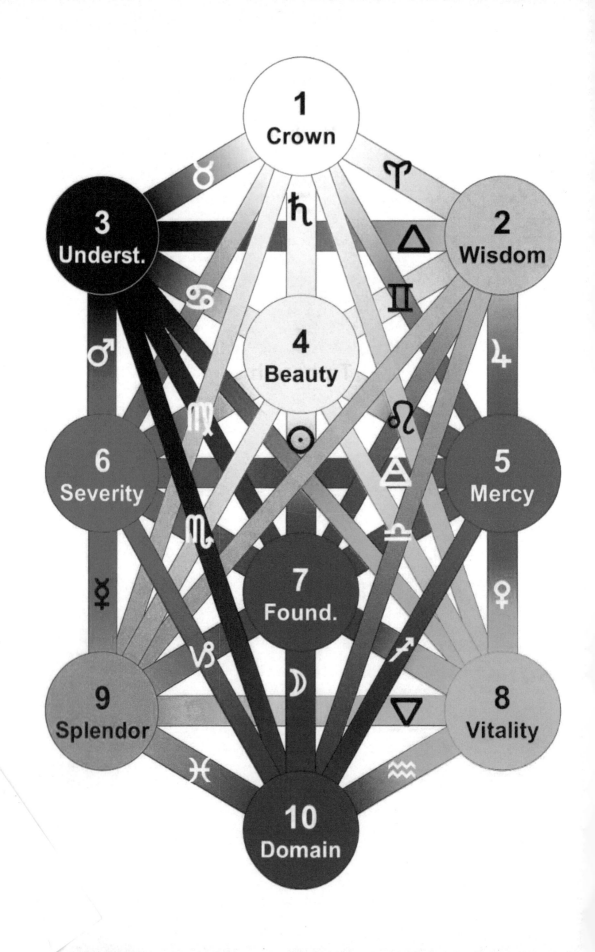

Made in the USA
Las Vegas, NV
04 December 2024

13345912R00136